Burgundy

the 90 greatest wines

Burgundy

« Grandeur Nature »
Collection

Collection based on an idea
by Marc Walter
© Marc Walter and Archipel
concept, 1999

Editor
Jean-Jacques Brisebarre

Art director
Marc Walter

Editorial assistant
Jeffrey Levy

Layout
Florence Cailly

Creation and production
Archipel concept
9, rue de la Collégiale
75005 Paris

Printed in Italy by
Milanostampa
September 1999

First edition
Bourgogne Grandeur Nature
Editions E.P.A. -
Hachette-Livre, 1998

© for this edition
1999 - Hachette-Livre
Dépôt légal : 7064
septembre 1999
ISBN : 2.85120.539.0
65/0799/0-01

James Turnbull

the 90 greatest wines

Photographs by
Daniel Czap

HACHETTE Livre

Contents

Introduction   6

Chablis

Domaine François Raveneau   10

Domaine Jean-Paul Droin   12

Domaine Louis Michel & Fils   14

Domaine de la Maladière   16

Domaine René & Vincent
Dauvissat   18

Côte de Nuits

Domaine Alain Burguet   20

Domaine Alain Hudelot-Noëllat   22

Domaine Alain Michelot   24

Domaine de l'Arlot   26

Domaine Armand Rousseau   28

Domaine Bachelet   30

Domaine Bernard Dugat-Py   32

Domaine Bruno Clair   34

Domaine du Clos de Tart   36

Domaine Comte Georges
de Vogüé   38

Domaine Confuron-Cotétidot   40

Domaine Daniel Rion & Fils   42

Domaine Denis Mortet   44

Domaine Dujac   46

Domaine Emmanuel Rouget   48

Domaine Faiveley   50

Domaine Forey   52

Domaine François Lamarche   54

Domaine Frédéric Esmonin   56

Note

Practical information concerning the estates and firms featured in this book –
their address and telephone number, directions for visiting them, and an
indication of the price of their wine and where to buy it – is given in the
address list on page 190.

So strong is worldwide demand, the majority of the estates have little if any
wine to sell to the passing visitor, who should instead call on the retail outlets
in order to purchase bottles. Some estates may be visited, in which case
common courtesy demands a telephone call before arriving, in order to make
an appointment. There are a multitude of tasks all making demands on the
vigneron's time, and receiving visitors is one of the less indispensable!

Domaine Georges Mugneret	58	
Domaine Georges Roumier	60	
Domaine Ghislaine Barthod	62	
Domaine Guy Coquard	64	
Domaine Henri Gouges	66	
Domaine Hubert Lignier	68	
Domaine Jacques-Frédéric Mugnier	70	
Domaine Jayer-Gilles	72	
Domaine Jean Grivot	74	
Domaine Jean-Jacques Confuron	76	
Domaine des Lambrays	78	
Domaine Leroy	80	
Domaine Méo-Camuzet	82	
Domaine Michel Gros	84	
Domaine Mongeard-Mugneret	86	
Domaine Pierre Gelin	88	
Domaine Ponsot	90	
Domaine René Engel	92	
Domaine Robert Arnoux	94	
Domaine Robert Chevillon	96	
Domaine Robert Groffier Père & Fils	98	
Domaine de la Romanée-Conti	100	
Domaine Rossignol-Trapet	102	
Domaine Sérafin Père & Fils	104	
Château de la Tour	106	
Domaine Trapet Père & Fils	108	

Côte de Beaune

Domaine Albert Morot	110
Domaine Bernard Morey & Fils	112
Domaine Bitouzet-Prieur	114
Domaine Blain-Gagnard	116
Domaine Bonneau du Martray	118
Maison Champy Père & Cie	120
Domaine Chandon de Briailles	122
Domaine Coche-Dury	124

Domaine Comte Armand	126
Domaine Comte Senard	128
Domaine des Comtes Lafon	130
Domaine Étienne Sauzet	132
Domaine François Jobard	134
Domaine Germain Père & Fils	136
Domaine Jacques Prieur	138
Domaine Jean Chartron	140
Domaine Jean-Marc Boillot	142
Domaine Jean-Noël Gagnard	144
Maison Joseph Drouhin	146
Domaine Joseph Matrot	148
Domaine Leflaive	150
Domaine Louis Carillon & Fils	152
Maison Louis Jadot	154
Maison Louis Latour	156
Domaine Marquis d'Angerville	158
Domaine Michel Colin-Deléger & Fils	160
Domaine Michel Gaunoux	162
Domaine Michel Lafarge	164
Château de Monthélie	166
Domaine de Montille	168
Olivier Leflaive Frères	170
Domaine Pavelot	172
Domaine Pierre Morey	174
Domaine Ramonet	176
Domaine Robert Ampeau & Fils	178
Domaine Rougeot	180
Domaine Roulot	182
Domaine Simon Bize & Fils	184
Domaine Tollot-Beaut	186
Domaine Vincent Girardin	188

Appendices

Domaines	190
Sales Outlets	192
Bibliography	192

Introduction

The wines of Burgundy have delighted the palates of connoisseurs since time immemorial with their incomparable fragrance, finesse and harmony, and today more than ever the greatest names command hushed attention and high expectation as their corks are drawn and as they are reverently savoured: Romanée-Conti, Chambertin, Clos Vougeot, Montrachet... In a growing world market for fine wine, the mythical names of Burgundy's Côte d'Or represent for many the summit of France's wine treasury, and are sought out with increasing avidity and difficulty as demand exceeds finite supply.

Time and tradition are the cornerstones of their formidable quality, and as for their undeniable uniqueness, that may be attributed to another, immutable, element: *terroir*. For at least a thousand years up until the Revolution, Burgundy's vineyards lay in the hands of local nobility and the Church. The Abbeys of Cluny and Cîteaux in particular benefited from numerous donations of land, and carefully tended their charges, refining methods of cultivation and wine-making. Observing, they noted the earlier ripening of fruit here than there, the different nuances of flavour between one plot and its neighbour, and the success of two particular grape varieties in Burgundy's climate and soil. These two noble varieties, Pinot Noir and Chardonnay, have evolved over the centuries into what they are today by natural selection, resulting in perfect suitability to their soils and microclimates. As for the wines' renown, that may be attributed to the Dukes of Burgundy, who vaunted their quality outside the region in the 14th and 15th centuries.

After a century of mixed fortunes in which wars, economic depressions and so-called advances in agriculture have all had their effect, the end of the millennium is witnessing a formidable renaissance. Wine-makers up and down the Côte, realizing that well-made, authentic *terroir*-driven Burgundy has a large market, but that *terroir* is the one quality which puts their wines in a different league to the Chardonnays and Pinots of the rest of the world, are reviewing their methods and sharing their knowledge. Thanks to work by luminaries such as the agronomic engineer Claude Bourguignon there is widespread recognition that much of Burgundy's prime vineyard land has been maltreated, its essential, teeming micro-organic life extinguished by years of treatments of chemical fertilizers, which progressively replaced manure from the 1950s onwards. Action to revivify and protect the soils and their environments is being taken to a greater or lesser degree – through reasoned treatment to biological, and even biodynamic, viticulture – by all self-respecting growers.

In the vatroom also experimentation and flexibility abound. Tradition and savoir-faire, passed down from father to son, are now better understood thanks to an oenology diploma, and are assessed in the light of visits to other wine regions and countries. Oenology though is still an alien concept in Burgundy, for most *vignerons* regard vinification as the crowning challenge of their art, and would not dream of contracting it out to a third party. However one independent advisor who has left his mark on Burgundian wine-making is the Lebanese agronomist-oenologist Guy Accad, who from 1975 onwards not only voiced the same anxieties as Bourguignon but also proposed solutions to the little-spoken but oft-held feeling that wines no longer had the richness of those of days gone by. His recommendations were highly controversial at the time, yet certain honest and courageous wine-makers adopted them, earning themselves vitriolic criticism from neighbours who then also quietly adopted at least their principal elements themselves. Nowadays one can taste the wines of Etienne Grivot, Philippe Senard and others and appreciate the great progress they have made.

To understand Burgundy, an understanding of its appellations and hierarchy is necessary. Burgundy is all about *climats*, vineyards with their own unique soil and microclimate, and *lieux-dits*, sections of a *climat* which are identified on the cadastre. There are also *clos*, those *climats* which in the Middle Ages were – and sometimes still are – walled. All these named vineyards are classified in a hierarchy, at the top of which are the Grands Crus, which are designated simply by their vineyard name on labels (Chambertin, Musigny, Montrachet). These come from the prime sites, those *climats* with the best orientation, drainage, soil and subsoil make-up and other factors. Occupying less favoured, yet nevertheless very good sites are the Premiers Crus, which are designated by the name of the vineyard preceded by that of its village (Gevrey-Chambertin Clos Saint-Jacques, Chambolle-Musigny Charmes). Less well-sited land simply has the right to its Village, or communal, name (Gevrey-Chambertin, Chambolle-Musigny), although wine from an individual *climat* enjoying the Village appellation may specify its origin (Gevrey-Chambertin En Motrot). Lastly come the Regional wines, which may be geographical, with varying degrees of precision (Bourgogne, Bourgogne Hautes

Côtes de Nuits, Bourgogne Epineuil), or may specify a grape variety (Bourgogne Aligoté) or a style (Crémant de Bourgogne).

There are some 4,500 *exploitations*, farming on average 4-5 hectares each and making perhaps as many different wines with them! Indeed Burgundy is today a mosaic of tiny vineyard holdings, a legacy of the Revolution and the Napoleonic Code, which obliges a *vigneron* to pass down his land in equal shares between all his children. Rare indeed is the *monopole*, the vineyard owned by a single estate. The relentless splitting up of vineyards has led to a multiplication of versions of what is ostensibly the same wine, and thus, inevitably, to consumer confusion: how to know which of a dozen offerings of a wine is the best, and which to avoid? The answer, of course, is to taste, to read, to discuss, and once one has found a grower who is competent to remain loyal to him; Burgundy is best bought by the grower's or producer's name, rather than any prestigious vineyard name.

Who then are the finest wine-makers? Who are those who are pushed incessantly to experimentation, and those who faithfully adhere to time-honoured family traditions, and is one better than the other? What are the histories of their estates? Who are those who have adopted biological or biodynamic viticulture, indeed what exactly are they? This book presents the men and women who make the finest wines, and reviews their growing and wine-making techniques, and the styles of wine achieved. By buying a bottle of their Burgundy the wine-lover is highly likely to be delighted with its quality. The selection was made on the basis of two criteria, quality and regularity, assessed over many comparative tastings. The estates reviewed are listed by region – Chablis, the Côte de Nuits and the Côte de Beaune – and by alphabetical order within each region.

S mall in size it may be, but Domaine François Raveneau makes quintessential Chablis of world-wide renown. Its wines are delicious young, yet more than any others they repay long keeping, developing magnificently complex flavours over the years. So limited is supply compared with demand that Raveneau wines are difficult to come by, yet anyone wanting to discover authentic Chablis should make the effort to find and taste a bottle. He or she will be anything but disappointed.

Careful traditional craftsmanship François Raveneau founded the estate with vines from both his parents' families, and his sons Jean-Marie and Bernard have succeeded him with great talent. There are no particular innovations or sleights of the hand to explain the quality of their wines, simply the basic priorities with which all good *vignerons* are in agreement – good healthy grapes and minimal intervention but maximum surveillance during fermentation. The vineyards are cared for by *lutte raisonnée* – biological as far as is possible, yet not rejecting out of hand the use of artificial treatments, for nature occasionally throws up situations when the bare choice is between using them or losing one's crop.

Yields are kept down by acting at the onset of vegetation, pruning short and debudding, never by lopping off bunches in July, and normal, not excessive, grape ripeness is sought. The alcohol/acidity balance is all-important, and to this end Jean-Marie Raveneau would prefer to harvest a little early, rather than have over-ripe fruit; for him chaptalisation is infinitely preferable to acidification.

Perfectly-defined terroir characteristics Grapes are fermented at 22°, mostly in vat but 10% in barrel, and the wines then undergo their malo-lactic fermentations. They are left in vat long enough to clarify themselves, then are transferred to barrel for ageing, which lasts roughly one year. That way little deposit forms in the barrel, and the wines can usually be bottled without filtration.

What sets Raveneau Chablis apart from nearly all others is the purity and intensity of the fruit and the perfect definition of *terroir* characteristics. When young La Forest is generally fresh, elegant and floral, Butteaux more ample and mineral, and Montée de Tonnerre leaner, tauter and flinty; Blanchots is more reserved, manly and structured and Les Clos somehow combining the latter's robustness with enormous refinement and elegance. After bottling these wines can be very dumb for a while, yet as they age they take on a whole range of tertiary aromas encompassing honey, mushrooms, seaweed, moss, fern and various minerals.

Chablis Valmur Valmur has the power and dimension of the true Grand Cru, with a splendid mineral flavour with an unmistakable iodine side to it, and behind all that, hints of the vegetal... This great Chablis throws up images of a plate of seafood, served on a bed of seaweed, and indeed the two are highly complementary at table. A mature Raveneau Valmur makes a magnificent partner for grilled lobster, and also lends itself to fish or white meat dishes in cream sauce.

• Other white wines:
Grand cru:
Les Clos, Blanchots.
Premier cru:
Montée de Tonnerre, Chapelot, Vaillons, Montmains, La Forest, Butteaux.
• Owner: Raveneau family
• Wine-makers: Jean-Marie & Bernard Raveneau
• Combined vineyards: 7.5 hectares
• Production: 45,000 bottles
• Exports: 30 %
• Take-away sales: No
• Visits: No

Wine selected:
Chablis Valmur

• Classification: Grand Cru
• Area cultivated: 0.75 hectares
• Soil type: Kimmeridge clay
• Average vine age: 30 years
• Average annual production: 4,500 bottles

DOMAINE JEAN-PAUL DROIN

The energetic and articulate Jean-Paul Droin has a superb 20-hectare estate spread over many of the most coveted slopes of Chablis. Droin is an unrepentant user of new oak, and is criticized by some for swamping *terroir* characteristics with the wood's opulent vanilla flavours. He accepts this criticism with the answer that he and his numerous clients like their wines that way. Whether one is for or against oaked Chablis, no one would deny that Droin follows his leanings with consummate talent.

A feel for tradition and an analytical character The Droins are probably the senior family of viticulteurs in Chablis, with lineage which Jean-Paul, the town archivist and a great lover of history, has traced back until 1640. He is the 12th generation to follow the family trade, and started working in the vineyards alongside his father and grandfather at the age of 14, eventually assuming total responsibility when his father retired in 1982.

This practical and analytical man is not afraid to swim against the purist tide when he judges it worthwhile. Not only as regards new oak but equally with regard to mechanical harvesters – he would happily use them even in his Grands Crus if they were not so steep, for they do not lead to any greater fruit oxidation than the deep harvest baskets used by previous generations, nor do they damage the vines.

Irreproachable fruit and new oak In many other aspects he is in perfect sync with all the other top Chablis growers. Pruning short, debudding (*essoumachage* is the local term), *rognage* (trimming and thinning growth to facilitate aeration), ecological vineyard practices, even experimentation such as *confusion sexuelle* to combat *grappe de ver* and the vine's other various enemies... all these are necessary in order to obtain fruit of irreproachable quality, so much so that yields of up to 70 hl./ha. in good years are capable of producing great wines, and that fruit selection is unnecessary.

Since 1986 Grands and certain Premiers Crus have been fermented in oak, a mixture of new and 1-, 2- and 3-year barrels, the choice and the amount of new wood being dependent on the vintage characteristics, while the remaining wines are fermented in vat. About 1 month after malolactic fermentations the wines fermented in barrel are racked off their lees, and the vat-fermented wines are transferred to these barrels, to benefit from the lees. All wines in barrel are given *bâtonnage* every 10-15 days.

Chablis Montée de Tonnerre Which wines one prefers in Droin's range is naturally a question of one's tolerance of new oak. While the Grand Cru Grenouille is undoubtedly a finely-crafted wine, it could easily be mistaken for a steely Condrieu. Vaudésir and Blanchots bring the taster nearer to home, yet more recognizable are the superb Les Clos and the exceptional Premier Cru Montée de Tonnerre, concentrated, taut and expressive, of medium-weight and with a perfectly-balanced blend of gun-flint, citrus fruit and wood flavours. This fine wine needs some 8-10 years for the mineral side to assert itself fully, and when ready is a superlative match for *écrevisses à la nage*.

- Other white wines:
Grand cru:
Valmur, Vaudésir, Grenouille, Les Clos, Blanchot.
Premier cru:
Vaillons, Montmains, Vosgros, Fourchaume, Côte de Léchet, Vaucoupin.
Village:
Chablis, Petit Chablis
- Owner: Droin family
- Wine-maker:
Jean-Paul Droin
- Combined vineyards:
20 hectares
- Production:
150,000 bottles
- Exports: 60%
Take-away sales:
By appointment
- Visits: By appointment

Wine selected:
Chablis
Montée de Tonnerre

- Classification:
Premier Cru
- Area cultivated:
1.76 hectares
- Soil type:
Kimmeridge clay
- Average vine age:
35 years
- Average annual production:
14,000 bottles

1996   1996

PRODUCT OF FRANCE

Chablis Premier Cru
Montée de Tonnerre

APPELLATION CHABLIS PREMIER CRU CONTRÔLÉE

Mise en bouteilles à la propriété par

JEAN-PAUL DROIN

Propriétaire-Viticulteur à Chablis - Yonne - France

ome Chablis is made by growers who are pro new wood, some by those who are pro old wood, and some who are resolutely against wood all together. One of the most fervent disciples of the stainless steel school, producing wine which is the absolute antithesis of that of its neighbour Jean-Paul Droin, is Domaine Louis Michel. This is the source of rapier-clean, fruity and vibrant Chablis which, no less than wooded versions, needs time to come round.

Measures against the dreaded frost The Michel estate was founded in 1850, and since then 5 generations have succeeded each other through times of prosperity and difficulty. Jean-Loup Michel has been at the helm since 1988, and very well remembers tobogganing on the lower slopes of Les Clos, which were left unplanted as recently as the 1960s, so regular and great were the frost ravages. Today, the ready market for all categories of Chablis and the progress in combatting Nature's spitefulness would make it financial folly not to plant all these slopes. Whenever the thermometer in his most vulnerable vineyard has sounded off the alarm on his bedside table, he telephones his vineyard workers and rushes out and lights up the numerous burners placed along the rows of vines. Others spray their vines with water, but his are too far from the reservoir or the river to do that. The latest idea in vogue is to enclose the vines in a tent of plastic sheeting with fine perforations; the greenhouse effect is highly desirable, and gives greater uniformity of flowering, yet the risk of it flying away with the wind is great, and as for the cost... the burners' days are not yet numbered!

Stainless steel for terroir definition The Michels firmly believe that terroir characteristics can only be successfully brought out in a wine by vinifying in a neutral environment, which for them is preferably stainless steel. Wood flavours and oxidation mask the different vineyards' true personalities. The Michel vatting hall contains an impressive battery of gleaming steel, and it is in these that all wines in the range spend their entire natal and postnatal period up until bottling.

After a gentle pressing in the two pneumatic Buchers, musts are left overnight to settle and are then transferred to vat, where they ferment at 18-20°. Malo-lactic fermentations follow; these are traditional in Chablis, for the wines would be outrageously unbalanced by the swingeing malic acidity if they were prevented. The wines are subsequently left on their fine lees, still in stainless steel, for 8 months in the case of village wines and 12 in the case of Premiers and Grands Crus, before fining when necessary and bottling.

Chablis Grenouilles Sporting the habitual green-tinged gold, the Louis Michel Grenouilles is very aromatic even in its youth, with a fine mix of the mineral and vegetal. On the palate it is rich and plumper than some of the other Grands Crus, yet has all the acidity it needs, half hidden in its fleshy folds, to keep it alert and vigorous over many a long year. This is a fine advertisement for the stainless steel school, a spokesman who is inspired to great eloquence in the company of distinguished friends like Scallop Carpaccio.

• Other white wines:
Grand cru:
Les Clos, Vaudésir.
Premier cru:
Montée de Tonnerre,
Montmain, Vaillons,
Forêts.
Village:
Chablis, Petit Chablis
• Owner: Michel family
• Wine-maker: Jean-Loup Michel
• Combined vineyards:
22 hectares
• Production:
160,000 bottles
• Exports: 90%
• Take-away sales: Yes
• Visits: By appointment

Wine selected:
Chablis Grenouilles

• Classification:
Grand Cru
• Area cultivated:
0.54 hectares
• Soil type:
Kimmeridge clay
• Average vine age:
25 years
• Average annual production:
2,800 bottles

1996

PRODUCE OF FRANCE

MISE EN BOUTEILLES AU DOMAINE

Chablis Grand Cru

GRENOUILLES

APPELLATION CHABLIS GRAND CRU CONTROLÉE   750 ml

LOUIS MICHEL & FILS, PROPRIÉTAIRES A 89800 CHABLIS - FRANCE

W illiam Fèvre is one of the most ardent defenders of traditional Chablis and one of the region's greatest wine-makers. At his Domaine de la Maladière, in the centre of Chablis, a long list of wines is produced which reflect the characteristics of their *terroir* with great precision.

Grower, négociant and defender of the appellation Over the last 40 years Fèvre has patiently built his domaine up to what it is today, not quite the largest yet certainly the best-endowed, with holdings in 6 of the 7 Grands Crus and 6 Premiers Crus, as well as a large quantity of Village land. Of the vineyards that he does not own Fèvre buys raw material from a number of growers, and between his domaine and *négociant* businesses can thus boast the entire range of Chablis crus.

His time is not only filled with making wine, but also with promoting Chablis and looking after its interests around the world. He has always been a staunch opponent of the extension of the Chablis vineyards, and as President of the Syndicat de la Défense de l'Appellation Chablis, it was he who led the fight against the extensions in the 1970s, arguing that true Chablis could only be made on slopes with a subsoil of Kimmeridge marl, as it has been for centuries. In the event his opponents, contending that factors such as orientation, altitude and microclimate were equally important, won that battle in 1976, yet Fèvre is still a formidable hurdle to anyone who is thinking of tampering with the region's traditions and reputation.

A fervent believer in the importance of oak A visit to the Domaine de la Maladière is not easily forgotten, so impressive are its extensive and modern installations with their ranks of medium-sized stainless steel vats, their five-high rows of oak barrels and their banks of maturing bottles.

All the Grands Crus and most of the Premiers are fermented in barrel, after which they are usually transferred to vat for their malo-lactic fermentations, before being put back into barrel for *élevage*. Their maker is a fervent believer in the importance of the contribution of oak to bring out the true Chablis character, and generally renews one quarter of his barrels every year. However unlike certain of his peers Fèvre does not believe in rousing the wines' lees by *bâtonnage*.

Chablis Les Clos The first slope planted was in all probability what is today called Les Clos, the superb slope which faces one as one leaves Chablis and crosses the Serein in the direction of Tonnerre. Les Clos is the largest of the Grands Crus, and is in many locals' opinion the finest. Certainly William Fèvre's offering is a very distinguished wine, rich and profound, yet lean and firm of physique. In youth its oakiness can be a little obtrusive, yet it is not made for drinking young; after a decade the aromatic palette is beautifully balanced between mineral, lemon and wood flavours, with a touch of honey. This deserves a rather special dish: lobster *émincé* served with fresh duck's *foie gras* makes a fine choice, and the match between wine and food will leave the diner congratulating himself on his gastronomic connoisseurship!

• Other white wines (Domaine):
Grand cru:
Vaudésir, Grenouilles, Valmur, Preuses, Bougros.
Premier cru:
Montée de Tonnerre, Vaulorent, Beauroy, Les Lys, Vaillons, Montmains.
Village:
Chablis Champs Royaux, Petit Chablis
• Owner: William Fèvre
• Wine-maker: William Fèvre
• Combined vineyards: 44.7 hectares
• Production: 350,000 bottles
• Exports: 90%
• Take-away sales: 9 a.m.-6 p.m., Wed. - Sun.
• Visits: Yes

Wine selected:
Chablis Les Clos

• Classification: Grand Cru
• Area cultivated: 3.41 hectares
• Soil type: Kimmeridge clay
• Average vine age: 25 years
• Average annual production: 24,000 bottles

Chablisien | Chablis

1997

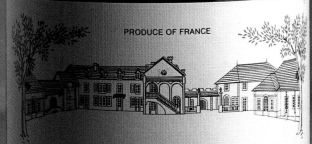

PRODUCE OF FRANCE

CHABLIS LES CLOS
grand cru
APPELLATION CHABLIS GRAND CRU CONTRÔLÉE

MIS AU DOMAINE DE LA MALADIÈRE
A CHABLIS - FRANCE

CHABLIS

DOMAINE R. & V. DAUVISSAT

Chablis, Burgundy's northern outpost, produces white wines which have a unique and unmistakable steely, mineral character. Vineyard sites are all-important of course, and the finest wines come from the most prestigious Grand Cru slopes with a subsoil of Kimmeridge marl. Yet the ambition and skill of the wine-maker also play an essential role, and there is a large gulf in quality between the wines of the most talented and their run-of-the-mill equivalent. Some of the very best bottles the region has to offer are the work of Vincent Dauvissat.

Observation, experimentation and reflection The Dauvissats have been growing vines in the region since the 17th century, and there are now a handful of different family branches making wine. In 1931 Robert Dauvissat decided to cease selling his wine to the Chablis *négoce* and to bottle and sell it himself, and thanks to him and then successively his son René and his grandson Vincent, this branch has over the intervening period gained itself an international reputation for the quality of its produce.

Since 1989 the lean, smiling Vincent Dauvissat has been in charge. Vincent's wine-making is brilliantly empirical, all he knows was learnt in a dozen years at his father's side, for he has never set foot in a wine school. That period involved much experimentation by the father-and-son team, which laid the foundations of the young man's habit of regular reflection on what he is doing, which no doubt explains the stunning quality of his wines today.

A succession of little details Making good wine is a succession of little details, the visitor is modestly informed. Sensitivity towards the vine, its soil and its environment, intimate knowledge of one's vineyards in order to know what is ready for harvesting, low yields of ripe and healthy grapes from vines which know no stress... Vinification also involves habitual practices but not fixed rules. A very gentle pneumatic pressing, a short period of settling, then fermentation, partly in vat and partly in barrel; one quarter of the barrels are new, but certain years this might be increased to 60%. A rapid start to fermentation is preferred, which sometimes necessitates seeding with a little cultured yeast, but generally the indigenous variety is preferred. Fermentation is lengthy, after which maturation over 6-12 months, or even more, takes place in old barrels and *feuillettes*, the small local barrels containing 132 litres. Bottling is by gravity, and is preceded by a light filtration if necessary.

Chablis Les Preuses Existing clients of Vincent Dauvissat no doubt count themselves privileged – as do those of his cousins the Raveneaus – to be able to buy a few bottles of his different *crus*, for excessive demand means that new clients can not be accepted. Les Preuses is a fine example of Dauvissat's art, a sumptuously full-bodied, full-flavoured and complete wine which in the better vintages takes 12-15 years to reach perfection. Concentration, finesse and a wonderful mineral side make this a textbook Chablis, which would be honoured by the presence of a lobster, fricasseed in Chablis wine.

Other white wines:
Grand cru:
Les Clos.
Premier cru:
La Forest, Sechet, Vaillons.
Village:
Chablis, Petit Chablis
• Owners: René & Vincent Dauvissat
• Wine-maker: Vincent Dauvissat
• Combined vineyards: 11 hectares
• Production: 80,000 bottles
• Exports: 50%
• Take-away sales: To existing clients
• Visits: By appointment

Wine selected:
Chablis Les Preuses

• Classification: Grand Cru
• Area cultivated: 0.96 hectares
• Soil type: clay and limestone over Kimmeridge marl
• Average vine age: 28 years
• Average annual production: 6,000 bottles

By dint of conviction and tenacity Alain Burguet, a self-taught individualist, has seen his excellent, no-compromise Gevreys recognized for what they are: consummate examples of their kind, made for the long-term. Burguet has built up his estate from scratch, the majority of his vines are share cropped, and until recently he had nothing better than village land. This *vigneron* proves that, contrary to received wisdom, land is not everything!

The young individualist goes it alone Burguet left school at 14 and gained his first experience alongside his father, who owned a couple of hectares. Soon the young man decided to go it on his own. He entered into a crop-sharing arrangement with a *vigneron* who was on the point of retiring – it was only a little over 2 hectares, but it was a start – and started work.

Having observed and noted from his earliest days working in the vineyard, Burguet had fixed ideas about what was and was not for him, and a clear idea of the type of wine he wanted to produce: a wine for the long haul, which took time to come round. Too bad if it wasn't drinkable in the first few years of its existence! He has obeyed his insticts pretty much unswervingly over the years, with just the occasional refinement of method, and time has proved them utterly reliable.

Wine-making with minimal intervention Healthy grapes, obtained by viticultural methods based on non-treatment, low yields and old vines are his priorities. He generally destalks all his fruit, and then once in vat the wine gets on with its own life with minimal intervention on his part. He prefers to go for a short fermentation at a high temperature rather than a protracted affair; there is no cold maceration before fermentation, no temperature regulation and no use of sulphur dioxide nor cultured yeast: since the various parcels all have different indigenous yeast, each vat starts its alcoholic fermentation in its own time.

Burguet is now aided by his two long-haired, earringed and *sympathiques* sons, which must be a relief during thankless jobs such as forcing the floating caps of solids down into the liquid for extraction, which they do by hand with a *pigeou*. As soon as the alcoholic fermentation is over they then transfer wines to barrel for *élevage*. In earlier years he placed scant importance on wood, but nowadays treats all his wines to a certain percentage of new oak every year; yet so finely judged is the balance that his wines never have new oak flavours. He expresses a preference for woods from the Tronçais or other central France forests, with a very fine grain.

Gevrey-Chambertin Vieilles Vignes Burguet started off making just one wine, his Vieilles Vignes, and although today he produces five, including the Premier Cru Champeaux, the original remains his best-known. It is an intense, rich mouthful, with a lot of structure, freshness and natural, perfumed, spicy fruit, which largely vindicates its creator's wine-making methods. The Vieilles Vignes needs a good 6-8 years in the cellar before it finds its voice, but when it does, what poetry! At table give it room to express itself, with unadorned red meat of quality. Châteaubriands maître d'hôtel are eminently suitable.

* Other red wines:
Premier cru:
Gevrey-Chambertin Les Champeaux.
Village:
Gevrey-Chambertin En Billard, GC En Reniard.
Régional:
Bourgogne
* Owner: Alain Burguet
* Wine-maker: Alain Burguet
* Combined vineyards: 6.3 hectares
* Production: 25,000 bottles
* Exports: 90%
* Take-away sales: No
* Visits: No

Wine selected:
Gevrey-Chambertin Vieilles Vignes

* Classification: Village
* Area cultivated: 2.5 hectares
* Soil type: Clay and limestone
* Average vine age: 60 years
* Average annual production: 9,000 bottles

Côte de Nuits | Gevrey-Chambertin

From the estate which he patiently built up over the years, comprising vineyards mostly around the villages of Vosne-Romanée and Chambolle-Musigny, Alain Hudelot-Noëllat makes deliciously fragrant and sensual wines. Self-effacing and modest by nature, he is a master of his art, and his wines inspire great loyalty among his clients.

A young entrepreneur goes it alone The Hudelots have lived in Chambolle and laboured in the fields and vineyards since before the Revolution. Alain Hudelot himself left school at the tender age of 14 to start working among the vines, for his father and also for the *négociants* Drouhin and Champy and others. By the time he was 20 the young entrepreneur had leased some parcels from his father in order to start his own exploitation, and then invested in a tractor and hired it and himself out to other *vignerons*. Tractors of course were still a novelty in Burgundy even then, and he managed to earn himself enough money to acquire further vineyards. Several years later his father gave him some of his vines in Clos Vougeot. The fledgling domaine was becoming sufficiently large to enable him to earn a decent living.

Hudelot married a Vosne girl, a member of the well-known Noëllat family. However the girl's family were against the marriage and refused to allow her access to her rightful dowry, which was made up of very desirable parcels of Vosne-Romanée vineyards. The unfortunate newlyweds found themselves locked in a long and costly conflict with her family which was only resolved more than a dozen years later, all in order to gain possession of vineyards which were rightfully theirs.

Aromatic, seductive and silky Alain Hudelot works in more or less the way his father and grandfather did before him. He reveres old vines, and works his vineyards as naturally as possible, rotating treatments to increase their efficacy and ploughing to keep weeds at bay.

He abhors green-pruning, and if the standard methods of yield reduction have not had the desired result, he prefers to give his vats a *saignée*. He generally destalks some 75% of the grapes, and gives his grapes a vatting of 15-18 days, preferring to macerate before rather than after fermentation. Maturing wines then enjoy exclusively new oak, if they have the luck to have been born Grand Cru, or one third or one quarter for the less illustrious members of the family. Since 1990 they have been neither fined nor filtered. Hudelot-Noëllat wines are aromatic, seductive and silky, with rich, intense fruitiness and body and structure.

Chambolle-Musigny Charmes Although he is best known for his Vosne-Romanées and his Clos Vougeot, Hudelot has vines in Chambolle-Musigny's largest Premier Cru, Les Charmes, halfway up the slope between Vougeot and Chambolle, which give a wine in which one finds all the finest characteristics of the village's wines: exquisite perfume, richness and at the same time delicacy, harmony and structure, and great finesse... how aptly named this irresistible wine is! It illustrates perfectly the man's wine-making prowess, and is delicious to savour on its own, or at table with the simple, unadorned perfection of a roast leg of lamb.

• Other red wines:
Grand cru:
Clos de Vougeot, Richebourg, Romanée-Saint-Vivant.
Premier cru:
Vosne-Romanée Les Malconsorts, VR Les Suchots, VR Les Beaumonts; Vougeot Les Petits Vougeots; Nuits-Saint-Georges Les Murgers.
Village:
Vosne-Romanée, Chambolle-Musigny, Nuits-Saint-Georges.
Régional:
Bourgogne
• Owner: Alain Hudelot
• Wine-maker: Alain Hudelot
• Combined vineyards: 10 hectares
• Production: 46,000 bottles
• Exports: 60%
• Take-away sales: By appointment
• Visits: By appointment

Wine selected:
Chambolle-Musigny Les Charmes

• Classification: Premier Cru
• Area cultivated: 0.3 hectares
• Soil type: Clay and limestone
• Average vine age: 80 years
• Average annual production: 1,500 bottles

A large archway on the main road through Nuits-Saint-Georges leads into the trim, gravelled courtyard of Domaine Alain Michelot, the source of as fine a range of Nuits-Saint-Georges wines as one could wish for. One may have trouble finding bottles, though those who frequent France's top restaurants do not, but once enjoyed, a Michelot wine is difficult to forget!

A superlative line-up of Nuits Premiers Crus The domaine is young. Michelot's grandfather was a vineyard worker, but did not own any land. It was Alain's father who started constituting an estate in the inter-war years, when vineyards came up for sale regularly and could often be had for a song. Alain Michelot took over the estate after his father's premature death in 1966, and several more plots came the domaine's way when he married.

At the heart of the estate is its superlative line-up of Nuits Premiers Crus, which make up one half of the holdings. Seven different wines, divided between the northern, Vosne section of the commune and the southern section, provide a fascinating and varied group of individuals, each with their own story to tell.

The skilled hand of a past master To encourage all these individuals to express themselves a skilled hand is required in the vineyard and the vatroom, and Michelot is a past master at coaxing the finer nuances of *terroir* into the bottle. In truth he is not one for keeping his yields to the low levels of some of his fellow-*vignerons*, claiming that a more relevant figure is that of yield per vine, and his wines are perhaps not as concentrated as some. However balance, harmony and *terroir* expression are never lacking. Some 10% of the fruit is left on its stalks, for their physical properties rather than their tannin, as they help the juice pass through the cap of solids. The wines then undergo a cold maceration of some three days before the natural yeast gets to work. Michelot favours a slow rise in temperature, which is not permitted to exceed 30°, and to that end chaptalisation is carried out in several stages, which has the added advantage of prolonging the process. There are two *pigeages* per day, and the total vatting time lasts up to three weeks.

After blending free-run and press wine there is a whole month's settling before wines go into cask. The amount of new oak varies, but is in general 30% for the Premiers Crus, which then spend 18 months of peace and quiet, uninterrupted by any racking, before bottling with a light filtration.

Nuits-Saint-Georges Les Saint-Georges The *climat* Les Saint-Georges, reckoned by many the commune's finest, was already planted in the year 1000, and later belonged to one Brotherhood of St. George, founded in 1470, which left it its name. Touching the commune of Prémeaux, its stony russet-coloured soil combines with Michelot's wine-making talent to produce a sumptuous, velvety wine with all the attributes that quality implies: pure fruit, tannin, acidity and alcohol, all in balance, and then a long finish... this is a complex and complete wine, which has the wherewithal to grow old and wise. Young vintages are delicious with a fillet of Charolais beef *en brioche*, older ones find the company of a haunch of venison more stimulating.

• Other red wines:
Premier cru:
Nuits-Saint-Georges Les Vaucrains, NSG Les Cailles, NSG Les Porêts-Saint-Georges, NSG Aux Chaignots, NSG La Richemone, NSG Aux Champs-Perdrix; Morey-Saint-Denis Les Charrières.
Village:
Nuits-Saint-Georges, Morey-Saint-Denis.
Régional:
Bourgogne
• Owner: Alain Michelot
• Wine-maker: Alain Michelot
• Combined vineyards: 8.15 hectares
• Production: 50,000 bottles
• Exports: 35%
• Take-away sales: Yes
• Visits: No

Wine selected:
Nuits-Saint-Georges Les Saint-Georges

• Classification: Premier Cru
• Area cultivated: 0.19 hectares
• Soil type: Clay and limestone
• Average vine age: 20 years
• Average annual production: 1,200 bottles

As one drives south through Prémeaux on the RN74, a steep, walled vineyard may be seen on one's right. This is the Clos de l'Arlot, and the fine cluster of buildings just next to it constitute the Domaine de l'Arlot. This estate was created from the ashes of the Jules Belin estate in 1987, and with impressive rapidity it has established a reputation for wines of very high quality.

Jean-Pierre de Smet and AXA team up The Clos de l'Arlot was walled off by Jean-Charles Vienot, a Nuits *négociant* and grower, at the end of the 18th century. From 1891 it belonged to another *négociant*, Jules Belin, yet the various wines produced by his firm gradually declined in quality as the decades rolled by. Then Jean-Pierre de Smet appeared in the area.

De Smet was originally an accountant, but a passion for wine had drawn him to Burgundy, and he had worked for Jacques Seysses of Domaine Dujac from 1977 and attended Dijon university to complete his education. That done, he started looking for his own property, and heard about the Belin estate. By chance he then met Claude Bébéar, AXA's Chairman and Managing Director, who had recently invested in Château Pichon-Longueville at Pauillac and wished to diversify into Burgundy, and drew his attention to the domaine. Bébéar was interested, and in 1987 de Smet arranged the purchase. He formed a company with AXA to exploit it, taking on the roles of manager and wine-maker himself.

Biological viticulture and cool fermentations Since then the partnership has worked to perfection, de Smet proving just what a talented wine-maker he is, aided in his quest for quality by AXA's financial muscle, which has also enabled several vineyard acquisitions since 1987. His viticultural practices are biological, and weedkiller has long been dispensed with, as have synthetic soil-enriching products. The problem of yields is addressed at the beginning of the season, although a green harvest is also undertaken if it is really necessary.

De Smet avoids destemming before vatting, and favours fermenting whole grapes, which he believes increases the eventual complexity of the wine. He cools the fruit before pumping it into the vats, yet there is no cold pre-fermentation maceration, this cooling merely retarding the onset of fermentation for several days. It does however mean that fermentations do not rise above 32°, which is felt to preserve aromatic finesse. Wines are matured in approximately 40% new oak for 15-18 months, then bottled after fining but without filtration.

Nuits-Saint-Georges Clos de l'Arlot Rather atypically for a Nuits-Saint-Georges from the Prémeaux sector, the Clos de l'Arlot is a wine of relative softness and elegance, quite different from the domaine's other monopole, the Clos des Forêts-Saint-Georges. Quite light in colour and perfumed on the nose, it is a wine for medium-term cellaring, and affords an exquisite glass when *à point*. Sweetbread with morels, or Bresse hen in a cream sauce with chanterelle mushrooms, these are the style of dishes with which it gets on best.

• Other red wines:
Grand cru:
Romanée-Saint-Vivant.
Premier cru:
Nuits-Saint-Georges Clos des Forêts-Saint-Georges (monopole); Vosne-Romanée Les Suchots; Beaune Grèves.
Village:
Nuits-Saint-Georges.
Régional:
Côte de Nuits Villages Clos du Chapeau
• White wine:
Premier cru:
Clos de l'Arlot (monopole)
• Owners: Jean-Pierre de Smet & AXA Millésimes
• Manager: Jean-Pierre de Smet
• Wine-maker: Jean-Pierre de Smet
• Combined vineyards: 15 hectares
• Production: 60,000 bottles
• Exports: 80%
• Take-away sales: Yes
• Visits: By appointment

Wine selected:
Nuits-Saint-Georges Clos de l'Arlot
(monopole)

• Classification: Premier Cru
• Vineyard size: 2 hectares (red wine)
• Soil type: Clay and limestone
• Average vine age: 42 years
• Average annual production: 7,500 bottles

MIS EN BOUTEILLE AU DOMAINE

DOMAINE DE L'ARLOT

NUITS SAINT GEORGES

PREMIER CRU

1993

CLOS de L'ARLOT

APPELLATION NUITS ST GEORGES 1er CRU CONTROLÉE

VIN NON FILTRÉ - DÉCANTATION RECOMMANDÉE

MONOPOLE

DOMAINE de L'ARLOT - PREMEAUX

NUITS SAINT GEORGES (CÔTE D'OR)

PRODUCE OF FRANCE

750 ml

J ust as it has its young super-stars, the Côte d'Or has a sprinkling of senior estates which have long enjoyed a reputation for producing the very finest quality, making benchmark wines against which new estates measure themselves. Domaine Armand Rousseau is one such. If there is one estate which has consistently over a half-century offered the finest available Gevrey-Chambertin, this is it.

Synonymous with the best Gevrey-Chambertin The young Armand Rousseau was a broker in Gevrey before the Great War. Following the devastation caused by the passage of the phylloxera louse, it was not rare for vineyard land to come onto the market, and he gradually started piecing together his own estate. At first he sold his wine in bulk, but encouraged by Raymond Baudoin, founder of the *Revue du Vin de France* and consultant to a number of France's finest restaurants, he started bottling his best *cuvées,* and the restaurants were eager customers. Their clients became his clients, and then soon he had an American agent. The name Rousseau was becoming synonymous with the best Gevrey-Chambertin.

Charles Rousseau suddenly found himself in charge after losing his father in a car crash in 1959. Since then he has continued to build on his father's foundations, delighting ever more wine-lovers with manly, rich wines and continuing to enlarge the estate as and when suitable parcels have come onto the market. Today his son Eric works by the side of this courteous, honest gentleman, yet Charles is always available with advice and encouragement to anyone in need of it, and unfailing modesty and good humour.

Experience and feeling Rousseau wines are made more by experience and feeling than modern oenological science. On paper the basic recipe is simple: fine land, old vines, low yields, draconian sorting and long fermentations. Vines are left in production as long as they are remotely productive, for they contribute great complexity as well as acting as yield-reducers. At harvest-time Rousseau demands extreme selectivity from his pickers, and the ground has been known to be carpeted with discarded fruit in difficult years. Vatting itself starts with destalking some 80% of the fruit and a short, natural maceration until the indigenous yeast get to work on the grape-sugar. Once their work is done the rich, dark liquids are transferred to barrel for maturation. Only the Chambertin and Clos de Bèze are permitted 100% new oak, for in the Rousseaus' view oak flavours can too easily dominate a wine. After 20-22 months' ageing, wines are lightly fined with egg white, lightly filtered and then bottled.

Chambertin The Rousseau Chambertin is one of Burgundy's greatest wines, a heady, rich and powerful beast, which has great aromatic complexity once it has matured... black fruit, liquorice, leather, cinnamon, undergrowth: every vintage has its character, and the lesser vintages are usually as interesting, if less long-lived, than the great ones. The latter have great longevity – in a good cellar 30 years is possible – and may be decanted shortly before serving. As for a suitable dish, *coq au chambertin* or a truffled fillet of beef followed by l'Ami du Chambertin are eminently suitable.

- Other red wines:
Grand cru:
Chambertin Clos de Bèze, Ruchottes-Chambertin Clos des Ruchottes (monopole), Charmes-Chambertin, Mazy-Chambertin, Clos de la Roche.
Premier cru:
Gevrey-Chambertin Clos Saint-Jacques, GC Premier Cru.
Village:
Gevrey-Chambertin
- Owner: Charles Rousseau
- Combined vineyards: 14 hectares
- Production: 65,000 bottles
- Exports: 90%
- Take-away sales: No
- Visits: By appointment

Wine selected:
Chambertin

- Classification: Grand Cru
- Area cultivated: 2.15 hectares
- Soil type: Clay and limestone
- Average vine age: 45 years
- Average annual production: 6,000 bottles

Without doubt the smallest of Burgundy's top estates, Domaine Bachelet nevertheless has a large reputation among those who have heard of it. Because of its size its wines are naturally rare and difficult to find – and that applies to the estate as well! – but the young craftsman who fashions them has an innate feel for his art, and his bottles should be enthusiastically tracked down. Who knows? Sometimes he has some for sale on the premises.

From wine school to operational responsibility Denis's family has been around Gevrey for a long time, indeed Bachelet must be one of the commoner names in Burgundy, although it is found more frequently further south, on the Côte de Beaune in Dezize, Saint-Aubin, Chassagne... His grandparents built up the estate, the 5 hectares of which were split in two between the young man's father and his aunt. Denis finished his studies and started putting them into practice straight away in 1983, his father being professionally occupied elsewhere, and is helped out by his wife when needed.

In the manner of previous generations The estate's 3.07 hectares produce one Grand Cru, one Premier Cru, one Village and two Regional wines, as well as an Aligoté, and the vines which give the first three wines have impressive ages – there are even some centenarians in the Grand Cru – which act as a natural brake on yields, and contribute great aromatic intensity and complexity. Many would uproot them and replant, citing commercial unviability, for with higher yields they could make more wine and sell it at the same price, but Denis would never do that; low yields produce the sort of wine of which he is really proud, wine worthy of its superb *terroir*.

The domaine cannot afford the luxuries of some of the trappings which some more fortunate wine-makers now take for granted, but that just ensures that Denis remains on his toes. Temperature control equipment, for instance, would certainly make his life easier, yet he knows how to work without it, as did previous generations. Indeed his wines are born as were theirs, with minimal intervention from the *vigneron*. After severe selection of the fruit, there is maceration until the fermentation gets going, and then long maturation in order to derive maximum benefit from lees. He retains a lot of CO_2 in the wines and thus needs little sulphur to protect them, which ultimately contributes to greater purity. After *élevage* wines are fined, left for a month or so and bottled by hand without filtration.

Charmes-Chambertin The Charmes-Chambertin *climat*, which generally gives a richly elegant wine without excessive power, produces in Denis's hands a splendidly intense, smooth and aromatic bottle of very pure fruit, thoroughly harmonious and with excellent definition. This is a very fine example of its appellation, one of the very best, a wine of great breeding. Difficult though it might be, it should be resisted for 8-10 years, before being served with a tasty shoulder of veal stuffed with wild mushrooms.

• Other red wines:
Premier cru:
Gevrey-Chambertin
Les Corbeaux.
Village:
Gevrey-Chambertin.
Régional:
Côte de Nuits Villages,
Bourgogne Rouge
• White wine:
Régional:
Bourgogne Aligoté
• Owner: Bachelet family
• Wine-maker: Denis
Bachelet
• Combined vineyards:
3.07 hectares
• Production:
15,000 bottles
• Exports: 95%
• Take-away sales:
By appointment
• Visits: By appointment

Wine selected:
Charmes-Chambertin

• Classification:
Grand Cru
• Area cultivated:
0.43 hectares
• Soil type:
Clay and limestone
• Average vine age:
75 years
• Average annual
production:
1,800 bottles

Burgundy domaines come in all sizes and qualities, although large is unusual. One of the smallest of note, a domaine with no history which is making ripples thanks to the outstanding quality of its wines, is that of Bernard Dugat-Py. Dugat is the quintessential crafts-man, unsung and largely unknown, a young man set on making the very finest examples of his appellations possible.

A young entrepreneur invests Dugat bought his first vine-yard in 1973 at the tender age of 15 and made his first wine, a village Gevrey, two years later. Gradually over the years he has acquired other land – his father gave him some Gevrey and some Charmes-Chambertin in 1987, and he has acquired some Chambertin, Mazis-Chambertin and Premiers Crus since – which brings the area of his estate, still reso-lutely stuck inside the village boundaries, up to 5.6 hectares. Dugat works with his wife Jocelyne from a house at the top of the village, a building which sits over three cellars, the most recent a 1980s construction, the oldest genuine 12th-century, when it was used for housing lepers.

Interfering as little as possible Like all of his *confrères* who are producing the best Burgundy today, Dugat treats his vineyards and vines in as respectful a manner as possible, working the soil naturally for maximum plant health and to encourage roots to penetrate deep down under the surface. His family have been vine nurserymen, and their experience no doubt helps when selecting the best plant material for the different *terroirs*. He goes for extremely low yields, training his vines by the low-yield-producing *Guyot simple*, pruning short and debudding in the spring.

Fruit is discarded in the vineyard if it is substandard, and thereafter wine-making is relatively uncomplicated, Dugat's principal rule of thumb being to interfere as little as possible in the process. Vatting lasts as long as necessary, and fermen-tations are prolonged by limited chaptalisations towards the end of the process in order to keep it going, resulting in a more substantial texture. Then wines are matured in a finely-judged proportion of new oak, for a length of time which again is adapted to the vintage: 50-100% new oak for 14-18 months in the case of Grands Crus.

Up until 1989 there was little domaine bottling, and Leroy and other *négociants* came and removed the wines in barrel. Nowadays, however, they still have the first option on young vines and less *recherché* plots, but all that is in the least in demand is bottled on the estate.

Charmes-Chambertin Like his other Grands Crus, and indeed his whole range, Dugat's Charmes-Chambertin has to be tasted to be believed. Beautifully deep in colour, its noble, rich aroma can take the taster aback, such is its purity and definition, and on the palate the impression is just as posi-tive! It is perfectly balanced, and so ripe is the tannin which contributes its significant structure that one is easily tempted to drink it young. Resist, and let it grow old and wise! Then, when the moment is right, bring it up from the cellar, for an uninterrupted exchange with some perkily eloquent quails, stuffed and seasoned with blackcurrants.

• Other red wines:
Grand cru:
Chambertin, Mazis-Chambertin.
Premier cru:
Gevrey-Chambertin Fonteny, GC Lavaux Saint-Jacques.
Village:
Gevrey-Chambertin Vieilles Vignes,
GC Cœur de Roy,
GC Les Évocelles.
Régional:
Bourgogne
• Owners: Jocelyne & Bernard Dugat-Py
• Wine-makers: Jocelyne & Bernard Dugat-Py
• Combined vineyards: 5.6 hectares
• Production: 25,000 bottles
• Exports: 80%
• Take-away sales: No
• Visits: No

Wine selected:
Charmes-Chambertin

• Classification: Grand Cru
• Area cultivated: 0.5 hectares
• Soil type: Clay and limestone
• Average vine age: 20 years
• Average annual production: 1,500 bottles

1996

CHARMES-CHAMBERTIN

Grand Cru

APPELLATION CHARMES-CHAMBERTIN CONTROLÉE

Bernard DUGAT-PY

Propriétaire - Viticulteur à

GEVREY - CHAMBERTIN
FRANCE

Mis en bouteille à la Propriété

Alc. 14% vol.   750 ml

I n 1985 the news spread like wildfire around the Côte d'Or: a sizeable part of the large and much-admired Clair-Daü estate, which had been in the throes of family strife and quarrel for a number of years, had been sold to Maison Louis Jadot, signalling the effective break up of the estate. At the time this seemed tragic, yet the demise of Clair-Daü gave rise to the foundation of Domaine Bruno Clair, which has proved itself a top-class domaine and worthy successor.

The rise of two great estates All started in 1919, when Joseph Clair married Marguerite Daü. Marguerite and her sister had inherited 8 hectares of vines in Marsannay, which Joseph started looking after, and that same year he came up with a brilliant invention, a rosé wine made with Pinot Noir, which subsequently brought great prosperity to the village.

Over the decades Clair invested in land and built up a fine domaine, and was joined by his son Bernard in 1939. During the 1960s and 1970s Clair-Daü enjoyed its finest hour, a worthy standard-bearer for a region which was producing at the time many substandard wines. After the break up Bruno Clair, Bernard's son, started making wines on his own account. He took on Philippe Brun as wine-making associate, and the pairing has proved inspired.

Elegant wines from a talented team Clair's viticultural methods are basically organic, with much attention paid to the state of the soils. However above all there is flexibility, and his intimate knowledge of his various parcels enables the growth of fine fruit, and harvesting at exactly the right moment.

When the grapes arrive at Marsannay they may or may not be destalked, all depends on the condition of the wood, and there is a short cold maceration before the onset of fermentation. A prolonged vatting period is preferred, for maximum extraction of structure, colour and aroma. Temperatures are allowed to climb up to 32°, and there are regular *pigeages*. Press-wine is incorporated into the free-run wine, and the wines are then matured, the Village appellations in oak *foudres* as well as barrel, and the more prestigious wines exclusively in barrel, some third of which are renewed each year. Then they are bottled, which may or may not be preceded by fining and filtration – as usual, there are no fixed rules, each year requires new decisions.

Chambertin Clos de Bèze The estate farms one whole hectare of the magnificent Clos de Bèze, the doyen of Burgundy's *clos*, which has existed as such since 640, when the Duke of Burgundy donated it to the Abbey of Bèze. Neighbour of Le Chambertin and ranked on at least an equal footing, in Bruno Clair's hands this wine is a masterpiece of richness, power and breeding, with a magnificently opulent and seductive character; it has the impressive structure which one would expect, but also great finesse, one of the hallmarks of Clair wines. It needs a decade to mature, after which it accompanies a savoury braised partridge perfectly.

Côte de Nuits | Marsannay

- Other red wines:
Premier cru:
Gevrey-Chambertin
Les Cazetiers, GC Clos
du Fonteny (monopole),
GC Clos Saint-Jacques,
GC La Petite Chapelle;
Savigny-lès-Beaune
La Dominode.
Village:
Marsannay Les
Vaudenelles,
M Les Longeroies,
M Les Grasses Têtes;
Gevrey-Chambertin,
Chambolle-Musigny
Les Veroilles, Morey-
Saint-Denis En la Rue de
Vergy, Vosne-Romanée
Les Champs Perdrix,
Aloxe-Corton.
Régional:
Bourgogne
- White wines:
Grand cru:
Corton-Charlemagne.
Village: Marsannay,
Morey-Saint-Denis
En la Rue de Vergy.
Régional:
Bourgogne, Bourgogne
Aligoté
- Rosé wine:
Village:
Marsannay
- Owner: Bruno Clair
- Wine-maker:
Bruno Clair
- Oenologist: Philippe
Brun
- Combined vineyards:
21 hectares
- Production:
100,000 bottles
- Exports: 60%
- Take-away sales: Yes
- Visits: 9-12 a.m., 2-6
p.m., by appointment

Wine selected:
**Chambertin
Clos de Bèze**

- Classification:
Grand Cru
- Area cultivated:
0.98 hectares
- Soil type:
Clay and limestone
- Average vine age:
80 years
- Average annual
production:
3,500 bottles

At the southern end of the Morey-Saint-Denis vineyards lies the walled Clos de Tart, one of Burgundy's oldest. This vineyard is a *monopole*, having never during its long history been split up. Over the last half-century the wine has not enjoyed unanimous critical approval, for regularity has not been one of its greater qualities, yet since the 1980s progress has been evident, and the most recent vintages, the work of a new manager who has reviewed viticultural and vinification practices, are sumptuous.

The wine of the Cistercian nuns The origins of the vineyard go back to the early 12th century, when it was known as Climat de la Forge. In 1141 the *climat* was sold by the friars of Maison-Dieu de Brochon to the newly-founded Cistercian convent Notre Dame de Tart, a dependency of Cîteaux Abbey. The *clos* remained in the hands of the church until the Revolution, when it was sold to Nicolas-Joseph Marey, whose family subsequently remained owners throughout the 19th century until selling it to the Mommessin family, owners of the large Mâcon *négociant* firm, in 1932. It is still in the Mommessins' hands today.

Old vines and low yields Over the years the Clos de Tart has been run for its owners by a succession of managers, notably Henri Perraud, who took retirement in 1996 after 27 years of loyal service. Perraud has been succeeded by wine-maker and author Sylvain Pitiot, who has drawn up a programme of ameliorations destined to make the wine live more fully up to its Grand Cru standing.

The vineyard is now managed by *lutte raisonnée*, and the use of treatments eschewed whenever possible. Yields are kept down to around 30 hl/ha. One of the vineyard's particularities is that it is planted in rows which are horizontal to the slope. This serves the dual purpose of increasing exposure to the sun's rays and preventing the erosion of the calcareous clay soil as a result of downpours. The *clos* contains some very elderly vines, and gradual replanting is carried out, by *sélection massale*, taking cuttings of the most robust vines.

Once the fruit is in, it is sorted through closely, then destemmed entirely before undergoing a long pre-fermentation maceration for extraction of colour, tannin, aromas and acidity. When the fermentation is well under way the liquid is transferred into barrel to finish the process, and there it undergoes its malo-lactic fermentation. The wine is matured for 18-24 months entirely in new oak, and is bottled with no filtration.

Clos de Tart Silkiness, elegance and refinement have always been the Clos de Tart's qualities, but the wine has often lacked the element of richness which is a prerequisite in a Grand Cru. Pitiot is aiming for more concentration, for a cross between Chambertin and Musigny – which is as it should be, given the vineyard's position. Morello cherries, raspberries, sometimes violets, then with time spice, liquorice, undergrowth... such is the flavour of Clos de Tart. The latest vintages are beautifully crafted and intensely flavoured, and call out for good red meat: a shoulder of lamb with morels, served with a mushroom *feuilleté*, provides a fine partner for this noble wine.

- Other red wine:
Premier cru:
Morey-Saint-Denis
La Forge
- Owner: Mommessin family
- Manager: Sylvain Pitiot
- Wine-maker:
Sylvain Pitiot
- Combined vineyards:
7.53 hectares
- Production:
27,000 bottles
- Exports: 60%
- Take-away sales: Yes
- Visits: By appointment

Wine selected:
Clos de Tart
(monopole)

- Classification:
Grand Cru
- Vineyard size:
7.53 hectares
- Soil type:
Calcareous clay, marl
- Average vine age:
50 years
- Average annual production:
25,000 bottles

1995

Produce of France

Clos de Tart

GRAND CRU
APPELLATION CONTRÔLÉE

MOMMESSIN
Seul Propriétaire
MOREY ST-DENIS (CÔTE D'OR) FRANCE

Mise du Domaine

S ilk and lace are two epithets frequently used to describe the wines of Chambolle's greatest vineyard, Le Musigny, and few of its incarnations demonstrate these qualities as well as that of the Domaine Comte Georges de Vogüé. This historic estate is a byword for top-quality Chambolle-Musigny.

From the Musignys to the Vogüés Nineteen generations separate the first known owner of what was to become the de Vogüé estate and his descendant, the current owner! The granddaughter of Jean Moisson, a benefactor of Chambolle who endowed the village with its church, married a Dijon merchant by the name of Millières in 1528, and took as dowry some vines, among which was a plot which bore the name of its 14th-century owners, the Musigny family. After a half-century the vineyards passed by marriage into the Bouhier family, of which successive generations farmed them for two centuries until 1766, when the last descendant, Catherine Bouhier, married Cerice François Melchior de Vogüé. From 1925 until his death in 1987 Comte Georges de Vogüé ran the estate, and since then his daughter, Baronne Bertrand de Ladoucette, has shouldered responsibilities.

A change of team For most of the 20th century the domaine has had a manager. The Roumier family held the post over three generations, until the retirement of Alain Roumier in 1986, following which the Baronne appointed a new team, with François Millet as wine-maker. Alain Roumier and Comte Georges de Vogüé between them made numerous fine vintages, such as the 1959, 1969 and 1972, yet after the latter vintage the wine became lighter and less distinguished over the ensuing years.

No one has conclusively put their finger on reasons for the perceived decline, but increased filtration to satisfy the American market is suggested by some. Millet, a consultant oenologist with wide experience up and down the Côte, felt his way into the job, and the return to form was seen from the 1988 vintage onwards, since when not a single wine has been less than remarkable. His basic philosophy, inhabitual for a trained oenologist, is to take every year as it comes, and to meet every situation with a suitable solution; he is against hard-and-fast rules in wine-making.

Musigny Vieilles Vignes The sublime quality of Millet's work is no doubt principally the result of strict control of yields, achieved by debudding in the spring and a 'green harvest' if necessary, as well as the old age of the vines and minimal interference in the vinification process.

The Musigny Vieilles Vignes has a deceptively light colour, which would certainly be deemed anaemic in many other regions, yet there is nothing weak about its flavour: on the nose magnificently fragrant, it has great intensity, great class and exquisite balance, and an airy personality which is not in the least fleeting! Great vintages improve over two decades or more, and give a tasting experience one does not forget in a hurry. Musigny is a superb wine to sip on its own, and gives endless thrills as one wallows in its enthralling aromas, but is also a perfect match for delicately flavoured meats such as poultry or veal served with morels.

- Other red wines:
Grand cru:
Bonnes-Mares.
Premier cru:
Chambolle-Musigny
Les Amoureuses.
Village:
Chambolle-Musigny
- White wine:
Grand cru:
Musigny Blanc
- Owner: Baronne Bertrand de Ladoucette
- Commercial Manager: Jean-Luc Pépin
- Wine-maker: François Millet
- Vineyard Manager: Eric Bourgogne
- Combined vineyards: 12.5 hectares
- Production: 40,000 bottles
- Exports: 80%
- Take-away sales: No
- Visits: 9-12 a.m., 2-5 p.m

Wine selected:
**Musigny
Vieilles Vignes**

- Classification: Grand Cru
- Area cultivated: 7.2 hectares
- Soil type: Clay and limestone
- Average vine age: 35 years
- Average annual production: 10,000 bottles

MUSIGNY

GRAND CRU
APPELLATION MUSIGNY CONTROLÉE
CUVÉE VIEILLES VIGNES

Domaine Comte Georges de VOGÜÉ
CHAMBOLLE - MUSIGNY (CÔTE-D'OR)

Georges de Vogüé

Réserve numérotée

1994

1% vol.   750 ml   PRODUCE OF FRANCE

Mis en bouteilles
au domaine
par SD Comte Georges de Vog...
Chambolle-Musigny - Fra...

A large, unremarkable house in one of the roads leading down from Vosne's *mairie* to the RN74 is the source of a range of wines which are anything but unremarkable. This is where Jack Confuron, one of the village's most conscientious wine-makers, lives and works with his wife and two sons. His wines are slowly and carefully made, and require many years to become fully ready to drink. When they are, each one is invariably among the finest of its appellation.

Evaluation of new ideas and old traditions The Confuron-Cotétidots have lived in Vosne and made wine since the mid-19th century, passing down expertise from generation to generation and building up family traditions. Jack, the late Jean-Jacques Confuron's nephew, is very much one for carefully evaluating the pros and cons of any new idea or long-established tradition, and is not afraid to change if convinced that that is the right thing to do.

One radical and courageous decision was to call in the consultant agronomist and oenologist Guy Accad. Confuron was one of the first on the Côte to do so, taking Accad's advice from 1977 to 1990, and this relationship was of great benefit to his vineyards and wines. Certain Accad recommendations are now thoroughly integrated into the domaine's ways, others have been modified somewhat, but one may be sure that integrated, modified or even discarded, much thought went into the matter before the final decision was taken.

Made by hand by a family team Having planted clones and been unsatisfied, Confuron is utterly opposed to them, and is one of the very few growers to select his own plants and do his own grafting. His vineyards contain a very large proportion of old vines, and are run ecologically, with many steps taken to reduce yields and achieve the greatest fruit quality possible.

Confuron would never be seen harvesting grapes that were not perfectly ripe, whatever risk the wait might entail. In the vatroom he does not destem them but vats whole bunches. They are cooled and sulphured, although far less than was advised by Accad, and spend several days of cold maceration before the start of fermentation. Fermentation temperatures are not allowed to rise above 28°, and in order to attain the required extraction, three *pigeages* per day are carried out. These are serious affairs, involving Confuron and his two sons getting in up to the neck to tread, a thoroughly dangerous pastime given all the ambient CO2.

Little new oak is used for *élevage*, for the wealth of stalks contributes the necessary tannin, and the wines are aged for longer than is usual, generally around 2 years. When they are ready they are bottled by hand, with neither fining nor filtration.

Clos de Vougeot For maximum extraction the Confurons vatted their Clos de Vougeot 1996 for 35 days, and the result is a monument of a wine, dense, powerful and with a thick layer of rich, ripe black fruit held in a rigid tannic girdle. This is one of the very best of the numerous Clos Vougeots made every year and one of the fullest-bodied, and will need a good dozen years to soften and reveal the true extent of its complex aromatic palette. Whatever the quality of the vintage, this wine makes a good companion for a haunch of venison.

- Other red wines:
Grand cru:
Charmes-Chambertin,
Mazis-Chambertin,
Échézeaux.
Premier cru:
Gevrey-Chambertin
Lavaux Saint-Jacques,
GC Petite Chapelle,
GC Craipillot; Vosne-
Romanée Les Suchots;
Nuits-Saint-Georges
Premier Cru.
Village:
Gevrey-Chambertin,
Vosne-Romanée,
Chambolle-Musigny,
Nuits-Saint-Georges.
Régional:
Bourgogne
Passetoutgrain,
Bourgogne
- Owner: Confuron-
Cotétidot family
- Wine-makers: Jack,
Jean-Pierre & Yves
Confuron
- Combined vineyards:
11 hectares
- Production:
40,000 bottles
- Exports: 60%
- Take-away sales: Yes
- Visits: By appointment

Wine selected:
Clos de Vougeot

- Classification:
Grand Cru
- Area cultivated:
0.3 hectares
- Soil type:
Clay and limestone
- Average vine age:
60 years
- Average annual
production:
700 bottles

1996

Clos de Vougeot

Grand Cru

APPELLATION CLOS DE VOUGEOT CONTROLEÉ

13% vol.
750 ml

MIS EN BOUTEILLE AU DOMAINE

J. CONFURON-COTETIDOT

PROPRIÉTAIRE A VOSNE-ROMANÉE (COTE-D'OR) FRANCE

LCV 95

D aniel Rion moved to Prémeaux from Vosne, where his family had lived for generations, after his marriage to a local girl, and created his own estate in 1955 with 2 hectares of Vosne land left to him by his father's father. The estate is now in the hands of his three sons, and thanks to ever-improving standards in recent years, it may be counted on for very high-quality wines.

Bottling and the development of export markets Until 1973 the estate's entire production was sold in bulk to the *négociants*, however Rion gradually started bottling it, and spurred on by the economic crises of the 1970s he started making great efforts to find export customers. That same year he got under way the construction of a large winery, and was joined by his two elder sons in the business. Patrice, the eldest, who had gained his oenology diploma at Beaune, started making the wine. By 1980 the construction was finished, the first crates were leaving for foreign destinations and Daniel's third son had come to join his brothers in the firm.

Wines of balance, fruit and colour As the years have gone by the three brothers have reflected a great deal and refined their techniques. Their aim is to grow fruit of such quality that the subsequent wine-making will require as little manipulation as possible. In the vineyard the vines are trained some 30 cms higher than the norm, for this leads to a greater degree of photosynthesis and thus in the end greater ripeness and health. Yields are kept under control by debudding in the spring, and at harvest-time grapes are sorted through both in the vineyard and on a sorting table in the reception area. The bunches are all destalked, for what the brothers aim for is balance, fruitiness and colour in their wines, rather than structure.

Vinification, which takes place in stainless steel vats, preferred for their hygiene and ease of temperature control, starts with 6-7 days of maceration at around 12°, before 10-12 days of fermentation at 32°. Press-wine may be added, depending on the quality of the vintage, and wines are then matured in oak. For village and superior wines, half of the barrels are renewed every year, the other half having served once, and the maturing wines are given *dodinage*, the red-wine equivalent of *bâtonnage*, 3-5 times before the malo-lactic fermentations, to increase their richness and stimulate better harmony between oak and wine. Racking is carried out as late as possible, for the lees nourish the wine, and the wines are eventually bottled without fining but with filtration if it is deemed necessary.

Nuits-Saint-Georges Clos des Argillières Lying next to the Clos de l'Arlot, the Clos des Argillières has little of the solidity of the Nuits wines of the Prémeaux sector, displaying instead great finesse and elegance, attributable to its particular pink limestone. When young it is redolent of black fruit flavours, blackberry in particular, and is well-nigh irresistible, yet it becomes progressively more complex over the years. After a dozen years it makes a fine table mate for simple grilled red meats, followed by Epoisses, Livarot and Pont-l'Evêque cheese.

• Other red wines:
Grand cru:
Clos Vougeot.
Premier cru:
Nuits-Saint-Georges
Les Hauts Pruliers,
NSG Les Vignes Rondes,
NSG Les Terres Blanches;
Vosne-Romanée
Les Chaumes,
VR Les Beaux-Monts;
Chambolle-Musigny
Les Charmes.
Village:
Nuits-Saint-Georges
Les Grandes Vignes,
NSG Les Lavières,
NSG Vieilles Vignes,
Vosne-Romanée,
Chambolle-Musigny.
Régional:
Côte de Nuits Villages,
Bourgogne Pinot Noir,
Bourgogne
Passetoutgrain
• White wines:
Premier cru:
NSG Les Terres Blanches.
Régional:
Hautes Côtes de Nuits,
Bourgogne Chardonnay,
Bourgogne Aligoté
• Owner: Rion family
• Wine-maker:
Patrice Rion
• Combined vineyards:
18 hectares
• Production:
95,000 bottles
• Exports: 80%
• Take-away sales:
By appointment
• Visits: By appointment

Wine selected:
**Nuits-Saint-Georges
Clos des Argillières**

• Classification:
Premier Cru
• Area cultivated:
0.72 hectares
• Soil type:
Clay and limestone
• Average vine age:
45 years
• Average annual
production:
3,500 bottles

NUITS-ST-GEORGES

Clos des Argillières

PREMIER CRU

1996

Domaine Daniel Rion & Fils

T horoughness, commitment and passion are among the forces at work in the Denis Mortet vineyards and cellar, giving birth to a supremely exciting range of wines centred around Gevrey-Chambertin. Were there a hundred and one tasks to see to, this restless perfectionist would see to them all, for the second-rate and the average are abhorred... His wines eloquently bear testimony to that!

A new source of Burgundy The name Denis Mortet has not yet graced many labels and vintages, yet the progress and the quality of what has been made to date have attracted the excited attention and plaudits of the world's specialized press. Domaine Denis Mortet has existed since his father Charles took retirement in 1991 and split his estate between his two sons. Since its début vintage in 1992 this small estate has grown larger with the arrival of various plots of land on leasing or sharecropping arrangements, and now covers 10 hectares, although unfortunately the production does not meet the strong demand.

Handmade for greater quality To make good wine, Mortet is convinced, as many of the numerous vineyard and vat-room jobs as possible must be carried out by hand. He is fortunate in that his average vine age is high, and by hoeing the vineyards the vines are obliged to bury their roots deeper, giving better juice; chemicals are never used. Yields are kept ruthlessly down by pruning short and debudding, and it therefore usually follows that the grapes become perfectly ripe without any undue waiting, and are harvested with impressive degrees of potential alcohol. As a result there is little need for chaptalisation, giving even greater aromatic purity.

At harvest-time the picked fruit is sorted through twice, once by the harvesters and then on a conveyor belt in the winery, for great wine does not tolerate the imperfect grape. The fruit is always destalked, and receives a 4-5 day cold maceration before fermentation takes place. This is a longish affair, conducted by the fruit's own yeast, with 3 or 4 *pigeages* per day at its height. Once it is over the necessary press wine is added and a long period of *élevage* commences, in a mixture of different oaks – Vosges wood is preferred for the Grands and Premiers Crus, but having a dozen red wines must make cask management something of a problem! Since 1988 the wines have been bottled unfiltered.

Every wine in the range has its characteristics and personality, and it is interesting to note that these are evident from the most recent vintage in barrel through to bottled vintages of different ages, which unfortunately is not the case at all Burgundian domaines!

Gevrey-Chambertin Lavaux-Saint-Jacques One of Mortet's most recent acquisitions is a superb 1.2-hectare plot of Lavaux Saint-Jacques, populated with vines of up to 70 years of age. This wine is a masterpiece of understated elegance and finesse, with beautifully defined aromas, concentration and perfect balance. Firmness and breeding characterize it, rather than the robustness and power of some of its colleagues, and as such it makes a perfect dining partner for a rack of lamb, or indeed pigeons, cooked *en cocotte à la bonne femme*.

- Other red wines:
Grand cru:
Chambertin,
Clos Vougeot.
Premier cru:
Gevrey-Chambertin
Les Champeaux;
Chambolle-Musigny
Aux Beaux-Bruns.
Village:
Gevrey-Chambertin
En Champs, GC Au Vellé,
GC En Motrot
(monopole), Gevrey-
Chambertin; Marsannay
Les Longeroies.
Régional:
Bourgogne Rouge,
Bourgogne
Passetoutgrain
- White wines:
Régional:
Bourgogne Chardonnay,
Bourgogne Aligoté
- Owner: Mortet family
- Wine-maker:
Denis Mortet
- Combined vineyards:
10.5 hectares
- Production:
55,000 bottles
- Exports: 75%
- Take-away sales: No
- Visits: No

Wine selected:
**Gevrey-Chambertin
Lavaux Saint-Jacques**

- Classification:
Premier Cru
- Area cultivated:
1.2 hectares
- Soil type:
Clay and limestone
- Average vine age:
20-70 years
- Average annual
production:
5,600 bottles

1996

MIS EN BOUTEILLE
À LA PROPRIÉTÉ

PRODUCE OF FRANCE

Gevrey-Chambertin
1er Cru - Lavaux St-Jacques
APPELLATION GEVREY-CHAMBERTIN 1er CRU CONTRÔLÉE

Mis en bouteille par

DOMAINE DENIS MORTET
PROPRIÉTAIRE-VITICULTEUR À GEVREY-CHAMBERTIN (CÔTE-D'OR) FRANCE

Alc 13% by vol

750 ml

A mere three decades have passed since the creation of Domaine Dujac, yet its reputation has been established and international for almost as long, such is the wine-making talent of its founder and owner Jacques Seysses. Dujac wines are among Burgundy's most aromatic, pure and elegant.

A young man finds his vocation His family did not come from a wine-making environment, yet Jacques' father Louis Seysses was a dedicated Epicurean, and at his table his son learnt from a young age what great wine and food were all about, tasting many a classic inter-war vintage from top châteaux and domaines. In 1966 and the following year Jacques worked in Volnay at Domaine Pousse d'Or during the harvest, and decided that wine-making was the path he wished to follow. A year later Domaine Marcel Graillet in Morey came onto the market, and this was just what he was looking for.

Seysses quickly managed to place his wines in a number of top French restaurants, found an American agent and received a flattering review in Gault & Millau, which triggered the arrival of a large French clientèle. He and his American wife felt optimistic about the future, and settled in Morey for good.

Study and experimentation in the vineyard From the start he regarded raw material as of primary importance, and got down to much study and experimentation. Clones were introduced in 1978 and the estate now has a wide variety of them. In 1987 Seysses took on Christophe Morin as vineyard manager, since which time the estate has even finer fruit to work with. Morin uses all four permitted methods of pruning and training, adapting the choice to the age of the vine. There is short pruning to 6 buds per plant, followed by debudding and green-harvesting if necessary. The vineyards themselves are cultivated by *lutte raisonnée*, in order to promote as great a health of vine and soil as possible while maintaining the possibility of adequate protection in case of sudden climatic or insect problem.

In his wine-making Seysses is inspired principally by the way things were done in days gone by, and reserves modern oenological knowledge for problematic situations; his broad outlook is to leave the wine alone while keeping a close eye on its development. There is no destalking, for longer fermentation and thus better extraction, and little temperature control during fermentation. Seysses appreciates the oxygenation afforded by oak barrels, and his Grands and Premiers Crus are matured exclusively in new wood. The wood itself, from the Allier, is dried naturally by air on the estate for 2 years, and given a light toast. Wines are occasionally fined but never filtered.

Clos de la Roche The wine for which Domaine Dujac is best known is probably its Clos de la Roche, for reasons of size as well as quality. This is as exquisite a bottle of Burgundy as one could wish for, combining structure and firmness with the Dujac purity, elegance and black fruit fragrance; a wine which takes 10 years to open up and will last another 10 or more in a good vintage. This wine, Rosalind Seysses advises, makes a delicious accompaniment to chicken with morels, truffle-based dishes, and just about any red meat.

• Other red wines:
Grand cru:
Clos Saint-Denis, Échézeaux, Bonnes-Mares, Charmes-Chambertin.
Premier cru:
Morey-Saint-Denis Premier Cru; Chambolle-Musigny Premier Cru; Gevrey-Chambertin Aux Combottes; Vosne-Romanée Les Beaumonts.
Village:
Morey-Saint-Denis, Chambolle-Musigny
• White wine:
Village:
Morey-Saint-Denis
• Owner: Jacques & Rosalind Seysses
• Wine-maker: Jacques Seysses
• Cellar-master: Christophe Morin
• Vineyard manager: Christophe Morin
• Combined vineyards: 12.5 hectares
• Production: 60,000 bottles
• Exports: 90%
• Take-away sales: No
• Visits: By appointment

Wine selected:
Clos de la Roche

• Classification: Grand Cru
• Area cultivated: 1.95 hectares
• Soil type: Clay and limestone
• Average vine age: 20 years
• Average annual production: 6,000 bottles

CLOS DE LA ROCHE

GRAND CRU

APPELLATION CLOS DE LA ROCHE CONTROLÉE

1995

DOMAINE DUJAC

PROPRIÉTAIRE A MOREY - ST. DENIS - FRANCE
PRODUCE OF FRANCE

The somewhat taciturn Emmanuel Rouget was educated in wine-making by the greatest of teachers, his uncle, the great Henri Jayer. As Jayer approached retirement age his nephew started looking after his vines on a sharecropping basis, and this arrangement has continued since Jayer's retirement in 1995. Rouget also has some vines of his own and others which he rents. The young man has learnt well, and his wines show consummate craftsmanship.

Guidelines for quality   Henri Jayer's philosophy, adopted and practised by his nephew, is disarmingly simple: fruit should be grown naturally, harvested neither too early nor too late, and then turned into wine in as traditional a way as possible, without trying to hurry the process. Naturally, behind these generalizations there are a host of little details which all have their importance. Yields should be kept rigorously low, for dilution becomes glaringly obvious in Pinot Noirs harvested at over 40 hl/ha; if the fruit quality is lacking before it is transformed into wine, no amount of compensatory measures will give the wine the quality it lacks. Vine age is of great importance, for old vines are less productive, and the quality of their grapes is therefore better.

Unhurried fermentation and luxury maturation   There are some trades in which one never retires, as many senior *vignerons* will testify, and Jayer is always on hand after harvest time. Rouget's vinifications are carried out either in Jayer's vatroom in Vosne or in his own in Flagey; which wine is made where depends on the origin of the fruit, for they seek to avoid too much transportation.

After totally destalking the fruit Rouget gives it a 5-7 day cold maceration, essential for extracting the finest aromas and colours. Fermentation is delayed by cooling to 15°, then when the time is right the must as allowed to warm, and the grapes' indigenous yeast start the fermentation. The total vatting time is some 15-20 days. When the cap of solids has stopped floating on top of the liquid, indicating the absence of the carbon dioxide and the ending of fermentation, wines are blended with press-wine and then transferred to barrel for maturation. Rouget uses nothing but new oak for his top wines, which are so rich and structured that they can digest it without it dominating. Finally, after some 18 months the wines are given a light fining and bottled without filtration.

Vosne-Romanée Cros Parantoux   The Premier Cru Cros Parantoux, lying above Les Richebourgs, is little seen, for it covers just 1.1 hectares and has two owners, Méo-Camuzet and Henri Jayer, the latter's 77 ares being sharecropped by Emmanuel Rouget. The soil is virtually nonexistent and the old vines struggle to force their roots down through the rock for nutrients, which may sound cruel but is the recipe for glorious wine! Velvet, opulent refinement, concentrated and explosive, blackberry and spice with toasted wood aromas in its youth, this wine is a match for many a prestigious Grand Cru. The lucky wine-lover who tracks down a bottle could serve it with *entrecôtes charolaises*, which it matches very well.

• Other red wines:
Grand cru:
Échézeaux.
Premier cru:
Vosne-Romanée
Les Beaumonts.
Village:
Vosne-Romanée,
Nuits-Saint-Georges,
Savigny-lès-Beaune.
Régional:
Bourgogne Rouge,
Bourgogne
Passetoutgrain
• Owner: Emmanuel Rouget
• Wine-maker: Emmanuel Rouget
• Combined vineyards: 7 hectares
• Production: 17,000 bottles
• Exports: 80%
• Take-away sales: No
• Visits: No

Wine selected:
Vosne-Romanée Cros Parantoux

• Classification: Premier Cru
• Area cultivated: 0.77 hectares
• Soil type: Clay and limestone
• Average vine age: 50 years
• Average annual production: 3,000 bottles

DOMAINE FAIVELEY

I ts 124 hectares of vineyard on the Côte d'Or and the Côte Chalonnaise make Faiveley one of the largest estates in Burgundy, yet its size in no way compromises the quality of the firm's output, which is invariably among the Côte d'Or's very best. The name Faiveley is a guarantee for authentic, well-made Burgundy with great potential for development over time.

Six generations build up the estate Founded in 1825, the firm is today run by the youthful and cultivated François Faiveley, the sixth generation of the family to do so. Successive generations had the enlightened idea of reinvesting in real estate when times were good, creating an edifice admired (and envied, no doubt) throughout Burgundy, and François Faiveley has continued that policy. However growth is not one of his preoccupations, indeed he would rather limit the firm's expansion in order to remain in total control of its quality processes.

The magnificent patrimony accumulated by his forebears is centred around Nuits-Saint-Georges and Gevrey-Chambertin and comprises a great number of Grands and Premiers Crus, and extends to a fine Mercurey estate built up by his father; however Faiveley has little 'ordinary' land for sourcing his generic wines, and buys some 20% of his raw material every year to bridge this gap. The domaine's wines are predominantly red, yet it does possess a small plot of Corton-Charlemagne, with which he makes a yardstick example, and its range is widened with Chablis and the classic Côte d'Or whites made from purchased grapes.

The soft and sensual aroma of Pinot Faiveley places great store on the aromatic qualities of his wines, and this colours his wine-making technique: high quality grapes from low yields, picked at perfect ripeness, and vinified gently, slowly and insistently, in order to extract all their aromatic qualities and finesse – that is what is needed.

Although different growths are naturally treated differently, the operative methods of Faiveley wine-making generally follow the following pattern: picking over the grapes, drying if necessary in a wind tunnel and total destalking; pressing with a pneumatic press, cold maceration for several days with treading and then a long, unhurried fermentation with indigenous yeast at a relatively low 26°; transfer into barrels (50-60% new for Grands Crus, 33% for Premiers Crus) for 16-18 month's maturation, with racking by gravity when necessary; and then equalization (again if necessary), fining with egg white and bottling – by hand, directly from the barrel, in the case of all the best wines.

Corton Clos des Cortons Faiveley An enclave lying in the Le Rognet et Corton vineyard in the commune of Ladoix is the source of a particularly distinguished wine. The Corton Clos des Cortons Faiveley is always deep-coloured, rich and tasty, fleshy and concentrated, with fruity blackberry opulence in its youth, and more complex aromas of leather, liquorice and spice as it matures, with, whatever its age, perfect balance and great length. This wonderful Burgundy deserves the company of noble game – a haunch of venison will do nicely!

• Other red wines:
Grand cru:
Chambertin Clos de Bèze, Mazis-Chambertin, Latricières-Chambertin, Musigny, Clos de Vougeot, Échézeaux.
Premier cru:
Gevrey-Chambertin La Combe aux Moines, GC Les Cazetiers, GC Champonnet, GC Craipillot, GC Les Issarts; Chambolle-Musigny La Combe d'Orveau, CM Les Fuées; Nuits-Saint-Georges Clos de la Maréchale (monopole), NSG Les Saint-Georges, NSG Les Porêts-Saint-Georges, NSG Aux Chaignots, NSG Les Vignerondes, NSG Les Damodes.
Also Village and Regional wines.
• White wines:
Grand cru:
Corton-Charlemagne.
Premier cru:
Meursault Poruzots; Chassagne-Montrachet Caillerets; Chablis Vaillons.
Also Village and Regional wines.
• Owner: François Faiveley
• Wine-maker: Régis Surrel
• Combined vineyards: 124 hectares
• Production: 800,000 bottles
• Exports: 55%
• Take-away sales: No
• Visits: No

Wine selected:
Corton Clos des Cortons Faiveley
(monopole)

• Classification: Grand Cru
• Vineyard size: 2.97 hectares
• Soil type: Brown calcareous clay
• Average vine age: 36 years
• Average annual production: 13,000 bottles

T here is unfortunately far too little of Régis Forey's wines to satisfy demand, for the lucky clients who discovered this talented young man when he started out at the beginning of the 1990s have remained steadfastly loyal, rarely foregoing their yearly allocation. Tasting his range and listening to him quietly explaining how he goes about his work one quite understands their loyalty - Forey is a consummate craftsman.

Wine-making by different arrangements The Forey family have been wine-makers since 1870, the year great-grandfather François bought some of the Vosne Premiers Crus Les Gaudichots and Les Chalandins. Régis's grandfather was given the privilege of looking after La Romanée - France's smallest AOC at 84.5 ares - and the Premier Cru Aux Reignots for their owners, the Liger-Belair family. Every year the barrels of these wines are collected after their malos by Bouchard Père & Fils for maturation and bottling, and Régis carries on this arrangement, which is due for review around 2005. Besides their Vosne holdings, the family have acquired or look after by *fermage* or *metayage* vineyards at Nuits, Flagey-Echézeaux and Prémeaux.

The family only started bottling as recently as 1983, and this year can be given as the date of foundation of Domaine Forey. After finishing school Forey worked alongside his father, and the 1989 vintage was the first for which he was entirely responsible.

Experimentation to protect soil and vine As with all the more thoughtful growers of his generation, Forey is well aware of the fragility of his land and of the importance of protecting its subsoil, and has operated his vineyard by *lutte raisonnée* since 1993. In 1996 he stopped weeding, and two years later put in operation a programme of 'sexual confusion' in the vineyard – in order to prevent the reproduction of the butterflies which cause *grappe de ver*, capsules which give off the odour of the female were placed in the vineyard in order to trap their male partners. Results of this have been very positive.

Vinifying for flavour and structure In order to give his wines the required richness, colour and structure Forey prefers to destem totally and then give his wines two days' cold maceration followed by a long fermentation, generally some 23-28 days, finishing with a slight temperature increase to fix the colour. When they have settled for 2 days, wines are transferred to barrel, where they spend 18 months in all. New wood is used for ageing the Grand and Premiers Crus, with the exception of the Perrières, and after the malos have finished Forey gives them a monthly *bâtonnage*, and then bottles with neither fining nor filtration.

Vosne-Romanée Les Petits Monts Lying above Richebourg and besides Cros Parantoux, Les Petits Monts is a lesser-known Premier Cru of which Forey is particularly proud. This *climat* gives a wine of great intensity, with elegance and finesse and great breeding, as well as a structure which requires 6-8 years in order to blend seamlessly into the wine. The succulent and deeply-coloured liquid conveys all the majesty of its exceptional site, and adores toying with a saddle of hare, prepared *à la bourguignonne*.

Côte de Nuits | Vosne-Romanée

- Other red wines:
Grand cru:
Échézeaux.
Premier cru:
Vosne-Romanée Les Gaudichots ; Nuits-Saint-Georges Les Perrières, NSG Les Saint-Georges.
Village:
Vosne-Romanée, Nuits-Saint-Georges.
Régional:
Bourgogne Rouge
- White wine:
Régional:
Bourgogne Blanc
- Owner: Régis Forey
- Wine-maker: Régis Forey
- Production:
40,000 bottles
- Exports: 30%
- Take-away sales:
By appointment
- Visits: By appointment

Wine selected:
**Vosne-Romanée
Les Petits Monts**

- Classification:
Premier Cru
- Area cultivated:
0.18 hectares
- Soil type:
Clay and limestone
- Average vine age:
30 years
- Average annual production:
1,000 bottles

1996

PRODUIT DE FRANCE

VOSNE-ROMANÉE

1ᵉʳ CRU - LES PETITS MONTS

Appellation Vosne-Romanée 1ᵉʳ Cru Contrôlée

S.C.E. Domaine Forey Père et Fils

PROPRIÉTAIRE À VOSNE-ROMANÉE (CÔTE-DOR) FRANCE

Mis en bouteille au Domaine

FILIBER A NUITS

It must be quite a feeling owning Grand Cru vineyard land on the Côte de Nuits... but just what must it feel like having an entire Grand Cru to oneself in Burgundy's most hallowed village?! Such is the fortune of the Lamarche family, who give their all every year to prove themselves worthy of their heritage, making wines which express their prestigious origins perfectly.

A fine vineyard accedes to its rightful rank With parts of four Vosne Premiers Crus and three Grands Crus, and their own *monopole* La Grande Rue, François and Marie-Blanche Lamarche have an enviable vineyard patrimony, which can be attributed to the industry and careful purchases of previous generations; the Grande Rue vineyard itself was given to François' father Henri as a wedding present in 1933.

This long, narrow vineyard, which could not be better situated in all of Burgundy, surrounded as it is on three sides by Romanée-Conti, La Tâche and Romanée-Saint-Vivant, has been referred to in enthusiastic terms ever since the first known document to mention it, in 1450. Surprisingly, it has only enjoyed the rank of Grand Cru since the 1991 vintage, the reason being that at the moment of the original classifications in the middle of the 1930s there was little price differential between Premiers and Grands Crus, and Henri Lamarche thought that extra taxes would probably outweigh any benefit in being one of the *crème de la crème*. In those days it was sold as "Romanée Grande Rue".

Wines which show Vosne's true hallmarks François Lamarche aims to produce wines as he likes them, rather than wines that will win international tasting competitions... and it is just too bad if they do not correspond to a trend in certain markets for extreme extraction and 100% new oak! He likes his Vosnes to have that elegance, finesse and class that are the true hallmarks of the village's wines, and tailors his vinifications to achieve that style.

Low yields naturally are at the root of the quality of his wines, and perfect ripeness and stringent selections are the next factors. After all the fruit has been destalked it is given a cold maceration, and the temperature is then allowed to rise and fermentation to start in its own time. The whole process takes place in traditional open wooden vats, and regular *pigeages* are an important feature of the 16-18 days' vatting. The wine is then run into barrel and installed in the cellar, where it will remain for 18-20 months. Finally, after fining with egg white it is bottled without filtration.

La Grande Rue All the breathtaking finesse, refinement and *noblesse* of Vosne's best soils are to be found in a glass of La Grand Rue. Relatively deep in colour, it gives up a superbly intense, fragrant aromatic mix, in which both red and black fruit jostle for front of stage, with pepper and other spices playing a supporting role. It is not a powerful wine, indeed what makes it so distinguished is its perfect mix of refinement, intensity, dimension and completeness. The Lamarches suggest serving La Grande Rue with roast beef or pheasant, followed by Cîteaux, Comté, Roblochon or Epoisses cheeses.

• Other red wines:
Grand cru:
Clos de Vougeot, Grands Échézeaux, Échézeaux.
Premier cru:
Vosne-Romanée Les Suchots,
VR Les Malconsorts,
VR Les Chaumes,
VR La Croix Rameau.
Village:
Vosne-Romanée.
Régional:
Bourgogne Hautes Côtes de Nuits, Bourgogne Rouge, Bourgogne Passetoutgrain
• Owner: G.F.V. Domaine François Lamarche
• Wine-maker: François Lamarche
• Oenologist: Jean-Pierre Bruley
• Combined vineyards: 10 hectares
• Production: 50,000 bottles
• Exports: 80%
• Take-away sales: Yes
• Visits: 8-12 a.m., 2-5 p.m. by appointment

Wine selected:
La Grande Rue
(monopole)

• Classification: Grand Cru
• Vineyard size: 1.65 hectares
• Soil type: Clay and limestone
• Average vine age: 30 years
• Average annual production: 6,300 bottles

1995

La Grande Rue
GRAND CRU MONOPOLE
APPELLATION CONTROLÉE

Domaine François Lamarche
Viticulteur à Vosne Romanée (Côte d'Or) France
PRODUCE OF FRANCE
MIS EN BOUTEILLE A LA PROPRIÉTÉ
750 ML.
LGR95

From their spacious property in the quiet Rue du Chêne on the Morey side of Gevrey, the father-and-son team of André and Frédéric Esmonin go about making absolutely delicious wines from the raw material of some very prestigious vineyards, and in a short period have made a great name for themselves. Their estate is small, and their production sells out extremely quickly... Burgundy-lovers take note, and do not miss the opportunity, should it present itself, of tasting a Frédéric Esmonin wine!

The foundation of a family business The estate is very young, having been founded by André Esmonin in the 1970s. André, as indeed did his brother Michel, whose Domaine Michel Esmonin & Fille has followed a somewhat similar course, learnt his trade alongside his *vigneron* father. He was contracted by the Hospices de Beaune to look after their Mazis-Chambertin, but he also wanted to found his own *exploitation*. Not only did he buy a little land when suitable plots came up for sale, he also leased some and entered into sharecropping agreements, and proceeded to produce very good wines, which he sold in barrel to Louis Jadot and Leroy – a reference if ever one was needed!

The year 1988 was significant in the domaine's development, for it was that year that André's son Frédéric, having studied in Beaune, came to join his father, and that same year that they more or less ceased selling in bulk and started bottling themselves. Frédéric then formed a *négociant* company called Les Estournelles in order to be able to buy in fruit to augment their supplies.

Terroir and high quality fruit Nothing is particularly revolutionary in the Esmonins' methods, and the quality must be put down to two basic elements: prestigious *terroir* and high quality fruit. They are certainly well-equipped for the first, having no less than three Grands Crus and two Premiers, as well as Village land, all in Gevrey-Chambertin. The second involves a host of minute details: vine age, yield restriction, vine health, harvesting at the right moment, and sorting through the fruit; and then vinification to get the most out of the raw material: the Esmonins destalk all their fruit, and ferment it at a high 35°. Maturation takes place in some 50% new oak and lasts from 14-17 months, depending on the quality of the vintage, before bottling without filtration.

Mazy-Chambertin From the very finely situated Mazis (for that is its usual spelling) vineyard, lying just below Ruchottes and alongside Clos de Bèze, the Esmonins fashion an extremely powerful, rich and complex wine, which has sufficient structure to guarantee it a long life. In its youth the better vintages are invariably somewhat muscle-bound, and time alone will work the necessary magic in the bottle to transform them into balanced, refined masterpieces. Then when they are finally mature, jugged hare will provide a fine repartee to their complex spicy, leather, red fruit aromas.

• Other red wines:
Grand cru:
Ruchottes-Chambertin, Griottes-Chambertin.
Premier cru:
Gevrey-Chambertin Estournelles Saint-Jacques, GC Lavaux Saint-Jacques.
Village:
GC Clos Prieur,
GC Les Chapponnets
• Owner: Esmonin family
• Wine-maker: André Esmonin
• Combined vineyards: 7 hectares
• Production: 38,000 bottles
• Exports: 95%
• Take-away sales: No
• Visits: By appointment

Wine selected:
Mazy-Chambertin

• Classification:
Grand Cru
• Area cultivated:
0.3 hectares
• Soil type:
Clay and limestone
• Average vine age:
50 years
• Average annual production:
1,200 bottles

Côte de Nuits | Gevrey-Chambertin

T he late Doctor Georges Mugneret was one of Vosne's most respected wine-makers, the creator of wonders of perfumed refinement which were sought out by Burgundy-lovers far and wide. Before his premature death in 1988 his two daughters trained at his side, and they have maintained the domaine's standards with great flair. The female touch *chez* Mugneret is sure, the wines exquisite.

Awaiting an improvement in Burgundy's fortunes The young Georges Mugneret combined work on his parents' Vosne estate with medical studies, and went on to practise ophthalmology at Dijon, rising to become one of the country's leading specialists. He bought the fine 19th-century house in Vosne at an auction in 1930, and the price paid for this and his first plots of vines reflected the hard times and generally felt pessimism with regard to the future of the region's wine industry. It was the success of his practice which enabled him to keep the unprofitable estate afloat while awaiting an improvement in Burgundy's fortunes.

Today his daughters Marie-Christine, Marie-Andrée and their mother Jacqueline are in fact nominally in charge not of one but of two estates: Domaine Georges Mugneret comprises vineyards bought by the doctor, while Domaine Mugneret-Gibourg was the estate founded in 1928 by his parents André Mugneret and Jeanne Gibourg. The women would like nothing more than to unite these two under one name, yet for absurd fiscal reasons this is apparently proving well-nigh impossible, so the two estates continue to coexist.

Two sisters exact their standards Since 1966 certain of the estate's vineyards have been looked after by *metayers*, and today 3.5 hectares are worked by that arrangement, the crop being shared after the harvest. The rest of the vineyards are looked after by *tâcherons*, who are paid an annual fee to cultivate specific plots. Whatever the arrangement, the Mugneret sisters liaise closely with their vineyard workers to ensure that fruit is of as fine a quality as possible; short pruning and green harvesting are regular features of the estate's viticultural calendar.

In the cellars the sisters, who are both qualified *oenologues*, subject the fruit to a quality check on a sorting table, and then destem it totally before giving it a cold maceration which lasts 2-4 days. Fermentation follows, then the wines are matured in oak for 15 months. A quantity of the oak is renewed every year, generally 20% for village wines and 70-80% for Grands Crus. After maturation their husbands are drafted in to help with the physical job of racking, and the wines are then fined with egg white and bottled.

Ruchottes-Chambertin The Mugnerets are one of the few to make the little seen Ruchottes-Chambertin, from the 3.3-hectare vineyard which lies above Mazis-Chambertin near the village of Gevrey. Their old, low-yielding vines produce a sumptuous wine of concentrated blackcurrant and spice flavours, rich in tannin and alcohol and of great breeding. Its great purity and finesse are witness to the wine-makers' mastery of their art. This noble wine needs a good dozen years to develop its complex bouquet, and, the Mugneret ladies suggest, may be enjoyed with a fillet of beef in a mushroom crust, or stewed rabbit.

Côte de Nuits | Vosne-Romanée

• Other red wines:
Grand cru:
Clos Vougeot.
Premier cru:
Nuits-Saint-Georges
Les Vignes Rondes,
NSG Les Chaignots;
Chambolle-Musigny
Les Feusselottes.
• Domaine Mugneret-Gibourg:
Grand cru:
Échézeaux.
Village:
Vosne-Romanée.
Régional:
Bourgogne
• Owners: Jacqueline, Marie-Christine & Marie-Andrée Mugneret
• Wine-makers: Marie-Christine & Marie-Andrée Mugneret
• Combined vineyards: 8.87 hectares
• Production: 25,000 bottles
• Exports: 50%
• Take-away sales: Yes
• Visits: By appointment; closed Wednesdays

Wine selected:
Ruchottes-Chambertin

• Classification: Grand Cru
• Area cultivated: 0.64 hectares
• Soil type: Clay and limestone
• Average vine age: 45 years
• Average annual production: 2,500 bottles

1995

RUCHOTTES-CHAMBERTIN

Grand Cru

APPELLATION RUCHOTTES-CHAMBERTIN CONTRÔLÉE

Mis en bouteille à la propriété par

DOMAINE GEORGES MUGNERET

VOSNE-ROMANÉE - FRANCE

PRODUIT DE FRANCE

The quiet little village of Chambolle has long been recognized for the quality of the vineyards which crowd round it, yet its wine-makers have not always in recent decades delivered the mesmerizing wines of which their lands are capable. One estate which always has, yet which today is nevertheless managing to surpass its previous high standards, is that founded by Georges Roumier.

Three generations of continued quality At the origin of the estate, as was so often the case, was a marriage. In 1924 Georges Roumier, a lad from near Saulieu, married a local girl, Geneviève Quanquin, and soon found himself running her family's estate, which owned parcels of Les Amoureuses, Les Fuées and Bonnes Mares. Roumier soon enlarged their production by becoming *métayer* of a plot of Musigny. From 1945 he started bottling all the production on the estate, and from the start bottles of Roumier wines gained a fine reputation – "classics of depth and harmony", Hugh Johnson judged them. The 1950s brought considerable further enlargement when he acquired one third of another estate, which included some Clos Vougeot and Bonnes Mares, and subsequently the entire Clos de la Bussière, in the commune of Morey.

It was Jean-Marie, the third of five sons, who eventually took over in 1961 on his father's retirement. In 1968 he gave himself a new challenge by acquiring some Corton-Charlemagne, and 10 years later managed to buy the plot of Musigny which the family had been sharecropping since the 1920s. His own son Christophe studied oenology at Dijon, and started working with him in 1982. This young man is a highly talented wine-maker with an inquiring and open mind, and the new impetus he has brought to the estate has taken it from the very good to the outstanding level.

Translating terroir into wine The essence of his philosophy is that Nature and *terroir* stamp grapes from different *climats* with different characteristics, and that the wine-maker's job is to translate these as faithfully as possible into wine. The fruit itself is merely the vehicle, and wines which are merely fruity can not be considered of great interest. To carry *terroir*'s message, vines must be old, in perfect health – the Roumier vineyards are run by *lutte raisonnée* – and must produce little fruit. After that, vinification methods must be tailored to each different *terroir*; at Domaine Roumier there are no set rules, each year requires deep reflection and suitable action.

Bonnes Mares The Roumier parcel of Bonnes Mares, the estate's flagship (if not its most prestigious) wine is made up of different geological entities, from which Christophe Roumier makes 4 different wines which he later blends together. Essentially there are *terres rouges*, Bathonian clay and limestone which give power, structure and flesh, and *terres blanches*, Bajocian marl giving finesse and complexity. However the whole is greater than the sum of its parts, a fleshy, chewy wine of great richness and breeding. It usually needs a decade to show its true colours, and will live a long adult life thereafter, before being summoned to a feast with marinated game and ripe, odorous Burgundian cheeses.

• Other red wines:
Grand cru:
Musigny, Clos Vougeot.
Premier cru:
Chambolle-Musigny
Les Amoureuses,
CM Les Cras ; Morey-
Saint-Denis Clos de la
Bussière (monopole).
Village:
Chambolle-Musigny.
Régional:
Bourgogne
• White wine:
Grand cru:
Corton-Charlemagne
• Owner: Roumier family
• Wine-maker:
Christophe Roumier
• Combined vineyards:
11.5 hectares
• Production:
45,000 bottles
• Exports: 70%
• Take-away sales: No
• Visits: No

Wine selected:
Bonnes Mares

• Classification:
Grand Cru
• Area cultivated:
1.45 hectares
• Soil type:
Clay and limestone
• Average vine age:
35 years
• Average annual
production:
4,800 bottles

An estate at the bottom end of the village of Chambolle provides proof of enlightened contemporary attitudes in the region, where a woman can run a business and make wines without incurring the chauvinistic male disapproval that she would have felt even as recently as 20 years ago. Ghislaine Barthod produces a fine range of Chambolles, all priced very reasonably, which are well worth discovering.

A young lady follows in her father's footsteps The estate was founded in the 1920s by Marcel Noëllat, who early on started bottling his own wine and selling it directly to his clients. Noëllat had two daughters, one of whom married Gaston Barthod, the other incidentally marrying into another, unrelated, Noëllat family in Vosne. Barthod worked alongside his father-in-law until the latter took retirement in 1977, and, if little-known outside the region, the wines had a very good reputation. His daughter Ghislaine attended the Beaune *lycée viticole* and duly joined her father at the end of her studies, and then took over responsibility for the estate in 1986. However her father and mother still help her out when necessary, in the cellar and the vineyard respectively.

Since that time the estate has been enlarged somewhat as the family have acquired a number of parcels of land, and now owns parts of no fewer than 9 different Chambolle Premiers Crus. Several years after Ghislaine's arrival the family also acquired larger premises in Rue du Lavoir, giving much-needed space for making and storing the increased quantities of wine.

Meticulous attention to detail Ghislaine Barthod's winemaking is run along traditional lines, but with all the meticulous attention to detail that separates the best from the rest. How else would it be possible, as she does, to produce a long list of Premiers Crus which each have detectable nuances? The essence of it all is in the quality of the fruit, which is attained by working the soil by hand, by low yields and by harvesting at exactly the right moment. When it comes to making the wine, some two thirds of the grapes are destalked, and there is brief cold maceration. Fermentation, with *pigeage* to extract colour, aroma and tannin, is allowed to rise to 32°. The wines are then matured for approximately 18 months, in casks of which one quarter are renewed each year.

Chambolle-Musigny Les Charmes It is a long way from being her largest Premier Cru parcel in size, but Les Charmes, lying halfway down the slope towards Vougeot, makes what is arguably the most distinguished Barthod wine. Displaying all the softness, sensuality and finesse that characterize Chambolle's wines, this wine nevertheless manages to provide an extremely concentrated and rich mouthful of flavour, and enough structure to see it through a quarter of a decade or more in the cellar. This wine's succulence makes it a suitable partner for offal dishes, such as veal kidneys with mushrooms, or charolais veal liver.

• Other red wines:
Premier cru:
Chambolle-Musigny Les Cras, CM Les Beaux-Bruns, CM Les Véroilles, CM Les Baudes, CM Les Châtelots, CM Les Fuées.
Village:
Chambolle-Musigny.
Régional:
Bourgogne Rouge, Bourgogne Passetoutgrain
• White wine:
Régional:
Bourgogne Aligoté
• Owner: Barthod-Noëllat family
• Wine-maker: Ghislaine Barthod
• Combined vineyards: 6.64 hectares
• Production: 32,000 bottles
• Exports: 60%
• Take-away sales: Yes
• Visits: By appointment

Wine selected:
Chambolle-Musigny Les Charmes

• Classification: Premier Cru
• Area cultivated: 0.25 hectares
• Soil type: Clay and limestone
• Average vine age: 40 years
• Average annual production: 1,200 bottles

1996

Chambolle=Musigny

1er CRU LES CHARMES

APPELLATION CHAMBOLLE-MUSIGNY 1ER CRU CONTROLÉE

13 % vol.

75 cl

Mis en bouteilles par

Ghislaine BARTHOD

Propriétaire-Récoltante à Chambolle-Musigny (Côte-d'Or) France

PRODUCE OF FRANCE

Burgundy has its share of high profile estates, with their long histories and world-wide reputations, yet despite receiving the lion's share of publicity they merely form the surface of a very rich pool of unsung but talented and industrious *vignerons*. Conscientiousness and devotion to their *métier* and traditions drive numerous lesser-known wine-makers to excel themselves. One such is Guy Coquard.

The transmission of tradition and know-how Nothing is particularly remarkable about the Coquard story. It was Guy's grandfather who settled in Morey, acquired a few vines and started making his own wine. His son followed in his father's footsteps, himself adding several parcels to the family holdings, and in turn handed the estate on to his own son Guy in 1962. The young Coquard had learnt his trade working with his father, initially as a lad helping out in the school holidays and then progressively playing a fuller role. Thus are traditions and accumulated know-how passed down the generations and continually enriched up and down the Côte. Coquard himself acquired several more parcels of vineyard as and when finances and availability permitted, bringing the holdings to their present extent of 6 hectares.

Delicate and fragrant wines of great purity Coquard cultivates his vineyards by traditional means, turning the soil to keep weeds at bay, giving vines the very minimum of treatments necessary to protect them from cryptogamic and insect depredations, and giving the soil just the occasional, organic enrichment. In such a way the soil's microorganisms can live and work. Yields are kept at a satisfactorily low level by debudding in the spring, and as soon as the crop is sufficiently ripe it is harvested by hand and given a quality control in the vineyard.

Some 50% is destemmed, and then fermentations start, by means of the fruit's own yeast. Vinifications are carried out in stainless steel vats, with *pigeage* twice per day and *remontages*, and after blending of the free-run and press wine the liquids are transferred to barrel for ageing. Premier and Grand Cru wines are aged exclusively in new wood, which seems a little excessive when the wines are tasted young, for these are delicate, fragrant souls and do not have particularly big structures, yet with time the wood always becomes perfectly integrated into the wine. When the time comes for bottling, they are not fined, but receive a light filtration if the vintage requires it.

Morey-Saint-Denis Les Blanchards Lying just below the village, the Blanchards *climat* gives a wine of great finesse, which is enhanced by Coquard's vinification style. Of medium-deep colour, it gains a great deal in flesh and fullness over the years, and reaches its magnificent, refined and perfumed best after 8-10 years. At that age it is a unbeatable example of delicate, exquisite Pinot, with none of the complication sometimes resulting from more exaggerated vinification techniques to please international judging panels. It is ideally suited to simply prepared red meats, and winged game such as partridge *à la mode bourguignonne*. Long live the unsung *vigneron*!

• Other red wines:
Grand cru:
Clos de Vougeot.
Premier cru:
Chambolle-Musigny
Premier Cru.
Village:
Morey-Saint-Denis,
Chambolle-Musigny,
Gevrey-Chambertin.
Régional:
Bourgogne Pinot Noir,
Bourgogne
Passetoutgrain
• White wine:
Régional:
Bourgogne Aligoté
• Owner: Guy Coquard
• Wine-maker: Guy
Coquard
• Combined vineyards:
6 hectares
• Production:
35,000 bottles
• Exports: 40%
• Take-away sales: Yes
• Visits: No

Wine selected:
**Morey-Saint-Denis
Les Blanchards**

• Classification:
Premier Cru
• Area cultivated:
0.3 hectares
• Soil type:
Clay and limestone
• Average vine age:
35 years
• Average annual
production:
2,400 bottles

1996

GRANDS VINS   DE BOURGOGNE

Morey=Saint=Denis 1er Cru

Les Blanchards
APPELLATION MOREY-SAINT-DENIS 1er CRU CONTROLÉE

Mis en bouteille par
Guy COQUARD
PROPRIÉTAIRE A MOREY-SAINT-DENIS (COTE-D'OR) FRANCE

PRODUCE OF FRANCE

Ever since its creation in 1925 the Henri Gouges estate has produced classic Nuits-Saint-Georges wines against which others have been measured. The quality of the wines stems in part from the fact that the estate has never been afraid to innovate, and recent experimentation has given them even greater finesse and *terroir* expression. This is one of the great estates of the Côte de Nuits.

The champion of Burgundy's reputation As a young man Henri Gouges inherited 9 hectares of vineyards from his father just after the Great War, and by adding other acquisitions between 1920 and 1934 gave the estate more or less the form it has today. With the Marquis d'Angerville and a clutch of fellow growers he set out to bring an end to the rampant fraud of the time involving large-scale blending of Burgundy with inferior wines, and started bottling his produce himself in 1933 and selling it direct to his customers. He was a champion of low-yielding Pinot Noir clones, and this obsession with tightly controlled yields, passed down from father to son, has contributed to the enduring quality of Gouges wines. Today his grandsons Christian and Pierre run the estate, looking after wine-making and the vineyard respectively.

A solution to the soil erosion problem One of the perennial problems on the steeper slopes of the Côte d'Or is soil erosion after storms, which presents the unfortunate grower with the arduous task of carrying soil back up the slope. In 1975 Pierre Gouges had the idea of planting grass between the rows of vines, and this *enherbement* has been highly successful, not only in pinning down the surface soil but also in contributing to weed prevention, reduced humidity and thus rot, and fruit quality and lower yields, since it obliges vines to bury their roots deeper. And what is more, this practice has led to greater *terroir* definition in the wines. This innovation has been responsible in large part for the outstanding quality of recent vintages.

Wine-making for long ageing In the cellars Christian Gouges prefers to destalk the entire crop. Fermentation with indigenous yeast and then maceration last some 20 days and take place in closed cement vats. Wines are then transferred to barrel for their malo-lactic fermentation, and are subsequently aged for 18 months in oak, of which at the very most 20% is renewed every year – the Gouges, unlike many, place new oak low on their list of priorities. Then wines are bottled, without filtration whenever possible.

Nuits-Saint-Georges Les Saint-Georges All the Gouges wines have definite personalities, which is a tribute to the vision of the young Henri Gouges as he went about building up his superb domaine. The greatest wine is probably Les Saint-Georges, a Grand Cru in all but title, which needs 10 years in bottle before it should be approached. This wine has the habitual tannic sturdiness of the southern Nuits vineyards, and with age develops a magnificent, powerful bouquet of leather, spice, burnt earth, meat or game. It calls for no-nonsense meat dishes: either marinated or roast game, or red meat, grilled or served in a red wine sauce, to be followed by medium-flavoured cheeses – these will set off a Les Saint-Georges to perfection.

• Other red wines:
Premier cru:
Nuits-Saint-Georges Les Pruliers, NSG Clos des Porrets-Saint-Georges (monopole), NSG Les Vaucrains, NSG Les Chênes Carteaux, NSG Les Chaignots.
Village:
Nuits-Saint-Georges.
Régional:
Bourgogne Pinot Noir
• White wines:
Premier cru:
NSG Clos des Porrets-Saint-Georges, NSG La Perrière.
Régional:
Bourgogne Pinot Blanc
• Owner: Gouges family
• Vineyard Manager: Pierre Gouges
• Wine-maker: Christian Gouges
• Combined vineyards: 15 hectares
• Production: 70,000 bottles
• Exports: 50%
• Take-away sales: Yes
• Visits: By appointment

Wine selected:
Nuits-Saint-Georges Les Saint-Georges

• Classification: Premier Cru
• Area cultivated: 1.08 hectares
• Soil type: Clay and limestone
• Average vine age: 40 years
• Average annual production: 5,000 bottles

1994

Mis en bouteille au Domaine

NUITS-St-GEORGES

LES SAINT GEORGES

APPELLATION NUITS-SAINT-GEORGES 1er CRU CONTRÔLÉE

Domaine Henri Gouges

Nuits-Saint-Georges France

D omaine Hubert Lignier is one of those small estates about which one hears good things but which it is difficult to confirm, since bottles are not easy to come by. The effort to find and taste the wine though is worthwhile, for its quality is excellent, and as at all good wine estates there is continual assessment of what is being done, with fine tuning and sometimes experimentation.

The devotion and talent of a father-and-son team Hubert bought out his two brothers when the three of them inherited the estate in the mid-1960s, and has in the intervening years doubled its size. He and his son Romain are hardworking, modest and friendly people, not the sort to seek publicity – they certainly do not need it, for loyal customers and word-of-mouth account for all they can produce. The young Romain is progressively taking over from his father as Hubert reaches retirement age, and since starting to work alongside him in 1988 he has instituted a number of changes of practice which have had an undeniably beneficial effect on the wines. They were very good before his arrival, for Hubert has never been one to let the vine overproduce nor to pick unripe grapes, yet these days there are solutions to perennial problems which had not even been dreamt of a few years ago.

Predators, scent diffusers and cold maceration Using predators to destroy other predators is one such advance: the yellow spider Tiphlodrome has been introduced into certain vineyards to eliminate the microscopic red spider, one of the vine's most redoubtable enemies. Biological confusion is another: the scent of the female Cochylis and Eudemis butterflies is diffused to confuse males, which can no longer find their mates; the resulting drop in fecundation means fewer caterpillars (*vers de la grappe*) which are instrumental in the development of grey rot.

Romain has modified wine-making methods somewhat also. He has taken to giving the musts a cold maceration for some 5 days before fermentation, which is then performed by natural yeast and takes place in concrete vats, the temperature being allowed to rise to 34°. Prior to this the grapes are all destalked, and to extract sufficient tannin, aroma and colour Hubert has always been one for getting into the vat and giving the pulp a good treading, helped by friends. The Lignier wines receive long ageing in wood, which has been the subject of trials to find which forests and which degree of toasting are best suited – a very wearying process, admits Romain! The best wines are aged equally in new and one-year oak, and have been bottled since 1992 with neither fining nor filtration.

Clos de la Roche The quality of the raw material sings out in the Ligniers' Clos de la Roche, a superbly rich, creamy and harmonious wine which reflects amply the talent and devotion the two men put into all of their wines. Structured for a long life, it is nevertheless enjoyable to taste even from the barrel thanks to the ripeness of its tannin and fruit and its fine aromatic definition. When young it is excellent with Cîteaux, Brie or Comté cheeses, when mature it deserves a red meat in wine sauce, such as tournedos of Charolais beef with a *marchand de vin* sauce.

- Other red wines:
Grand cru:
Charmes-Chambertin.
Premier cru:
Gevrey-Chambertin Les Combottes; Chambolle-Musigny Les Baudes; Morey-Saint-Denis Premier Cru.
Village:
Morey-Saint-Denis, Gevrey-Chambertin, Chambolle-Musigny.
Régional:
Bourgogne, Bourgogne Passetoutgrain
- White wine:
Régional:
Bourgogne Aligoté
- Owners: Hubert & Romain Lignier
- Wine-makers: Hubert & Romain Lignier
- Combined vineyards: 8 hectares
- Production: 40,000 bottles
- Exports: 80%
- Take-away sales: Stock permitting
- Visits: By appointment

Wine selected:
Clos de la Roche

- Classification: Grand Cru
- Area cultivated: 0.98 hectares
- Soil type: Clay and limestone
- Average vine age: 40 years
- Average annual production: 3,500 bottles

DOMAINE JACQUES-FRÉDÉRIC MUGNIER

For many years Domaine Jacques-Frédéric Mugnier, owner of the Château at the top of Chambolle-Musigny, was in a moribund state, condemned by the disinterest of its owners to the role of landowner, its wines swelling the vats of the *négociants* and its name forgotten. Then Frédéric Mugnier fell in love with the place. Since his arrival he has reclaimed the vines, and propelled their wines amongst the cream of Chambolle and of the Côte de Nuits.

An estate without an identity In the middle of the 19th century one François Mugnier founded a liqueur business in Dijon, which soon became very profitable. Mugnier became interested in wine, and bought some 9 hectares of prime Côte de Nuits vineyards from the Marey-Monge family, who in 1899 also sold him the Château de Chambolle-Musigny. Over the years Mugnier's estate was passed down from generation to generation, ending up in Jacques-Frédéric's hands in 1944. He was a lawyer and financier in Paris, and had no intention of changing his life and going to live down in Burgundy. He sold off the liqueur business to L'Héritier Guyot and rented out the vineyards. Jacques-Frédéric died in 1980, and the *fermage* contracts continued to be renewed.

A change of profession In 1984 his son Frédéric decided to take a sabbatical from his job as offshore oil engineer, and went to have a look at the family estate he hardly knew. He fell in love with it, turned his back on the oil industry and enrolled at Beaune for a 6-month crash course in wine-making, built up contacts and experience, and started making his wines. Yet the estate was hardly large enough to support a family, so he decided to indulge in another passion, aviation, and gained his pilot's licence in 1988. Nowadays he flies for 3 days a week, giving himself another source of income and enabling him to take slightly more risks with his wine-making.

Measures for quality at every stage Vineyard work is carried out by *tâcherons*, yet Mugnier supervises them closely and imposes his own quality measures; then, once the fruit arrives at the *cuverie*, the job is entirely his. There is extremely stringent sorting and rejection of substandard fruit, and then a cold maceration gets the wine-making under way. Fermentation is started by indigenous yeast, and maximum colour, aroma and tannin exchange between solids and liquid is attained by repeated *pigeages* – sometimes up to 5 per day. Departing from normal practice, press-wine is kept apart instead of being blended with free-run before *élevage*, and is only added just before bottling.

Musigny Looking down over the Clos de Vougeot, the two *climats* of Musigny and Petits Musigny combine to form one of the Côte de Nuits' greatest Grands Crus, giving birth to a wine of extraordinary fragrance and delicacy when in the best hands. Mugnier's exquisite offering is beautifully aromatic and ethereal, a triumph of intensity and balance as much as of refinement and aroma; irresistible in its youth despite a little rigidity, it is stunning after a dozen years, as Mugnier's first vintages, in particular the 1985, are now showing. This sumptuous wine may be savoured with a truffled Bresse hen.

- Other red wines:
Grand cru:
Bonnes-Mares.
Premier cru:
Chambolle-Musigny
Les Fuées,
CM Les Amoureuses.
Village:
Chambolle-Musigny
- Owner: Frédéric Mugnier
- Wine-maker: Frédéric Mugnier
- Combined vineyards: 4 hectares
- Production: 16,000 bottles
- Exports: 60%
- Take-away sales: By appointment
- Visits: By appointment

Wine selected:
Musigny

- Classification: Grand Cru
- Area cultivated: 1.13 hectares
- Soil type: Clay and limestone
- Average vine age: 45 years
- Average annual production: 3,500 bottles

PRODUIT DE FRANCE

1993   1993

MUSIGNY
GRAND CRU
APPELLATION CONTRÔLÉE

Jacques-Frédéric Mugnier
Propriétaire au Château de Chambolle- Musigny (Côte-d'Or)

MIS EN BOUTEILLE AU CHATEAU

The quiet and fertile slopes of the Hautes Côtes have seen the planting over recent years of large tracts of vineyard, much of which is destined to produce ordinary wine – one only has to drive around and observe how the vines are widely spaced and pruned high – which will mostly be sold to the *négociant* houses. Yet in the hands of conscientious and talented individuals these lands are capable of making wine of far greater achievement. Perhaps the best examples of quality Hautes Côtes wines, as well as others from more prestigious origins, come from the Jayer-Gilles family.

Robert Jayer starts out on his own A cousin of the much-renowned Henri Jayer, Robert Jayer gained his first practical experience working as a cellarhand at the Domaine de la Romanée-Conti. Having married a Gilles girl from Magny-lès-Villers, he set out on his own and rapidly gained a large and loyal following. His son Gilles studied viticulture and oenology and started working alongside him in 1980, and took entire responsibility for the estate in 1998 on his father's retirement.

Cold maceration and new oak Jayer-Gilles wines are made by traditional methods, flavoured by the teachings of the oenologist Guy Accad. When making the red wines, after being picked through on the sorting table some 70-80% of the fruit is destemmed, and a lengthy cold maceration of up to 8 days gets under way. The alcoholic fermentation then starts, and a morning *remontage* and evening *pigeage* help keep the cap of solid matter wet and extract colour, tannin, aromas and acidity. In all the *cuvaison* lasts 15-18 days, and the wine is then left to settle for 24 hours before transfer into new oak barrels.

The domaine makes unreserved use of new oak for maturing all of its red wines, a practice which very possibly had its origins in Robert Jayer's training at the Domaine de la Romanée-Conti. Some maintain that this is wildly excessive for Hautes Côtes de Beaune or Nuits, which Jayer ages in barrel for no less than 15 months, yet if any such regional wines can take it, these can. There is no disagreement, however, as regards the better reds, which are unquestionably capable of digesting 18 months' new oak with a smile. Once aged the wines are bottled with neither fining nor filtration.

Even the white Jayer-Gilles Hautes Côtes wines, which are a blend of 70% Pinot Blanc (the famous Pinot mutation found by Henri Gouges) and 30% Chardonnay, are fermented in 60% new oak and matured for a half-dozen months, yet in their case this treatment is thoroughly suitable, giving them great richness, texture and aroma, while at the same time retaining the necessary balancing acidity.

Echézeaux Low yields and old vines combine to give an Echézeaux which is eminently suited to the Jayers' vinification habits. This, their finest wine, is a very deep, dark red when young, and has a sumptuously rich and seductive black fruit flavour and great volume and structure in the mouth. It amply repays a dozen years' cellaring. This is one of the greatest and most elegant of all Echézeaux, and calls for a pheasant or lamb to offer it suitable homage at table.

• Other red wines:
Premier cru:
Nuits-Saint-Georges
Les Damodes.
Village:
NSG Les Hauts Poirets.
Régional:
Côtes de Nuits Villages,
Hautes Côtes de Nuits,
Hautes Côtes de Beaune,
Bourgogne
Passetoutgrain
• White wines:
Régional:
Hautes Côtes de Nuits,
Hautes Côtes de Beaune,
Bourgogne Aligoté
• Owner: Jayer-Gilles
family
• Manager: Gilles Jayer
• Wine-maker:
Gilles Jayer
• Combined vineyards:
11 hectares
• Production:
65,000 bottles
• Exports: 65%
• Take-away sales: No
• Visits: No

Wine selected:
Échézeaux

• Classification:
Grand Cru
• Area cultivated:
0.53 hectares
• Soil type:
Clay and limestone
• Average vine age:
50 years
• Average annual
production:
2,500 bottles

DOMAINE JEAN GRIVOT

The Grivot estate has an enviable patrimony of Grands and Premiers Crus in the communes of Vougeot, Vosne and Nuits, and has long made quintessential examples of each appellation. Yet the family laurels are never rested on, and reflection and experimentation are continual. From the village wines through to the Clos de Vougeot and Richebourg, intensity, balance and class sing out.

A fine estate is parcelled together After the Great War, Gaston Grivot determined to build a prestigious wine domaine, and started by selling off odd family vineyards to finance the acquisition of a large parcel of Clos Vougeot. Grivot was one of the first students of oenology at Dijon university, and was one of the first to bottle and sell his production himself. His bride brought him several parcels of Nuits-Saint-Georges as dowry, then his son Jean came into more vineyards on his marriage to a Jayer. In 1984 the estate's pride and joy, a parcel of Richebourg, was acquired.

Guy Accad is consulted Jean Grivot's son Etienne progressively took over responsibilities from his father in the early 1980s. This thoughtful young man had the feeling that, despite old vines, low yields and suitable fermentation methods, which were at the time enabling him to make elegant, harmonious and balanced wines, modern vintages had none of the sheer richness, power and structure of wines of the past. What was lacking? He happened to meet the oenologist Guy Accad, and found that their ideas went in the same direction. He asked Accad to counsel him, which was to earn him much jealous and uninformed criticism.

Revitalized soils and cooler fermentations The problem lay initially in the fruit, Accad diagnosed; the soils were dying of an excess of nitrogen, potassium and phosphorus, a legacy of excessive fertilizing over previous decades, and the fruit simply did not attain the ripeness of bygone days. Corrective measures and an organic regime were got under way. Fermentation methods were also called into question: Accad counselled a long period of maceration at a cool temperature, as naturally happened in the cold cellars of yesteryear, with liberal use of sulphur to retard fermentation, followed by fermentation itself at low temperatures.

After 5 vintages Grivot and Accad parted company, since when Grivot has practised a synthesis of all the best elements of Accad's and previous methods. As the years go by the Accad-influenced wines seem to be taking on the qualities which had been missing; Grivot's courage seems to be paying off, and the scars of all the hypocritical attacks of other wine-makers during this brief period are, thankfully, slowly healing.

Richebourg Generally recognized as occupying the third step of the podium after Romanée-Conti and La Tâche, the Richebourg vineyard produces for its fortunate dozen owners a wine of majesty, opulence, refinement and great structure, about which it is difficult to restrain the superlatives! With age its massive fruit may acquire a host of tertiary nuances, of the leather, meat, game and spice varieties, while its succulence is irresistible. The sumptuous Grivot Richebourg, a wine for very special occasions, appreciates the company of hare *à la royale*, or a succulent cut of Charolais.

• Other red wines:
Grand cru:
Clos de Vougeot, Échézeaux.
Premier cru:
Vosne-Romanée Les Beaumonts, VR Les Brûlées, VR Les Chaumes, VR Les Suchots, VR Les Rouges; Nuits-Saint-Georges Les Boudots, NSG Les Pruliers, NSG Les Roncières.
Village:
Vosne-Romanée, Chambolle-Musigny La Combe d'Orveau, Nuits-Saint-Georges.
Régional:
Bourgogne Rouge
• Owner: Domaine Jean Grivot
• Wine-maker: Etienne Grivot
• Combined vineyards: 14 hectares
• Production: 65,000 bottles
• Exports: 85%
• Take-away sales: By appointment
• Visits: By appointment

Wine selected:
Richebourg

• Classification: Grand Cru
• Area cultivated: 0.31 hectares
• Soil type: Clay and limestone
• Average vine age: 65 years
• Average annual production: 1,400 bottles

RÉCOLTÉ, ÉLEVÉ ET MIS EN BOUTEILLE AU DOMAINE

RICHEBOURG
GRAND CRU
APPELLATION RICHEBOURG CONTRÔLÉE

13.2% vol.   750 ml

1996

DOMAINE JEAN GRIVOT
VOSNE-ROMANÉE · 21700 · CÔTE-D'OR · FRANCE
PRODUCE OF FRANCE

DOMAINE JEAN-JACQUES CONFURON

E ver since its young owners finished wine school and
took on responsibilities a handful of years ago,
Domaine Jean-Jacques Confuron has been a hive of
activity. With every new vintage Alain and Sophie
Meunier refine their methods, with great success.
Fortunately for clients their youth means that there should
be many a great vintage of Jean-Jacques Confuron wines
over the next decades.

Putting education into practice Sophie, daughter of Jean-
Jacques and Andrée Confuron, met Alain Meunier at the
Beaune *lycée viticole*, where she was studying viticulture and
oenology at the same time as looking after the family estate
with her mother, and he was in charge of the *lycée's* agricul-
tural machinery. They married, Alain himself enrolled as a
student and learnt how to make wine, and in 1989 they produced their first vintage of the Domaine's wines together.

They were ambitious, and to put their ideals into practice they needed a new vatroom and new vinification equipment, and the barrel cellars needed extending. The vineyard
also needed a certain amount of attention. Knowing that he
would not be able to produce great wine with anything less
than impeccable grapes, Alain Meunier decided to introduce
a biological regime in the vineyard, in order to increase the
microorganic life in the soil and the vines' capacity to with-
stand illness.

Preserving the delicacy of the fruit Meunier sees his obliga-
tion as principally of preserving the delicacy of the fruit, and
has minutely refined his technique to that end. After sifting
through the bunches on his sorting table he gives his grapes
a cold maceration lasting 4-5 days, during which they
receive one gentle *remontage* daily. The grapes are not
crushed, and the fermentation is started by warming up the
vats somewhat, so that the wild yeast can get to work. His
vats have removable lids, in order to keep in as much aroma
as possible. After some 10 days the wine is transferred to
barrel, the solids pressed very gently and some of this press-
wine blended in, and the fermentation finishes in the wood.
Thereafter the wine is matured, with a healthy quantity of
new oak, and bottled after 14-18 months with neither fining
nor filtering.

Such is the quality of the Meuniers' wines that demand
exceeds supply, and to satisfy a greater number of prospec-
tive clients Alain has set up a *négociant* business, Féry-
Meunier, which enables him to buy grapes and make a wider
range of wines. These wines are made by exactly the same
methods as the Confuron wines, and in order to attain the
quality required no more than 10 *pièces* are made of each
wine, with an annual maximum of 150 *pièces* in all.

Romanée-Saint-Vivant The finest wine in the Confuron cellar is naturally the Romanée-Saint-Vivant. This is a magnificent demonstration of Burgundy at its best, a wine made
from very old vines and low yields, which is aged in nothing
but new wood. It is a splendid blend of exquisite perfume,
refinement and generosity, perfectly balanced and with the
structure, under its velvety exterior, for a long life. It is one
of the finest Romanée-Saint-Vivants made today. Depending
on its age it may be served with cold chicken, truffle ragout
or breast of veal stuffed with wild mushrooms.

Côte de Nuits | Prémeaux

• Other red wines:
Grand cru:
Clos Vougeot.
Premier cru:
Vosne-Romanée
Les Beaux-Monts;
Nuits-Saint-Georges
Les Chabœufs,
NSG Aux Boudots;
Chambolle-Musigny
Premier Cru.
Village:
Chambolle-Musigny,
NSG Les Fleurières.
Régional:
Côte de Nuits Villages
Les Vignottes, Bourgogne
Pinot Noir
• White wine:
Régional:
Bourgogne Aligoté
• Owners: Sophie & Alain
Meunier
• Wine-maker: Alain
Meunier
• Combined vineyards:
7 hectares
• Production:
32,000 bottles
• Exports: 80%
• Take-away sales: No
• Visits: By appointment

Wine selected:
Romanée-Saint-Vivant

• Classification:
Grand Cru
• Area cultivated:
0.5 hectares
• Soil type:
Clay and limestone
• Average vine age:
80 years
• Average annual
production:
2,000 bottles

ROMANÉE St-VIVANT

GRAND CRU

APPELLATION ROMANÉE St-VIVANT CONTRÔLÉE

RED BURGUNDY WINE

1996

Mis en bouteille à la propriété par

DOMAINE JEAN-JACQUES CONFURON

PROPRIÉTAIRE À PREMEAUX PAR NUITS-St-GEORGES (CÔTE D'OR).

Product of France

L ike its neighbour the Clos de Tart, the Clos des Lambrays has a long history and a chequered past. Having made some of the greatest Burgundies of the first half of the 20th century it went through decades of decline, before progressively coming to rights again. Recent vintages promise very great things from this superb Morey-Saint-Denis vineyard.

From the Middle Ages to the 20th century The oldest known document relating to the vineyard concerns its cession in 1258 by the Lambrays brothers to Cîteaux Abbey. It then went through long centuries of tranquillity in the ownership of the Cistercians until the Revolution stripped the Church of its lands. After this cataclysm the *clos* suddenly found itself shared between no less than 74 owners, and it could subsequently have become the most carved-up vineyard in the whole of Burgundy, had it not been for Louis Joly, a Nuits *négociant*. From 1836 Joly set about buying up others' plots, and Albert Rodier, who did likewise from 1865, had whittled the number down by 1879 to its present-day figure of a mere 4 owners. Rodier's grandson Camille, one of Burgundy's great personalities and co-founder of the Confrérie des Chevaliers du Tastevin, propelled the wine to mythical standards in the inter-war years.

Decline and renaissance Rodier sold the *clos* to a Parisian banker, René Cosson, in 1938, and there followed a 41-year gentle but inexorable decline as the property was neglected. The vines were extremely old but many were missing, and the odd random great wine, particularly later ones such as the 1964, 1969 and 1971, was the result of chance as much as anything else. When in 1979 the Saier brothers bought the estate, locals opined that it was more suitable for hunting in than growing vines!

The Saiers hired as *régisseur* a young Dijon oenologist named Thierry Brouin and invested heavily in refurbishing the fine residence and the wine-making facilities. In 1981 they replanted the northern part of the vineyard, and that same year the vineyard was promoted to Grand Cru status, a recognition of the land's quality. Brouin made great improvements with the wine, however the Saiers themselves were obliged to start looking for a buyer in 1994 as a result of business problems. In December 1996 salvation came in the form of Günter Freund and his son Hans-Joachim, from Coblentz.

Clos des Lambrays Proving a real desire to make a wine worthy of its Grand Cru classification, the Freunds encouraged Thierry Brouin to be thoroughly niggardly in his yields and stringent in his selections, both of fruit and of barrels destined for the final blend. Half of the 1994 vintage was declassified to Morey-Saint-Denis Premier Cru, as was some 40% of the excellent 1995 vintage. This stringency was lacking in the previous owners' time, and the difference is there to be seen. At last the real quality of Clos des Lambrays is there for all to appreciate: reasonably full-bodied yet elegant, with a succulent peppery black fruit flavour, with complex mineral, truffle and earthy notes and a slightly smoky character... This is a very fine Burgundy, and a splendid partner for truffled capon cooked in a coarse salt crust.

Côte de Nuits | *Morey-Saint-Denis*

- Other red wines:
Premier cru:
Morey-Saint-Denis
Premier Cru.
Village:
Morey-Saint-Denis
- White wines:
Premier cru:
Puligny-Montrachet
Les Folatières,
PM Clos du Cailleret
- Owner: Freund family
- Manager: Thierry Brouin
- Wine-maker: Thierry Brouin
- Combined vineyards: 11 hectares
- Production: 45,000 bottles
- Exports: 60%
- Take-away sales: Yes
- Visits: 8-12 a.m., 1.30-6.00 p.m

Wine selected:
Clos des Lambrays

- Classification: Grand Cru
- Area cultivated: 8.7 hectares
- Soil type: Clay and limestone
- Average vine age: 45 years
- Average annual production: 30,000 bottles

One of the highest profiles in the Burgundy wine world today is that of Lalou Bize-Leroy, a smallish, attractive and energetic woman with a strong personality and correspondingly strong convictions. This perfectionist makes wines of extraordinary quality, by viticultural methods which are decidedly risky, and then manages to sell them at outlandishly expensive prices.

A museum of Burgundy's finest   The name Leroy has long been revered by wine-lovers. In 1868 the *négociant* firm Maison Leroy was founded in Auxey-Duresses, and by the efforts of François Leroy, then Joseph, and then Henri, it came to be known as a source of quintessential Burgundies. In 1942 Henri Leroy bought a half-share in the Domaine de la Romanée-Conti, and the Leroys still share the estate with the de Villaine family today. Over the years Maison Leroy has kept back stocks of its wines, and today possesses a treasure-house of several million bottles, which has given rise to comparisons with the Louvre and the Bibliothèque Nationale. Since 1955 Henri's daughter Lalou has been at the helm, and has presided over the firm with astuteness and devotion.

In recent years, in common with other *négociants* Leroy has found it progressively more difficult to come across sufficiently good wine for sale, and in 1988 Mme. Bize-Leroy bought the Vosne domaine of Charles Noëllat, and subsequently that of Philippe Rémy at Gevrey, in order to provide a sure source of fruit.

Biodynamic viticulture and traditional wine-making   Her quest for *terroir* typicity and the most perfect fruit has led Mme. Bize-Leroy on a passionate crusade on the behalf of Burgundy's much abused vineyard soil, and this has led her to embrace biodynamic viticulture as a way of regenerating its microorganic life. This at the start caused many raised eyebrows and much scepticism, and her readiness to speak out against the unecological practices of others has not endeared her to everyone on the Côte. Biodynamics involve applying thoroughly ecological methods at precise moments, which are dictated by cosmic rhythms. Extremely low yields are another feature of Leroy wines, indeed they are situated at levels which would be commercially unviable for anyone not selling at the firm's exorbitant prices.

The Leroy vinification methods are tailored for making wines for the very long term. There is a stringent quality control of the fruit, no destemming, no temperature control, no *débourbage*, and then *élevage* in 100% new oak, followed by bottling with absolutely no filtration.

Romanée-Saint-Vivant   Every year the Leroy Romanée-Saint-Vivant is one of the very finest Burgundies, and in 1995 the domaine fashioned a stunningly beautiful wine of enormous finesse and perfume, from a pitiful yield of 13 hl/ha. With a magnificent ethereal fragrance of roses, black fruit and spice, it is exquisitely intense on the palate, precise, refined and infinitely long. This is a wine that can be laid down for one's children. So entrancing is it that it is a shame to break the spell with the foreign savours of any dish, yet were one to do so, hare *à la royale* could not easily be bettered.

• Other red wines:
Grand cru:
Chambertin, Latricières-Chambertin, Clos de la Roche, Musigny, Clos de Vougeot, Richebourg, Corton Renardes.
Premier cru:
Gevrey-Chambertin Les Combottes; Chambolle-Musigny Les Charmes; Vosne-Romanée Les Beaux Monts, VR Aux Brûlées; Nuits-Saint-Georges Les Boudots, NSG Les Vignerondes; Savigny-lès-Beaune Les Narbantons; Volnay Santenots.
Vins de village et régionaux également
• White wines:
Grand cru:
Corton-Charlemagne.
Village:
Auxey-Duresses
• Owner: Domaine Leroy
• Wine-maker:
Lalou Bize-Leroy
• Combined vineyards:
22.41 hectares
• Production:
55,000 bottles
• Exports: 85%
• Take-away sales: No
• Visits: No

Wine selected:
Romanée-Saint-Vivant

• Classification:
Grand Cru
• Area cultivated:
0.99 hectares
• Soil type:
Clay and limestone
• Average vine age:
50 years
• Annual production:
2,500 bottles

1995
Grand Cru
Appellation Contrôlée
Mis en bouteille au Domaine
PRODUCT OF FRANCE

One of Vosne-Romanée's greatest estates was unknown as recently as the beginning of the 1980s, for its vineyards were worked by sharecroppers, and the wine with which the estate was paid was sold off in bulk. Yet since 1983 much has changed at Domaine Méo-Camuzet, to the extent that it is today one of the highest fliers of Vosne and Burgundy.

A young man devotes himself to his estate The estate's history has little in common with that of most on the Côte d'Or. It was built up by Etienne Camuzet, who was *député* for the Côte d'Or to the Assemblée Nationale from 1902-1932, and mayor of Vosne towards the end of his life. Camuzet it was, incidentally, who bought the Château du Clos de Vougeot in 1920 and sold it to the Confrérie des Chevaliers du Tastevin for a nominal sum in 1945. He died in 1946 and left the estate to his daughter, but she died childless 13 years later, and the estate then passed to Camuzet's great-nephew Jean Méo. Not long before passing away Camuzet had approached the young Henri Jayer to ask if he was interested in operating a number of his vineyards on a sharecropping basis, to which Jayer agreed. Jean Méo was an eminent figure in business and politics and had neither the time nor the inclination to look after the estate, so other *vignerons* were then contracted to look after the remaining vineyards. They made the wine, and the estate sold off its share in bulk.

Jayer began bottling his wine at the beginning of the 1980s and rapidly made himself a name, before officially retiring in 1988. That same year saw the arrival of Méo's son Jean-Nicolas, who had decided to devote himself to the estate. Coincidentally several of the other *métayers* retired around the end of the decade, and the vineyards conveniently reverted to the domaine. Méo, seconded by Christian Faurois, who had worked at the estate alongside Jayer, and Jayer himself in an advisory capacity, formed a resolute team.

From vineyard to bottle Camuzet had bought his vineyards wisely, and the advanced age of many of the vines today only increases the superb quality of their wines. Méo and Faurois tend their vines as naturally as possible, using predators to eliminate the vine's predators where possible. Low yields, perfect ripeness and severe selection bring top quality raw material to the vatroom, and vinification thereafter is largely *à la* Jayer: total destalking, 3-5 days' cold maceration, fermentation with natural yeast to temperatures of 34-35°; *pigeage* as the vintage requires, little chaptalisation and some 18 months' *élevage* in barrel. Grands and Premiers Crus are matured in exclusively new oak, and Village and even Bourgogne Rouge have the luxury of 50% new wood.

Richebourg The greatest of the Méo-Camuzet wines is their Richebourg, a sublimely perfumed, opulent and sensual wine. It is always very subtle, with complex flavour nuances of beautiful purity, and it always impresses the taster with its great breeding. Ah! Fortunate indeed are the favoured clients who can reserve (and pay for!) this wine every year! This is as splendid a wine as can be found on the Côte de Nuits, an aristocrat which appreciates the company of cuisine of its standing: tournedos Rossini has the necessary class.

Côte de Nuits | Vosne-Romanée

- Other red wines:
Grand cru:
Clos de Vougeot, Corton, Échézeaux.
Premier cru:
Vosne-Romanée Les Chaumes, VR Les Brûlées, VR Cros Parantoux; Nuits-Saint-Georges Les Boudots, NSG Les Murgers.
Village:
Vosne-Romanée, Nuits-Saint-Georges.
Régional:
Bourgogne, Bourgogne Passetoutgrain
- White wine:
Régional:
Hautes Côtes de Nuits Clos Saint-Philibert
- Wine-maker:
Jean-Nicolas Méo
- Combined vineyards:
14.5 hectares
- Production:
60,000 bottles
- Exports: 75%
- Take-away sales:
Very little!
- Visits: No

Wine selected:
Richebourg

- Classification:
Grand Cru
- Area cultivated:
0.35 hectares
- Soil type:
Clay and limestone
- Average vine age:
40 years
- annual production:
1,200 bottles

Mis au Domaine

RICHEBOURG

GRAND CRU

Appellation Contrôlée

Domaine Méo-Camuzet

PROPRIÉTAIRE A VOSNE-ROMANÉE, COTE-D'OR, FRANCE

13 % vol.   PRODUCE OF FRANCE   75 cl

1996

DOMAINE MICHEL GROS

It is not easy for the outsider to understand who in the tentacular Gros family owns what and what is made by whom, and it is fortunate therefore that the quality of the wines of all branches of the family is very high. Gros is generally synonymous with excellence. Until 1995 Michel Gros made the wines of two estates, his own and that of his father Jean Gros, yet after the vintage that year Jean split his holdings amongst his 3 children and retired. Since then Michel Gros has concentrated his energies on his own, expanded estate. This man is a very talented wine-maker.

Taking every new year as it comes Gros started working alongside his father in 1975 once he had completed his studies at the Beaune *lycée viticole*. For him the vine-growing side of the business is of paramount importance and interest, and if he has an overriding philosophy it is to take every new year as it comes and adapt accordingly, for each vine behaves differently with each new season. He keeps his yields down by acting at the beginning of the yearly cycle, pruning short and eliminating excess buds, rather than taking rectifying measures later on, the efficacy of which is far more uncertain.

Once the fruit is picked and has arrived at the *cuverie* it is totally destemmed and then transferred to vat to begin its alcoholic fermentation. There is no pre-fermentation maceration, simply a cool start at 15° aided by selected yeast. Gradually the temperature rises, and once it has reached the 'hot phase' of around 32° it is held there, and two *pigeages* a day are effected to extract all the fruit's ingredients. At the end of the alcoholic fermentation the wine's temperature is raised to 38° for two days to fix the colour. There follows a gentle pressing, and this press-wine is blended with the free-run wine, and the resulting liquid run off into barrels for ageing. The duration of ageing and quantity of new oak used naturally depends on the wine and the vintage quality, but generally Michel Gros treats his Grands Crus to 100% and his lesser wines with less; thereafter he racks them once and bottles them after a light fining with egg white but no filtration. This way he manages to imprison all the finesse of the fruit with great intensity of flavour.

Vosne-Romanée Clos des Réas One of the finest of the Michel Gros wines comes from the triangle of land touching on the Nuits-Saint-Georges border called Clos des Réas, a *monopole* of higher quality than the neighbouring village wine Aux Réas. Planted to a density of 10,000 vines per hectare, its fruit is fermented in enamel-lined cement vats and then aged in barrel – roughly 80% is new for the Clos des Réas – for some 18 months before fining with egg white and bottling at the end of summer.

Clos des Réas offers up a sumptuous black fruit nose, and on the palate is sensual, refined and elegant, with lots of concentration and the structure for 5-6 years' improvement before reaching perfect harmony. While rich and eloquent it is not a powerful wine, and to fully appreciate its breeding and finesse it should be served with guinea fowl, roast pigeon or a leg of lamb.

• Other red wines:
Grand cru:
Clos de Vougeot.
Premier cru:
Vosne-Romanée Aux Brûlées; Nuits-Saint-Georges Premier Cru.
Village:
Vosne-Romanée; Nuits-Saint-Georges, NSG Les Chaillots; Chambolle-Musigny.
Régional:
Bourgogne Hautes Côtes de Nuits, Bourgogne Rouge
• White wine:
Régional:
Bourgogne Hautes Côtes de Nuits
• Owner: Michel Gros
• Wine-maker:
Michel Gros
• Combined vineyards:
17 hectares
• Production:
65,000 bottles
• Exports: 75-80%
• Take-away sales: Yes
• Visits: By appointment

Wine selected:
Vosne-Romanée Clos des Réas
(monopole)

• Classification:
Premier Cru
• Vineyard size:
2.12 hectares
• Soil type:
Clay and limestone
• Average vine age:
25 years
• Average annual production:
9,000 bottles

MIS EN BOUTEILLE AU DOMAINE
PRODUCT OF FRANCE

VOSNE-ROMANÉE 1er CRU
CLOS DES RÉAS
APPELLATION VOSNE-ROMANÉE 1er CRU CONTRÔLÉE

MONOPOLE

MICHEL GROS
Propriétaire-Viticulteur à Vosne-Romanée (Côte d'Or) FRANCE

1996

The Mongeards, one of Vosne's older families, produce wines of delicacy and fragrance from a fine portfolio of vineyard holdings centred around their own and the neighbouring villages. Much of the production is exported, but what remains is eagerly lapped up by a long list of private clients and restaurant owners. These wines are fine expressions of the delicate Pinot Noir.

Impeccable fruit and careful wine-making "Our job is not to extract the maximum, it is not Syrah" opines Vincent Mongeard, the latest heir to a family tradition stretching back over at least 8 generations, and to that end this perfectionist tries to be present at every stage of the growing and wine-making cycle, ensuring that fruit quality is impeccable and that it is vinified in order to best capture the fruit's delicate fruitiness, elegance and aroma. For Mongeard, a good Burgundy must at all moments be delicious, it must at any age be a delight to taste, with a development curve which is perfectly regular over the years.

Tradition, technology and trial Traditional ways, with the aid of a little modern insight and technology, combine to realize these aims. Pruning short and serious debudding enable yields to be held at some 30 hl/ha for Grands Crus and 40 hl/ha for village wines, and the vines are encouraged to give of their best in a healthy, organic environment in which they know little stress. Yet experimentation and trial are also part of this domaine's tradition: in 1982 the young Vincent Mongeard carried out his first green harvest, amid the mockery of other growers, one of whom even went and fetched his camera; today it is *confusion sexuelle* which he and other enlightened growers are using, spreading capsules in the vineyard which diffuse the scent of the female butterflies which produce the *ver de la grappe*, in order to confuse would-be suitors.

Putting the emphasis on fragrance and elegance Wine-making is traditional, with the emphasis put on fragrance and elegance rather than body and power. Grapes are entirely destalked, with the occasional exception of one quarter of the Grand Cru fruit, and a 48-hour cold maceration precedes fermentation, which is started with the aid of the grapes' natural yeast. This lasts no longer than necessary for the style required, some 10-12 days, after which wines are aged in oak for 18-24 months. They are racked twice and some are fined if necessary, but none but the regional appellations are filtered before bottling.

Echézeaux Vieilles Vignes The family's 2.73 hectares of the Flagey Grand Cru Echézeaux contain a parcel of 73 ares of very old vines which is vinified on its own, giving a wine of great intensity, sensuality and succulence. While the Mongeard vinification style gives it great attraction from youth onwards, this wine can nevertheless age gracefully over two decades or more, as the 1976 vintage showed with great aplomb when tasted at the estate in 1998, a cornucopia of exquisite mature Pinot aromas. Young or mature, it finds a well-matched dining partner in stuffed shoulder of veal.

• Other red wines:
Grand cru:
Grands Échézeaux, Clos de Vougeot, Richebourg.
Premier cru:
Vosne-Romanée Les Orveaux, VR Les Suchots, VR Les Petits Monts; Nuits-Saint-Georges Les Boudots; Vougeot Les Cras; Savigny-lès-Beaune Les Narbantons.
Village:
Vosne-Romanée, Nuits-Saint-Georges, Gevrey-Chambertin, Fixin, Savigny-lès-Beaune.
Régional:
Hautes Côtes de Nuits, Bourgogne Rouge, Bourgogne Passetoutgrain
• White wines:
Village:
Puligny-Montrachet.
Régional:
Bourgogne Aligoté, Bourgogne Blanc
• Owner: Mongeard family
• Wine-maker: Vincent Mongeard
• Combined vineyards: 25 hectares
• Production: 100,000 bottles
• Exports: 80%
• Take-away sales: Yes
• Visits: By appointment

Wine selected:
Échézeaux
Vieille Vigne

• Classification: Grand Cru
• Area cultivated: 0.73 hectares
• Soil type: Clay and limestone
• Average vine age: 70 years
• Average annual production: 2,500 bottles

1993

ECHEZEAUX

GRAND CRU

VIEILLE VIGNE

APPELLATION CONTROLÉE

mis en bouteille au Domaine

13% vol.   75 cl

MONGEARD-MUGNERET

PROPRIÉTAIRE-RÉCOLTANT A VOSNE-ROMANÉE (CÔTE-D'OR) FRANCE

PRODUCE OF FRANCE

T hree hundred years ago the wines from Fixin fetched a higher price than those of its neighbour, Gevrey-Chambertin, yet the latter has overtaken it at a canter and left it far behind in the intervening period. While no one would dispute the greater capacity of Gevrey's vineyard land to turn out great wine, Fixin nevertheless remains capable of excellent bottles, and a fine source for the clued-up wine-lover without limitless funds. Domaine Pierre Gelin is perhaps its finest exponent.

Rich wines for laying down The domaine is run by Stephen, son of the founder Pierre Gelin, who built up the nucleus of the vineyard holdings in the inter-war years. As a young man Stephen Gelin learnt his trade at his father's side, then took over when he died in 1978. Originally he worked in partnership with André Molin, who had helped Pierre make many a vintage, yet Gelin has had total responsibility for the domaine since Molin retired in 1995.

Gelin's style is for uncompromising, rich wines for laying down. This is attained by limiting yields, never harvesting before perfect ripeness, and a protracted fermentation in wooden vats at a high temperature, with much extraction of colour, tannin and aromatics by *pigeage* and *remontage*. Further extraction is then attained by the unusual measure of heating the vats to up to 45° for one night once fermentation is over, then after this the wines are transferred to barrel for ageing for suitably long periods.

In memory of the Emperor The Clos Napoléon is one of Fixin's many imperial reminders, which may all be ascribed to the wealthy Claude Noisot, a veteran of the Napoleonic imperial campaigns and the retreat to Elba, who lived out his later life in the village. Among other acts of devotion he commissioned the Dijon sculptor François Rude to carve a statue of the reclining Emperor called "The Emperor Awakening to Immortality" which sits in the Parc Noisot at the top of the village, and renamed the Les Cheusots *climat* after his idol. Noisot, a commander of the Imperial Guard, even wanted to be buried upright in front of the statue, but the ground was apparently too hard and the Emperor was left unprotected!

Fixin Clos Napoléon Stephen Gelin is the proud owner of the entire Clos Napoléon, indeed he also had another Fixin *monopole*, the Clos du Chapitre, to farm and vinify, until its owners sold it in 1985. Clos Napoléon is relatively powerful and structured, thanks to Gelin's vinification method and some 22 months in barrel before bottling, and requires a good 6-8 years to soften up. This is a delicious and flavoursome bottle with a lot of character. Stephen Gelin would recommend serving it with that Burgundian speciality eggs *en meurette*, or with *coq au vin* or a grilled rib of beef.

Côte de Nuits | *Fixin*

- Other red wines:
Grand cru:
Chambertin Clos de Bèze.
Premier cru:
Fixin Les Hervelets,
Gevrey-Chambertin Clos
Prieur.
Village:
Fixin, Gevrey-Chambertin.
Régional:
Bourgogne Pinot,
Bourgogne
Passetoutgrain
- White wine:
Régional:
Bourgogne Aligoté
- Owner: Gelin family
h Wine-maker:
Stephen Gelin
- Combined vineyards:
12 hectares
- Production:
65,000 bottles
- Exports: 90%
- Take-away sales: Yes
- Visits: 9-12 a.m.,
2-5 p.m., Monday until
Saturday midday.

Wine selected:
Fixin Clos Napoléon
(monopole)

- Classification:
Premier Cru
- Vineyard size:
1.8 hectares
- Soil type:
Clay and limestone
- Average vine age:
45 years
- Average annual
production:
9,000 bottles

Contributing to the generally high standard of wine-making in Morey-Saint-Denis today, Domaine Ponsot makes rich, aromatic wines by thoroughly traditional methods which merit the high reputation they enjoy. It is the largest proprietor of the Grand Cru Clos de la Roche, and the Ponsot Clos de la Roche can be one of the Côte de Nuits' greatest wines.

Helping refine the nascent Burgundian wine industry The estate's origins go back to 1870, when William Ponsot returned from the Prussian war and bought several parcels of vineyard and a house at Morey. He had no children, and eventually passed the small estate to his nephew Hippolyte Ponsot in 1920. Hippolyte played an important role in easing the Burgundian wine industry into the modern era, as one of the first, along with Henri Gouges, Armand Rousseau and others, to start bottling his own production as early as 1932, and also as an instigator of Burgundy's appellation laws in 1935/1936.

His son Jean-Marie started working alongside him in 1947 and took over from his father ten years later. Jean-Marie also made a vital contribution: he was a pioneer in clonal selection, contributing much valuable work in the early 1960s, and many of the most successful Pinot clones used today – including the 113, 114, 115, 667 and 777 – came from his cuttings in the Clos de la Roche, where the mother vines can still be admired today. Since 1983 Laurent, Jean-Marie's son, has made the wine, with all the conscientiousness and talent of the previous generations.

Tried, tested and proved to work As may be imagined, Jean-Marie in his time planted clones ideally suited to his vineyard soils and to their rootstock, and stopped fertilizing the soil very early on. As a result Laurent has radiantly healthy vines and soils to work with, giving very fine quality fruit. Severe yield reduction is routine on the estate.

In the vatroom the bunches of fruit are usually totally destalked before vatting, and the Ponsots then let the fermentation proceed without any initial cold maceration. The temperature and duration of fermentation vary, and if necessary a *saignée* is effected. There is no new wood in the cellars, for the family have always abhorred it, which enables the Ponsots to mature their wines for fully 2 years and yet suffer less ageing, thanks to the very limited oxidation. One sole racking over two years, no fining, no filtration, no addition of sulphur, and the wines are bottled. To enhance clarity, racking and bottling are always carried out during periods of high atmospheric pressure, when the moon is on the wane.

Clos de la Roche The Ponsot wine-making method gives powerful, rich, spicy and very perfumed wines, none more so than their Clos de la Roche. This is a wonderfully classy, opulent and heady wine with a superbly complex flavour palette, each vintage contributing its own colours, with all the concentration and depth that a Grand Cru should have. Great vintages need some 10 years to reveal their talent, and when the decade is up they make a wonderful match for tournedos with a sauce of morels.

- Other red wines:
Grand cru:
Clos Saint-Denis, Chambertin, Griotte-Chambertin, Chapelle-Chambertin.
Premier cru:
Morey-Saint-Denis Premier Cru Cuvée des Alouettes; Chambolle-Musigny Charmes.
Village:
Morey-Saint-Denis Cuvée des Grives, Gevrey-Chambertin Cuvée de l'Abeille
- White wine:
Premier cru:
Morey-Saint-Denis Clos des Monts Luisants
- Owner: Laurent Ponsot
- Wine-maker:
Laurent Ponsot
- Combined vineyards:
9 hectares
- Production:
25,000 bottles
- Exports: 90%
- Take-away sales: No
- Visits: No

Wine selected:
Clos de la Roche

- Classification:
Grand Cru
- Area cultivated:
3.4 hectares
- Soil type:
Clay and limestone
- Average vine age:
58 years
- Average annual production:
8,000 bottles

I t may not be particularly large in size, but the René Engel estate in Vosne-Romanée produces wines which are masterful examples of their appellations: aristocratic, full-bodied, richly flavoured and with structure for great longevity. This is an estate which has made great progress in recent years... yet its present owner, René Engel's grandson, is not about to rest on his laurels!

The heritage of a great Burgundian René Engel was a well-known figure in post-war Burgundy: Professor of oenology for 35 years at Dijon University, a man of letters – among other works his *Propos sur l'Art de Bien Boire* set out in print his philosophy – and one of the founders of the Confrérie des Chevaliers du Tastevin, he was unceasing in his promotion of the Côte d'Or. He inherited a 10-hectare estate and made many a glorious vintage before officially taking retirement in 1949. His son Pierre was of the same stamp, yet prolonged illness and disheartenment began to reflect in his wines, and the estate became progressively neglected. He died in 1981, five years before his father. Pierre's son Philippe, who had studied at Beaune's *lycée viticole* and gained experience at his side, took over control of the estate.

A young man asserts himself Philippe was determined from the start to halt the decline and produce the very finest wines possible. He asserted his authority in 1982 by removing his grandfather – well-meaning yet ever-present – by force from the cellars, and started doing things his way. First of all there were some essential improvements to be carried out, in both vineyard and vatroom. There had been no replacement of dead vines, and so the many spaces had to be filled; there had also been excessive fertilization with potassium-based products, and a programme of bringing the soils back to life had to be put under way. In the cellars there was much old wood to be discarded, and new to be bought.

Philippe Engel modified a number of the Domaine's wine-making techniques to bring about the improvements he envisaged: yields, although never excessive in his father's time, were reduced further, and selection of the raw material accorded greater importance; a sorting table was bought in 1990. Today there is a good deal more *pigeage* than previously, and fermentations are allowed to rise to 35°. Use of sulphur, racking and filtering have all been reduced to the bare minimum, and new wood is bought in the quantities needed for the wines. Engel's modifications had a rapid effect, and his wines were soon back amongst the best in the village.

Grands Echézeaux Lying on the west side of Clos de Vougeot, the 9.13 hectares of Grands Echézeaux give what Jean-François Bazin has described as "a wine for the erudite who appreciate nuances". Certainly Philippe Engel's wine will satisfy the most discerning connoisseur, offering as it does concentrated fruit, finesse, breed and balance, with the wherewithal in great vintages to develop a supreme aromatic complexity over 20 years. What is more this great Burgundy, ideally suited to game of both the winged and four-legged varieties, represents astonishingly good value for money compared with some of its more sought-after Grand Cru neighbours.

Vosne-Romanée

Côte de Nuits

• Other red wines:
Grand cru:
Échézeaux, Clos Vougeot.
Premier cru:
Vosne-Romanée Les Brûlées.
Village:
Vosne-Romanée
• Owner: Philippe Engel
• Wine-maker: Philippe Engel
• Oenologist:
Jean-Pierre Bruley
• Combined vineyards:
7 hectares
• Production:
26,000 bottles
• Exports: 70%
• Take-away sales: No
• Visits: 8-12 a.m.,
2-6 p.m., by appointment

Wine selected:
Grands Échezeaux

• Classification:
Grand Cru
• Area cultivated:
0.5 hectares
• Soil type:
Clay and limestone
• Average vine age:
75 years
• Average annual production:
2,000 bottles

PRODUCE OF FRANCE

1996

GRANDS-ÉCHEZEAUX

GRAND CRU

APPELLATION GRANDS-ÉCHEZEAUX CONTRÔLÉE

MIS EN BOUTEILLES À LA PROPRIÉTÉ

DOMAINE RENÉ ENGEL
À VOSNE-ROMANÉE, CÔTE-D'OR, FRANCE

CETTE CUVÉE AYANT DONNÉ 1500 BOUTEILLES   N⁰ 0282
CETTE BOUTEILLE PORTE LE

750 ML. 13,5% ALC. BY VOL.   L 40

T hings have been looking up at Domaine Robert Arnoux since the beginning of the 1990s, when Pascal Lachaux, the late Robert Arnoux's son-in-law, took on responsibility for the estate. The wines Arnoux himself made were good, but what can now be tasted is the hunger and ambition of the young tiger, who knows that if he really works on it, they could be brilliant. This is a fine estate, which is on its way to becoming one of the very finest.

Prestigious climats, old vines and a natural phenomenon...
The young Lachaux is helped in his mission by the quality of the vineyards at his disposal, which lie in the communes of Nuits, Vosne, Flagey and Vougeot and are crowned by 3 Grands Crus: Echézeaux, Clos de Vougeot and Romanée-Saint-Vivant. The old age of the vines which many of them contain is additionally conducive to quality, and the fact that some of the vines are regularly subject to the phenomenon of *millérandage* – when embryo bunches of grapes form but do not develop – is another factor in their favour, for this leads to lower yields, and, curiously enough, to extremely concentrated juice in the affected bunches. Stringent debudding, a regular springtime activity, is also very important in reducing yields.

Finesse and elegance with staying power Cellar practices are very much in tune with the latest trends, although Lachaux is certainly not one for lazily following these without reflecting and testing to verify their suitability in his particular case. The grapes are all destalked on arrival at the *cuverie* and are put to macerate at a cold temperature for several days in stainless steel vats. Then the various wines start to ferment, at temperatures which do not rise above 32°, and this period is interspersed with limited *pigeage* and *remontage*, the aim being to have good extraction of colour, tannin, acidity and aroma, yet to retain as much finesse and elegance as possible. Wines are subsequently matured in oak for 18 months, the quantity of new barrels varying according to the appellation between 30-100%. When they are ready they are bottled, with fining but without filtration.

Romanée-Saint-Vivant The finest wine in the Robert Arnoux cellar is the Romanée-Saint-Vivant. Here the 70-year-old vines produce a beautifully refined wine, balanced and complex, with all the exquisite breeding that comes from this magnificent site. Fragrant, hypnotic, seductive, its 100%-new-oak upbringing gives it a heavy accent in its youth, but its innate balance promises it many a year to soften this and reveal the poetry of its origins. No one has yet seen one of Pascal Lachaux's Grands Crus at full maturity, but they seem destined to become wines of reference. Saddle of hare in a cream sauce provides just the sort of dish to enable this masterpiece to express itself with all its wonderful fluency.

• Other red wines:
Grand cru:
Clos de Vougeot,
Échézeaux.
Premier cru:
Vosne-Romanée Les Chaumes,
VR Les Suchots,
VR Aux Reignots; Nuits-Saint-Georges Les Procès,
NSG Les Corvées Pagets.
Village:
Vosne-Romanée,
VR Les Hautes Maizières;
Nuits-Saint-Georges,
NSG Les Poisets.
Régional:
Bourgogne, Bourgogne Passetoutgrain
• White wine:
Régional:
Bourgogne Aligoté
• Wine-maker: Pascal Lachaux
• Combined vineyards: 12 hectares
• Production: 50,000 bottles
• Exports: 70%
• Take-away sales: Yes
• Visits: 8-12 a.m., 1.30-6.00 p.m.

Wine selected:
Romanée-Saint-Vivant

• Classification: Grand Cru
• Area cultivated: 0.35 hectares
• Soil type: Clay and limestone
• Average vine age: 70 years
• Average annual production: 1,200 bottles

W hile it is not unknown for wine-makers to get swollen heads as soon as a few articles have been dedicated to them in the press, others seem genuinely at a loss as to why any journalist should want to take an interest in them – even those with as big and well-established a reputation as Robert Chevillon. This consummate craftsman makes a wide and very fine range of Nuits-Saint-Georges against which others are and should be measured.

Generations in the service of wine Chevillon was born into a family which has plied the trade of *vigneron* for generations, although when he started working alongside his father Maurice in 1968 their own estate only covered 3 hectares. Yet gradually it grew, as vines were taken on a sharecropping basis, leased or bought, until reaching its present size of 13 hectares. By 1977 the bulk of the production was being sold in bottle, and Chevillon wines finally found their way to foreign shores for the first time in 1979. Maurice Chevillon's grandsons Denis and Bertrand are now working full-time with their father, learning the trade for the benefit of future wine-lovers.

Measures for better-quality fruit Some of the finer *climats* of the Chevillon estate are full of very old vines, including some centenarians, which goes some way to explaining the quality of their wines. Chevillon admires these senior citizens, who can expect to be looked after right up until their natural deaths; only then will their space in the row be filled by a bright new young plant, whose immature production will for a while be used to swell the vats of Village wine. An intimate knowledge of all his different parcels enables him to treat them individually in order to get the most out of them, taking preventive action against a susceptibility to illness or rot here, pruning shorter to neutralize a tendency to overproduce there... The vineyards also contain a smattering of white vines, which add a certain extra something to the reds, as well as producing a fine white Nuits-Saint-Georges.

A thoroughly traditional cellar In the cellar few wine-makers can be more traditional. Stainless steel vats with (little used) heat exchangers probably represent the most significant concession to late 20th-century technology. One quarter of the fruit is left on its stalks, and starts to ferment as soon as it likes; Chevillon judges cold maceration a passing fad, indeed it is clear that Accad has not put a foot in this cellar. Fermentations are allowed to rise to 35° before he will intervene, and maceration here takes place at the end of the process. Then the wines spend 18 months maturing in wood, of which one third at the very most is new, before bottling, which will have been preceded by fining and a light filtration.

Nuits-Saint-Georges Les Saint-Georges Chevillon's parcel in the prestigious Les Saint-Georges is occupied by 75-year-old vines, which have the very praiseworthy quality of restraint in their yields. The wine issuing from their fruit is splendidly rich, fleshy and profound, fairly powerful and structured for the long-term. This wine has character rather than breeding, which is probably due to its soil, yet also has finesse. At table it is happy to find itself confronted with jugged hare.

• Other red wines:
Premier cru:
Nuits-Saint-Georges Les Pruliers,
NSG Les Roncières,
NSG Les Chaignots,
NSG Les Perrières,
NSG Les Bousselots,
NSG Les Cailles,
NSG Les Vaucrains.
Village:
Nuits-Saint-Georges Vieilles Vignes.
Régional:
Bourgogne Rouge,
Bourgogne Passetoutgrain
• White wines:
Village:
Nuits-Saint-Georges.
Régional:
Bourgogne Chardonnay,
Bourgogne Aligoté
• Owner: Robert Chevillon
• Wine-maker: Robert Chevillon
• Combined vineyards: 13 hectares
• Production: 50,000 bottles
• Exports: 80%
• Take-away sales: Yes
• Visits: By appointment

Wine selected:
Nuits-Saint-Georges Les Saint-Georges

• Classification: Premier Cru
• Area cultivated: 0.62 hectares
• Soil type: Clay and limestone
• Average vine age: 75 years
• Average annual production: 2,800 bottles

NUITS-SAINT-GEORGES
LES SAINT-GEORGES
APPELLATION NUITS-SAINT-GEORGES 1er CRU CONTROLÉE

Domaine Robert CHEVILLON   750 M.

Viticulteur à Nuits-Saint-Georges (Côte-d'or) France

PRODUIT DE FRANCE

From their fine establishment in the centre of Morey-Saint-Denis the father-and-son team of Robert and Serge Groffier produces a selection of Chambolles and Gevreys – yet, quaintly, not a single drop of Morey – which are utterly seductive. Their wines are recognizable, for there is a Groffier 'style', yet in no way is it to the detriment of *terroir* expression. One could do worse than choose a Groffier wine to introduce a novice to the joys of Burgundy!

Four generations at work in the vines The foundations of the estate were laid by Jules Groffier, son of a vineyard worker named Frédéric Groffier, from the 1930s onwards, and by 1960, the year in which Jules handed it down to his daughter and two sons, it included some choice appellations, notably Chambertin Clos de Bèze, Bonnes Mares and Chambolle-Musigny Les Amoureuses. Robert Groffier's brother was not interested in wine, and fortunately he managed to buy him out, and has since further increased his holdings with a little extra Amoureuses.

Although his father had dabbled with estate-bottling, largely in frustration at the pittance paid by the *négoce*, the wines had generally been sold in bulk, and it was only in 1973, after some 8 years at the helm, that Robert started bottling the major part of his output every year. Nowadays all is sold in bottle, and worldwide demand following a subtle but significant rise in quality during the 1990s means that there is little on sale at the estate.

Robert's son Serge learnt the business working with his father, and now takes care of the lion's share of duties as Dad eases up a bit. Not that he has any intention of retiring just yet, though...

Maximum extraction of colour and structure The Groffiers like their wines to have deep colour and lots of structure, and they like to coat the latter in a soft, fleshy texture. To obtain all this they employ lots of maceration – both cold (20-25°!) for 5-6 days before fermentation and warmer for 5 days after it – and fermentation temperatures are allowed up to 35°. Throughout the process there are repeated *pigeages*, during which the Groffiers no doubt congratulate themselves on their investment in an automatic *pigeoir*. To obtain even more extraction, in 1996 they heated up their wines to 38° for two hours after fermentation. They like to prolong malolactic fermentations as long as possible, so maturation in oak, which for the top wines is 70-100% new, lasts roughly 18 months, and the subsequent bottling generally takes place after fining but without filtration.

Bonnes Mares The house style is perfectly represented by the sumptuous Bonnes Mares, a magnificently creamy and soft wine at first approach, which then reveals a chewy, structured physique which indicates that there is virility behind the charm. The low yields and the fine quality of the fruit give great intensity and refinement to the wine, which is delicious even in its youth. This succulent Bonnes Mares is shown to great advantage with a tournedos *forestière*.

• Other red wines:
Grand cru:
Chambertin Clos de Bèze.
Premier cru:
Chambolle-Musigny
Les Amoureuses,
CM Les Hauts-Doix,
CM Les Sentiers.
Village:
Gevrey-Chambertin.
Régional:
Bourgogne Rouge
• Owner: Groffier family
• Wine-maker:
Serge Groffier
• Combined vineyards:
8 hectares
• Production: 36,000 bottles
• Exports: 65%
• Take-away sales:
By appointment
• Visits: No

Wine selected:
Bonnes-Mares

• Classification:
Grand Cru
• Area cultivated:
0.98 hectares
• Soil type:
Clay and limestone
• Average vine age:
30 years
• Average annual production:
3,500 bottles

Côte de Nuits | Morey-Saint-Denis

Few wine-lovers get the chance in their lifetime to taste the legendary Romanée-Conti, although almost all have read about it, such is the wealth of print devoted to this mythical wine. Its extraordinary quality, combined with its extreme scarcity, unfortunately make it a luxury which only the inordinately well-off can afford. Romanée-Conti is the jewel in the crown of the domaine of the same name, a crown which is also set with other gems of stunning quality.

An unrivalled portfolio of vineyards The Domaine's vineyard holdings are of the very greatest quality: six red Grands Crus, at the qualitative pinnacle even of that exalted category, and one white Grand Cru, from Burgundy's finest white-wine vineyard. Plus 1.6 hectares of Vosne Premier Cru and a little Bâtard-Montrachet, which are never offered for sale.

The vines in all these vineyards are cosseted in a thoroughly ecological fashion. When they need to be replaced, it is done by *selection massale*, using grafts from 50 plants in the Romanée-Conti vineyard which are selected for their health, robustness, moderate yield, fruit quality and perfect regularity from year to year.

In preparation for a long life Yields are kept at an extremely low level, and only when peak ripeness is attained is fruit picked by the domaine's experienced pickers, who operate an initial quality control in the vineyard, before transportation to the pressroom.

After undergoing another inspection on a conveyor belt the fruit is lightly pressed and tipped into the fermentation vats, generally with its stems. For vinification the domaine uses both open, wooden vats and stainless steel ones. A lengthy fermentation and maceration give the wines the colour, tannin, acidity and intense fruitiness to see them through a period of up to two years maturation in new Tronçais oak and many subsequent years in bottle.

Romanée-Conti It was Louis François de Bourbon, Prince de Conti, who created the myth surrounding Romanée-Conti. Having purchased the Romanée vineyard in 1760 at ten times the rate for the finest vineyards, he withdrew it from the market and reserved it for his own glittering social events. Reclaimed as the property of the nation at the Revolution, the vineyard passed through the hands of several owners before in 1942 arriving at the present situation of being owned by the De Villaine and Leroy families. Today, such is demand that Romanée-Conti is sold singly in mixed dozens of the domaine's wines, both to satisfy a greater number of clients and as a measure against speculation.

The fabulous quality of Romanée-Conti lies in its great aromatic complexity, which evolves over the minutes in a truly awe-inspiring manner. Depending on the vintage and its age, its ethereal bouquet suggests roses, violets, cinnamon, leather, tobacco, coffee, caramel, hot earth, game...

While this wine is rich and opulent, it has an extraordinary degree of finesse, and is in no way a blockbuster. When sufficiently knowledgeable friends have been gathered, it should be enjoyed reverently, unhurriedly, and perhaps accompanied with a roast woodcock, followed by the monastic Cîteaux cheese. An indelible souvenir is guaranteed!

Vosne-Romanée | Côte de Nuits

- Other red wines:
Grand cru:
La Tâche (monopole), Richebourg, Romanée-Saint-Vivant, Grands Échézeaux, Échézeaux
- White wine:
Grand cru:
Montrachet
- Owner: SCI du Domaine de la Romanée-Conti
- Co-managers: Aubert de Villaine, Henry Frédéric Roch
- Wine-maker: Bernard Noblet
- Combined vineyards: 26 hectares
- Production: 80,000 bottles
- Exports: 70%
- Take-away sales: Yes, depending on stock availability
- Visits: No

Wine selected:
Romanée-Conti
(monopole)

- Classification: Grand Cru
- Vineyard size: 1.8 hectares
- Soil type: Clay and limestone
- Average vine age: 50 years
- Average annual production: 5,000 bottles

I n 1990 the Louis Trapet domaine was divided between Jean Trapet, who ran it, and his sister Mado, giving birth to a renamed Trapet Père et Fils and a completely new Rossignol-Trapet. The latter estate, created by Mado and her husband Jacques Rossignol, has in its short existence made some very fine wines, and has a vineyard patrimony many would envy. Today Nicolas and David Rossignol are progressively shouldering responsibilities.

A union with no shortage of traditions The Trapets originally came from Chambolle, and have made wine since the 18th century, the last century of which has been spent in Gevrey. As for the Rossignols, they have lived and made wine in Volnay since the 16th century. The union of the two families could not be said to be short of traditions!

There is a modern awareness on the estate of the fragility of the soil and of the dangerous abuses to which it has been subjected in previous, less enlightened times. To protect the vineyards' natural micro-fauna a thoroughly ecological outlook is the rule of the day, involving the sparing use of organic compost, manual weeding and the reduction to a strict minimum of treatments to protect against disease and parasites such as mildew and red spider. And when treatments there must be, spraying is carried out with great care, to direct them to the exact problem areas, as opposed to the haphazard blanket spraying of the past.

Yield limitation and quality control The Rossignol vines are trained low and planted densely, which restrains productivity, and are subjected to a green harvest if they are overladen with bunches in July. The Rossignols' pickers come back every year, and their experience enables judicious selectivity as they work their way along the rows of vines. The fruit also receives a close inspection as it is loaded into the trailer.

In the vatroom operations are more or less standard. Fermentations are carried out in open stainless steel vats (actually not so standard!), with emphasis placed on regular *remontage* and *pigeage* for maximum extraction of colour, aromas, acidity and tannin. A small percentage of grapes are left on their stalks, in order to extract their tannin, and the quantity is increased in weaker years when there is less potential structure in the skins. Wines are transferred to barrel for their malo-lactic fermentations, then spend 14 months maturing, before bottling with fining but usually without filtration.

Chambertin Thanks to a plantation density of 11,500 vines per hectare and the vines' great age, the Rossignols' finest wine, their Chambertin, is magnificently rich and powerful, with great intensity of flavour, impressive length and a structure to guarantee it a fine long life. Matured for 14-18 months in barrel depending on the vintage's characteristics, half of which is new, this wine requires some 7-8 years to round out and express itself with conviction, yet the longer it is kept, the more its voluptuous and rich flavours gain in depth! For one of France's great wines, game is called for: a haunch of wild boar, marinated and roasted, understands Chambertin's language perfectly.

Côte de Nuits | Gevrey-Chambertin

• Other red wines:
Grand cru:
Latricières-Chambertin,
Chapelle-Chambertin.
Premier cru:
Gevrey-Chambertin Petite
Chapelle, GC Clos Prieur,
GC Premier Cru; Beaune
Teurons.
Village:
Gevrey-Chambertin,
Morey-Saint-Denis Rue de
Vergy, Beaune Mariages,
Savigny-lès-Beaune.
Régional:
Pinot Noir de Bourgogne
• White wine:
Régional:
Bourgogne Chardonnay
• Owners: David &
Nicolas Rossignol
• Wine-makers:
David & Nicolas Rossignol
• Combined vineyards:
14 hectares
• Production:
65,000 bottles
• Exports: 70%
• Take-away sales: Yes
• Visits: 9.00-11.30 a.m.,
2-6 p.m., by appointment

Wine selected:
Chambertin

• Classification:
Grand Cru
• Area cultivated:
1.6 hectares
• Soil type:
Brown clay and limestone
• Average vine age:
50 years
• Average annual
production:
5,000 bottles

T he Sérafin domaine, located up at the top of the village of Gevrey below the Cazetiers vineyard, is little known, for its yearly output is small and is mostly bought by the Swiss, and the domaine does not have a very long history. The quality of its produce is very fine, and the rare bottle which comes one's way may be bought without the slightest hesitation.

A happier life for soil and vine The estate was founded by Sérafin *père* in 1947, and his son Christian eased himself into the driving seat in the 1960s. The family holdings started off with a patch of Gevrey village land, and have gradually increased over the years, after a half-century even extending themselves beyond the village, with parcels of Chambolle Les Baudes and Morey les Millandes!

Like a good many of his peers nowadays Sérafin is well aware of the importance of looking after his vineyard soils in order to promote happier vines and finer quality fruit. Vineyard operations are therefore as ecological as possible, with hoeing rather than weedkiller to keep weeds at bay and give the soil's microorganic life a chance to thrive, and with minimal treatments against the various pests and illnesses to which the vine succumbs from time to time... and, when a treatment is inevitable, it is done carefully; there is none of the blanket spraying still seen too often even in prestigious appellations.

Rich wines in the finest Gevrey tradition Old vines and low yields are an essential part of the Sérafin formula for quality, and the vines are pruned short and debudded in spring in order to control their enthusiastic productivity. If necessary a "green harvest" is carried out at the moment the grapes turn colour, and *verjus*, the second crop of grapes, are painstakingly cut from the plant in order to avoid a waste of valuable energy.

Vinification is aimed at producing rich, structured wines, in the finest Gevrey tradition. Some 70% of the raw material is destalked and the fruit is then given a cold maceration before fermentation gets under way in the stainless steel vats, with the aid of natural yeast. The fermentation is a protracted affair which takes place at up to 35°, a temperature which would send many into a cold sweat, and regular *pigeages* ensure that all the colour, aroma and tannin are transferred to the wine. New oak barrels then feature prominently in the ageing process – a little too prominently sometimes, it could be argued – and wines are bottled with neither fining nor filtration.

Charmes-Chambertin Heading the Sérafin price list is Charmes-Chambertin. This Grand Cru was acquired in several stages, and the bulk of the holding lies in Mazoyères-Chambertin, yet due to one those administrative anomalies Mazoyères may use the name Charmes, which is rather easier on the ear and no doubt also easier to sell, while the reverse is not permitted. This is a deliciously smooth and refined wine, packed with flavour and extremely elegant. Heavily oaked in youth, it needs some 10 years to develop its aromatic balance, and when it has done so may be served confidently with woodcock and foie gras paté, a combination which should delight all present.

Côte de Nuits | Gevrey-Chambertin

• Other red wines:
Premier cru:
Gevrey-Chambertin Les Corbeaux, GC Le Fonteny, GC Les Cazetiers;
Chambolle-Musigny Les Baudes; Morey-Saint-Denis Les Millandes.
Village:
Gevrey-Chambertin, GC Vieilles Vignes.
Régional:
Bourgogne
• White wine:
Régional:
Bourgogne Chardonnay
• Owners: Christian Sérafin & Jacqueline Goulley
• Wine-maker: Christian Sérafin
• Oenologist: Laboratoires SGS
• Combined vineyards: 5.3 hectares
h Production: 30,000 bottles
• Exports: 70%
• Take-away sales: No
• Visits: No

Wine selected:
Charmes-Chambertin

• Classification: Grand Cru
• Area cultivated: 0.31 hectares
• Soil type: Clay and limestone
• Average vine age: 54 years
• Average annual production: 1,400 bottles

1995

CHARMES-CHAMBERTIN

APPELLATION CHARMES-CHAMBERTIN CONTRÔLÉE

Grand Cru

13,5% vol.

MIS EN BOUTEILLE PAR

750 ml

SÉRAFIN PÈRE & FILS

PROPRIÉTAIRES A GEVREY-CHAMBERTIN · COTE-D'OR · FRANCE

PRODUCT OF FRANCE

With its 50.6 hectares and 82 owners, Clos Vougeot epitomizes the fragmented Burgundian vineyard. As a result of its large surface area and varying soil make-up as well as its multiplicity of proprietors, Clos Vougeot wines vary greatly in quality depending on the position in the *clos* of the vines and on the talent of the *vigneron*. The most important owner is Château de la Tour, whose vines are admirably sited and whose wine is equally admirable.

Making Clos Vougeot on site The château is actually situated inside the *clos*, hugging its northern side and lying below the historic Château du Clos de Vougeot. It was constructed in the late 1880s by the Beaune *négociant* Maison Beaudet Frères, who sold it and its vines to another *négociant*, Morin Père & Fils, in 1920. Eventually the estate passed into the hands of two sisters, Mesdames Labet and Déchelette, daughters of Jean Morin, and from the 1975 vintage Jacqueline Labet took an active part in the day-to-day running of the estate, then in 1986 her son François took over.

François Labet consults Guy Accad François Labet was convinced that the estate was not performing to its full potential, and got in touch with the oenologist Guy Accad to work out how to improve the wine. The work commenced in the vineyard, with soil analyses, which permitted them to keep a close eye on the vines' nutrition; rectifications have since been biological. Low yields were the next target, to attain which Labet started pruning shorter and doing some serious debudding in the spring, thus bringing to an end the green harvests and *saignées* in the vatroom which had been estate practice. It was considered that lower yields would give better acidities, and this meant that harvesting could be delayed for extra ripeness, without any detrimental heaviness.

The vatroom saw a good number of modifications also. Destalking of roughly half the crop became the norm, following which a prolonged maceration at 5°, retarding the onset of fermentation by the use of sulphur, enabled the extraction of the finest aromas, colour, tannin and acidity. When fermentation got under way it was initially maintained also at a low temperature of around 26°, although since Accad's departure Labet has allowed it to rise a little. Finally maturing wines were treated to rather more new wood than had been the practice, up to 50% in good years, followed by bottling with neither fining nor filtration.

Clos Vougeot Vieilles Vignes In exceptional years Labet isolates the fruit of the oldest vines to make a Vieilles Vignes wine which is truly exceptional. The 1995 vintage gave birth to one such wine. Harvested at 9 hl/ha, the fruit was macerated without destalking and after fermentation the wine spent 22 months in oak barrels, of which 75% were new. This will be a great wine, but owners of bottles will need a lot of patience! The 1989 Vieilles Vignes was starting to express itself forcefully and with great eloquence after 7 years, but more structured and 'classic' years need more time than that. When its day has finally come, enjoy it with venison, suggests Labet, in a Grand Veneur sauce.

- Other red wine: Clos Vougeot (cuvée normale)
- Owners: Labet and Déchelette families
- Wine-maker: François Labet
- Oenologist: Jean-Pierre Confuron
- Combined vineyards: 5.5 hectares
- Production: 21,000 bottles
- Exports: 50%
- Take-away sales: Yes
- Visits: 10 a.m.-7 p.m., Tues.-Sun., Easter until end of November

Wine selected:
Clos Vougeot Vieilles Vignes

- Classification: Grand Cru
- Area cultivated: 2 hectares
- Soil type: Clay and limestone
- Average vine age: 70 years
- Average annual production: 2,400 bottles

T he Trapets are an integral part of the Gevrey-Chambertin scenery, having lived there and made wine for six generations. Not only has this permanence enabled the family to build up a superb vineyard patrimony, it has also led to a great understanding of the different vineyard plots, enabling the Trapets to bring out their *terroir* characteristics with great talent. Trapet wines, particularly those made since 1990, are models of purity, finesse and balance.

A series of fine acquisitions Louis Trapet of Chambolle married a Gevrey girl in the middle of the 19th century and settled in the village. His son Arthur started buying vines on Village land in the 1870s, and bought some of the Premier Cru Petite-Chapelle in 1877, today blended with that of the Premier Cru Clos Prieur, acquired in 1893. But the serious purchases came at the turn of the century, when Pierre-Arthur Trapet bought some Latricières-Chambertin in 1904, and the Chambertin itself in 1919. Each generation has added to the family holdings, the latest acquisitions being a section of the wonderfully-named Marsannay *climat* Les Grasses Têtes in 1979 and some Le Poirier and a plot of Chardonnay shortly after.

Reducing the vines' yields Jean, the head of the house, has retired from active wine-making duties, which have been the province of his son Jean-Louis since 1990. The Trapet vineyards are the source of wonderful fruit, for many of the vines are old, and the vineyards are planted at an impressive density of 12,000 per hectare, which restricts their productivity. To further keep yields at a level conducive with quality, Jean-Louis debuds in the spring and if necessary also green harvests when the grapes turn colour. Viticultural practices are ecological and minimal, the principal aim being to revive the microorganic life in the soil which suffered in the post-war decades as a result of the vogue for potassium-based fertilizers, which take many years to work their way out of the soil.

Chambertin The finest wine produced by the Trapets is without doubt the Chambertin. This noble vineyard, which gained its name in the 13th century when it was a field lying alongside the Clos de Bèze and belonged to a certain Bertin (*le champ Bertin*), today mesmerizes wine-lovers the world over with its complex, manly character.

The Trapet Chambertin is made with the habitual devotion, starting with a double selection process to eliminate any imperfect fruit, once by harvesters in the vineyard and again on arrival at the vathouse. The perfection of the fruit imparts enormous intensity and depth of flavour to the wine, which acquires a fleshy, opulent feel and a tannic structure guaranteeing longevity, through long, gentle fermentation. Elegance, aromatic purity and class, these are the first words the Trapet Chambertin utters, and if he takes a moment the enchanted wine-lover soons discovers the depth, complexity and irresistible persuasiveness of this *seigneur*. A noble dish is called for: truffled fillet of beef, or perhaps jugged partridge, followed, naturally, by that especially delicious époisses, l'Ami du Chambertin.

• Other red wines:
Grand cru:
Chapelle-Chambertin,
Latricières-Chambertin.
Premier cru:
Gevrey-Chambertin
Clos Prieur, GC Petite
Chapelle.
Village:
Gevrey-Chambertin,
Marsannay.
Régional:
Bourgogne Pinot Noir
• White wines:
Village:
Marsannay.
Régional:
Bourgogne Chardonnay
• Owner: Trapet family
• Wine-maker:
Jean-Louis Trapet
• Combined vineyards:
12 hectares
• Production:
43,000 bottles
• Exports: 50%
• Take-away sales: Yes
• Visits: 9-12 a.m.,
2.30-5.30 p.m.,
by appointment

Wine selected:
Chambertin

• Classification:
Grand Cru
• Area cultivated:
1.9 hectares
• Soil type:
Clay and limestone
• Average vine age:
40-80 years
• Average annual
production:
5,000 bottles

DOMAINE TRAPET PÈRE & FILS
CHAMBERTIN
GRAND CRU
APPELLATION CONTRÔLÉE

1995

Jean & Jean-Louis TRAPET
PROPRIÉTAIRES A GEVREY-CHAMBERTIN, CÔTE-D'OR, FRANCE

MIS EN BOUTEILLE
AU DOMAINE

PRODUCT
OF FRANCE

75 cl

FILIGER A NUITS

T he wines of Beaune are rather less fashionable than those of the villages just south of the town, in particular Volnay and Pommard, and equally so with just about everything produced to the north. This is a shame, for there are some fine *climats* capable of producing very good, interesting wine, and at a more attractive price than the more fashionable appellations. One of the best addresses is Domaine Albert Morot.

The changing face of Albert Morot's legacy The estate was founded in 1820 and was initially a *négociant* business. After the phylloxera crisis Albert Morot's successors acquired the Beaune vineyards which they own today, principally from the descendants of Jean-Marie Duvault-Blochet, who in his lifetime owned 133 hectares of what are today Grands and Premiers Crus, crowned by Romanée-Conti. In the 1890s they built the Château de la Creusotte, on Beaune's outskirts, in which the domaine has been based ever since, and after the Great War extended their *négociant* activities and leased cellars in the centre of Beaune, and subsequently started selling abroad.

In 1952 Guy and Françoise Choppin inherited the firm, and over 30 years Guy made many a classic wine. Illness however gradually overtook him, to the extent that he eventually became an invalid. His sister Françoise took his place, looking after both him, neither of them being married, and the estate. From 1984 the *négociant* business was discontinued, and since then Françoise has made the Domaine Morot wines herself, displaying remarkable talent and consistency in doing so.

The great and the mediocre Old vines and low yields, these are the principal sources of quality as far as Mlle. Choppin is concerned, these make the difference between great and mediocre wine. Otherwise there are no special processes or tricks to explain the quality of her wines, simply a devoted adherence to traditional practice, without cutting corners, without being rushed. Grapes are entirely destalked and musts are given a traditional long vatting with indigenous yeast at a temperature going up to 33°, with regular *pigeage*. Free-run wine is mixed with press-wine and the resulting blends are matured for a year after the end of their malo-lactic fermentations, in barrels of which one half at the most is renewed annually. They are then bottled, usually without fining and always without filtration.

Beaune-Teurons The estate has 6 Beaune Premiers Crus, enabling a fine appreciation of the influence of *terroir* on wines. Which one prefers is a question of personal preference, for all have their qualities. Perhaps the most distinguished is the Teurons, a rich, medium- to full-bodied wine of great class. It has depth and structure and rather more refinement and less of the meatiness of the others. The more accentuated the meatiness, the better suited the wine is to meats in sauce; the Teurons therefore can be more fully appreciated with a more delicate dish, such as roast lamb. It reaches full maturity after some 8 years.

- Other red wines:
Premier cru:
Beaune Cent Vignes,
B Toussaints,
B Bressandes, B Grèves,
B Marconnets; Savigny-lès-Beaune Vergelesses
La Bataillère (monopole)
- Owners: Guy & Françoise Choppin
- Manager: Françoise Choppin
- Wine-maker: Françoise Choppin
- Combined vineyards: 7 hectares
- Production: 30,000 bottles
- Exports: 75%
- Take-away sales: Yes
- Visits: 10-12 a.m., 2-6 p.m

Wine selected:
Beaune-Teurons

- Classification: Premier Cru
- Area cultivated: 1 hectare
- Soil type: Clay and limestone
- Average vine age: 35 years
- Average annual production: 4,500 bottles

1993   1993

PRODUCE   OF FRANCE

TIRAGE DU   DOMAINE

Beaune-Teurons

APPELLATION BEAUNE 1er CRU CONTROLÉE

Mis en bouteilles par

Albert Morot

Négociant au Château de la Creusotte à Beaune (Côte-d'Or)

Ce vin n'est pas filtré

DOMAINE BERNARD MOREY & FILS

The Moreys are a large family with buildings and cellars spread all over their home village of Chassagne and around it, indeed there are even several distantly-related branches in Meursault. The general standard of wine-making is very high, particularly so *chez* Bernard and Jean-Marc Morey, and much of the credit for this must go to their father Albert Morey, who instilled all the right lessons into his two sons.

From generation to generation When Albert left his estate to his two sons on his retirement in 1981, they decided that instead of dividing every holding in half they would each take the entirety of certain holdings, rendering the wine-making more practical and reducing potential confusion for clients. Since then Bernard Morey has added the odd parcel and almost doubled his original inheritance, and today produces slightly more red wine than white, although the list of whites is longer.

Natural, rich and ripe wines Viticultural practices are natural and respectful of the soil and the vine's health on his estate. Fruit ripeness is accorded extreme importance, and every year involves a waiting game as Morey patiently surveys sugar levels and holds back from harvesting until the perfect degree of ripeness is reached. Only so can the wines have natural, ripe richness, without the forced aspect that is often the result of excessive chaptalisation of insufficiently ripe must.

Black grapes are all destemmed and then cold-macerated before starting their fermentation in cement vats, which are eminently preferred to wooden vats for their hygiene and easy maintenance. The fermenting liquids are allowed to rise to some 33°, giving fine, colourful wines, and this is increased by systematic *saignées* in order to increase the ratio of solid matter to liquid. Morey gives his reds a judiciously judged blend of new and used oak for maturation, which lasts as long as the wine and vintage require, then bottles without filtration.

As for the white wines, the grapes are delicately squeezed in a pneumatic press and the must is then chilled and transferred to cask, of which some 25% are renewed every year. There it ferments, enjoying regular *bâtonnage* every 15 days until the malo-lactic fermentations have finished, and then matures, before being fined, lightly filtered and bottled roughly 11 months after the harvest.

Chassagne-Montrachet Morgeot Lying near the dividing-line with Santenay, the Morgeot *climat* has rich soil which is suitable both to the Chardonnay and the Pinot, and this always results in whites of firmness, depth and dimension... particularly, as in Bernard Morey's case, when they are made from ultra-ripe grapes and lots of *bâtonnage*. This splendid, fat, concentrated wine improves over 8-10 years, but is in truth pretty irresistible at any age. At table it can be partnered with a good many dishes: fresh *foie gras*, poultry, veal or pork in cream sauces, salt-water fish, all combine admirably with it.

- Other white wines:
Premier cru:
Chassagne-Montrachet
Embrazées,
CM Caillerets,
CM Baudines,
CM Vide-Bourse;
Puligny-Montrachet
Truffière; Santenay
Passetemps;
Saint-Aubin Charmois.
Village:
Chassagne-Montrachet.
Régional:
Bourgogne Blanc
- Red wines:
Premier cru:
Beaune Les Grèves;
Santenay Passetemps,
Santenay Clos Grand
Rousseau; Maranges
La Fussière.
Village:
Chassagne-Montrachet,
CM Vieilles Vignes;
Santenay; Maranges
Côte de Beaune
- Owner: Bernard Morey
- Wine-makers: Bernard
Morey, Vincent & Thomas
Morey
- Oenologist: BIVB,
Beaune
- Combined vineyards:
14 hectares
- Production:
75,000 bottles
- Exports: 65%
- Take-away sales: Yes
- Visits: By appointment

Wine selected:
**Chassagne-Montrachet
Morgeot**

- Classification:
Premier Cru
- Area cultivated:
0.6 hectares
- Soil type:
Clay and limestone
- Average vine age:
25 years
- Average annual
production:
3,600 bottles

1996

PRODUCE OF FRANCE

Chassagne Montrachet

Morgeot 1er Cru

APPELLATION CHASSAGNE-MONTRACHET CONTROLÉE

MIS EN BOUTEILLE A LA PROPRIÉTÉ PAR

BERNARD MOREY ET FILS

VITICULTEURS A CHASSAGNE MONTRACHET (CÔTE D'OR) FRANCE

Those who like nothing more than a luscious glass of Meursault for their aperitif and with their first course, and a soft and refined Volnay with their meat dish, can pay a visit with confidence to the estate of Vincent Bitouzet-Prieur in Volnay. There they will be able to taste a range of both types of wine, and will no doubt wish to buy some bottles, for both whites and reds are of very fine quality.

A dowry presents a new challenge Bitouzet is not an internationally-known name, unlike those of some of his neighbours, yet the family are no newcomers, having been established in Volnay ever since Simon Bitouzet settled there in 1860. Vincent is the fifth generation to look after the family vines, of which he has been in charge since 1981. These were situated exclusively around the home village, and he learnt his trade making red wines, but the day he wedded a girl from Meursault, who brought dowry of some 3 hectares of white vineyards around that village as well as some red Beaune, his horizons were opened more than a little. However he duly took things in his stride, and the quality in the various bottles bears witness to his talent for both colours.

The elusive qualities of finesse and delicacy The Meursaults continue to be made in Meursault, in Vincent's father-in-law's house, by traditional methods. They are rich and pure, lively and well-balanced, without any excessive heaviness, and do not hide their *terroir* signatures. As for the red wines, Vincent aims above all for finesse and delicacy. Their fine quality is derived first from healthy, ripe fruit, obtained by low yields from healthy vines, grown in soils which are cultivated with respect, enabling their micro-organic life to live and thrive.

On arrival at the vatroom all the fruit is destalked, and during the initial maceration juice is pumped up from the bottom of the vat over the floating cap of solids. This *remontage* is replaced by twice-daily *pigeage* once fermentation has got under way, which does not take long, for Bitouzet's cellar is not equipped with cooling equipment. He likes to ferment his musts gently, for only so can those elusive qualities of finesse and delicacy emerge in the final wine. Once the alcoholic fermentation is over the wines then spend a long period in cask, for lees contact is sought for the depth and intensity of flavour it contributes. The casks themselves are renewed over four years, for new-oak flavours can too easily submerge Volnay's delicate aromas.

Volnay Caillerets "He without vines in Cailleret knows not what is Volnay" says a local adage, and indeed this *climat* is often said to sum up all that is best about Volnay, notably its elegance, finesse and breed. At 11,000 vines per hectare Bitouzet's tiny plot is densely planted, which obliges roots to bury themselves deeper in their quest for nourishment, and contributes greater *terroir* character and intensity to the final wine. His Caillerets is a suave, succulent, velvet delight, exquisitely perfumed with violets, sometimes roses even, with ripe tannin to fortify it in its confrontation with time. Such elegance is easily swamped by rich sauces, and a Caillerets is best enjoyed with simple roast beef.

Côte de Beaune | Volnay

- Other red wines:
Premier cru:
Volnay Clos des Chênes,
V Taillepieds, V Les
Pitures, V Les Aussy;
Beaune Les Cent Vignes.
Village:
Volnay.
Régional:
Bourgogne, Bourgogne
Passetoutgrain
- White wines:
Premier cru:
Meursault Perrières,
M Charmes,
M Santenots.
Village:
M Clos du Cromin,
M Les Cabrins,
Meursault.
Régional:
Bourgogne Aligoté
- Wine-maker:
Vincent Bitouzet
- Combined vineyards:
12 hectares
- Production:
66,000 bottles
- Exports: 30%
- Take-away sales: Yes
- Visits: By appointment

Wine selected:
Volnay Caillerets

- Classification:
Premier Cru
- Area cultivated:
0.15 hectares
- Soil type:
Clay and limestone
- Average vine age:
16 years
- Average annual
production:
900 bottles

1992

VIN FIN
DE BOURGOGNE

MIS EN BOUTEILLE
A LA PROPRIÉTÉ

VOLNAY CAILLERETS
PREMIER CRU
APPELLATION CONTROLÉE

BITOUZET-PRIEUR

VITICULTEUR A VOLNAY - COTE~D'OR - FRANCE

PRODUIT DE FRANCE

DOMAINE BLAIN-GAGNARD

L overs of rich, fleshy, classic white Burgundy may address themselves to the Blain-Gagnard estate in Chassagne without any qualms, for there tradition and modern oenology rub shoulders in perfect harmony, making wines which are both technically faultless and deliciously hedonistic. The expertise is applied to red wines as well as white, and these should certainly not be overlooked.

The transmission of a fine estate Jean-Marc Blain and Claudine Gagnard met while studying oenology at Dijon University. He came from Sancerre, and having seen the wine world from close up, decided that it was for him. Claudine came from Chassagne, where the Gagnards have long been one of the principal families. Her father Jacques Gagnard has a fine estate and a great reputation, and the same may be said for her uncle Jean-Noël at the other end of the village. Claudine was doing her studies prior to helping her father and eventually inheriting some of his vineyards.

The two went back to settle in Chassagne and married in 1980. Shortly afterwards Jacques Gagnard passed much of his estate down to Claudine and to her elder sister Laurence, who was later to marry Richard Fontaine, giving Burgundy-lovers some new names with which to familiarize themselves: Blain-Gagnard, Laurence Gagnard, and a little later Fontaine-Gagnard.

Making wines which improve with time Jean-Marc Blain is dedicated to quality, and well aware that it starts in the vineyard. Every spring sees him debudding his vines, in the aim of restricting his Chardonnay yields to a low 40-45 hl/ha, and his Pinot yields to significantly less. When vintage-time arrives, the size and closeness of the family is a definite advantage, as everyone goes off to pick this or that plot of Gagnard-Delagrange vines, or of Fontaine-Gagnard or Blain-Gagnard vines, depending on which parcel is ready for picking. This cooperation is extended to the next step, for sometimes the different families' produce is pressed together, and the juice distributed afterwards.

Blain-Gagnard sets out to make wines which improve with time, and his vinification methods are thoroughly traditional, involving lots of lees contact and *bâtonnage*, and ageing in oak for a year. He never uses more than 25% new barrels for his wines.

Criots-Bâtard-Montrachet Hugging one end of Bâtard-Montrachet, with village land on the other side, the tiny 1.57-hectare Criots (the word is a corruption of *craie*, chalk) is the smallest of all Burgundy's Grands Crus save La Romanée, and produces some 9,000 bottles annually of a sublimely perfumed, rich and elegant wine. Elegance above richness, for Criots wine is generally the least powerful of the Montrachet satellites – no doubt the chalk has something to do with this. The Blain-Gagnard offering is beautifully made, with perfect balance and definition and a slightly floral character, which calls for a dozen years in the cellar in good vintages, and may be served with a crawfish *feuilleté*.

- Other white wines:
Grand cru:
Bâtard-Montrachet.
Premier cru:
Chassagne-Montrachet
Clos Saint-Jean,
CM Boudriottes,
CM Morgeot,
CM Caillerets.
Village:
Chassagne-Montrachet
- Red wines:
Premier cru:
Chassagne-Montrachet
Clos Saint-Jean,
CM Morgeot; Volnay
Champans.
Village:
Chassagne-Montrachet,
Volnay, Pommard
- Owners: Jean-Marc &
Claudine Blain-Gagnard
- Wine-makers: Jean-
Marc & Claudine Blain-
Gagnard
- Combined vineyards:
7.6 hectares
- Production:
40,000 bottles
- Exports: 80%
- Take-away sales:
By appointment
- Visits: No

Wine selected:
**Criots-Bâtard-
Montrachet**

- Classification:
Grand Cru
- Area cultivated:
0.2 hectares
- Soil type:
Clay and limestone
- Average vine age:
45 years
- Average annual
production:
1,200 bottles

1994

GRAND CRU   de Bourgogne

Criots-Bâtard-Montrachet

APPELLATION CONTROLÉE

Mis en bouteille par

Blain-Gagnard

Propriétaire-Récoltant à Chassagne-Montrachet (Côte-d'Or) France

PRODUCE OF FRANCE

DOMAINE BONNEAU DU MARTRAY

The Pernand estate of Bonneau du Martray has two wines, a red and a white, which originate in neighbouring parcels on the Corton hill, north-east of Beaune. It is principally the white wine, the Corton-Charlemagne, which has given the domain its long-held world-wide reputation, and with reason, for this is a very fine example of its kind.

Stains on the Emperor's beard The land around Aloxe and Pernand is generally more suited to the production of red wine than white, and a legend explains the origin of the white wine: the Emperor Charlemagne, a man of great stature and equally great appetite, owned a vineyard on the Corton hill which supplied him with his favourite tipple. As the years went by his beard turned progressively whiter, and the copious draughts of red wine left stains which grew ever more visible. His wife Liutgarde considered they detracted from his dignity, and tried to persuade him to drink white wine, so in order to accommodate her and at the same time continue imbibing his Corton, Charlemagne had some of the vineyard replanted with white-grape vines.

Whatever the real origin of the white wine vineyard, the 18th-century historian Abbé Courtépée was of the opinion that the *clos* which Charlemagne donated to the collegiate church of Saulieu in 775 was that which much later belonged to M. Bonneau-Véry – and that which concerns us here. It is situated at the top of the hillside, where the clay soil has noticeably more limestone and is much better suited to the Chardonnay.

In 1969 René Bonneau du Martray, having no direct heirs, left the domain to his niece, Comtesse Jean le Bault de la Morinière. Today her son Jean-Charles runs the estate.

Fermentation in tank and barrel To make the Corton-Charlemagne, only pristine fruit, sorted for quality, will suffice. After crushing it gently in two membrane presses and letting it settle for a short while, he vinifies it in two mediums: fermentation is started in stainless steel, at a temperature of no more than 18°, and then the liquid is decanted by gravity into oak barrels to finish fermenting. The lees are stirred occasionally to keep them in suspension and thereby increase the wine's aromatic qualities, and the malo-lactic fermentation eventually takes place. When all activity is over and the wine has had enough wood contact, it is transferred into tank again for equalization, and is finally filtered and bottled.

Corton-Charlemagne Bonneau du Martray's Corton-Charlemagne is one of the steeliest, for its vines face south and south-west rather than east, as is the case of the great majority of its peers, and therefore receive a little less sunlight during the day. When young it is somewhat reserved, and really requires 10 years to reach its best. The citrus fruit, floral or peach aromas of its youth (every vintage has a different personality) tend to develop into honeysuckle, hazelnut and cinnamon flavours, while all through its life vigour, power and great length characterize it. Grilled lobster is a great friend, smoked fish and seafood are not, and it also gets on well with Bresse chicken *demi-deuil*.

- Red wine:
Grand cru:
Corton
- Owner: M. le Bault de la Morinière
- Combined vineyards:
11 hectares
- Production:
56,000 bottles
- Exports: 85%
- Take-away sales: Yes
- Visits: No

Wine selected:
Corton-Charlemagne

- Classification:
Grand Cru
- Area cultivated:
9.5 hectares
- Soil type:
Clay and limestone
- Average vine age:
40 years
- Average annual production:
48,000 bottles

CORTON-CHARLEMAGNE

GRAND CRU

APPELLATION CONTRÔLÉE

Bonneau du Martray

PROPRIÉTAIRE À PERNAND-VERGELESSES & ALOXE-CORTON (CÔTE-D'OR) FRANCE

Mis en bouteille
au Domaine

1994

PRODUCE OF FRANCE

T he Beaune *négociant* firm Champy, founded in 1720, underwent a slow decline in the late 20th century which was linked with the advancing years of its proprietor. After his death its vineyards were purchased by Louis Jadot and the firm resold. It might well have disappeared forever. Fortunately, however, it fell into the right hands and has not looked back since.

Purchased by a family of brokers The buyers were Henri and Pierre Meurgey and Pierre Beuchet. The Meurgeys are brokers, and their firm DIVA finds buyers for the wines of a large number of Burgundy estates. It might have appeared curious branching out into the *négociant* business at a time when merchant firms without their own vineyards are having problems sourcing good wine, yet thanks to his 35 years' experience and numerous contacts with growers, Henri Meurgey has been able to find a great many wines which would otherwise have been hard to come by.

A tight rein on the quality purchased The Meurgeys' first vintage was the 1990. At first they bought wines, and matured and bottled them themselves, yet now they are progressively concentrating their purchases on grapes in order to carry out the entire vinification themselves. They demand great conscientiousness from the growers under contract to them, particularly when it comes to yield limitation, pruning and methods of soil enrichment and vine treatment, which have to be as natural as possible.

When it is ready-made wine which is bought, the Meurgeys like to take possession as soon as is practicable, and to that end deliver their own barrels to the growers at harvest time. That way presents the advantage of ensuring that each wine is housed in the type and quality of wood required.

Made expressly for laying down Vinification and ageing are oriented uncompromisingly towards the production of *vins de garde*. For red wines, cold maceration for up to 6 days is followed by fermentation at a high 36° in open wooden vats. *Pigeage* and *remontage* are practised for extraction, then the vats are covered as the fermentation arrives at its end in order to retain heat and prevent oxidation. For maturation anything between 30-100% new oak is used, with a medium toast. Both reds and whites are left in barrel in Champy's fine 15th-century cellars for relatively long periods before bottling, and this final operation is carried out by gravity and without filtration whenever that is possible.

Corton Bressandes The Meurgeys' way of making red wine lends itself particularly well to those appellations which are normally structured and tannic, giving them much typicity. Such is the case with their Corton Bressandes. This wine, aged for 24 months before bottling, is rich and structured, yet with ample fruit and flesh to give it balance and attraction. Judging by the excellent 1995, the better vintages require some 8 years' keeping before they soften up, and when they are eventually summoned to the ultimate rendezvous express themselves most eloquently with red meats, grilled or in sauce, and most medium-flavoured cheeses. Champy wines are inexpensive for the quality proposed, and are well worth discovering.

• Other red wines:
Premier cru:
Beaune Grèves, B Clos des Avaux, B Champs Pimont, B Premier Cru; Savigny-lès-Beaune Les Peuillets, SlB Les Serpentières; Pommard Premier Cru; Volnay Premier Cru; Morey-Saint-Denis Premier Cru.
Village:
Savigny-lès-Beaune, Pommard, Volnay.
Régional:
Beaune Villages
• White wines:
Grand cru:
Corton-Charlemagne.
Premier cru:
Puligny-Montrachet Premier Cru; Chassagne-Montrachet Premier Cru.
Village:
Puligny-Montrachet, Chassagne-Montrachet, Meursault, Saint-Romain, Pernand-Vergelesses, Rully.
Régional:
Côte-de-Beaune
• Owners: Pierre Meurgey, Henri Meurgey, Pierre Beuchet
• Wine-maker: Michel Ecard
• Oenologist: Henri Meurgey
• Combined vineyards: 6 hectares
• Production: 440,000 bottles
• Exports: 76%
• Take-away sales: Yes
• Visits: Yes, tel. 03 80 24 97 30

Wine selected:
Corton Bressandes

• Classification: Grand Cru
• Soil type: Clay, limestone, stony marl
• Average vine age: 30 years
• Average annual production: 900 bottles

MAISON
FONDÉE
EN
1720

CHAMPY

1995
MAISON
FONDÉE
EN
1720

CO... ...BRESSANDES

GRAND CRU

APPELLATION CORTON-BRESSANDE... ...

MIS EN BOUTEILLES PAR

CHAMPY PÈRE & Cⁱᵉ

NÉGOCIANTS A BEAUNE CÔTE-D'OR · FRANCE

T he simple, classical elegance of the 18th-century country house of Domaine Chandon de Briailles, and the neat formality of the garden which Le Nôtre laid out behind it, deepens the sense of anticipation as the visitor arrives to visit the estate and taste the wines. And indeed the elegance, refinement and breeding are echoed in the domaine's *crus*, a fine range which is perfectly worthy of the elegant *monument historique* in which their creators reside.

Mother and daughter take charge of the estate Domaine Chandon de Briailles had a great reputation in the post-war period, when it furnished some of the capital's top restaurants and was already exporting its wine. On the death of its owner, the Countess whose name it bore, it was bequeathed to her grandson Count Aymard-Claude de Nicolay. Unfortunately the Count worked in Paris, where he owns a real estate business, and his wife Nadine was busy raising their young family; the estate inevitably started suffering through lack of close attention.

By the beginning of the 1980s however, with the children growing up, Nadine had time on her hands and needed to occupy herself constructively with something. Despite having the barest knowledge of how wine was made, she decided to settle in Savigny and put an end to the decline of the family estate. Her third daughter Claude also felt the call, and enrolled at Dijon University to study viticulture and vinification. Having taken her Diploma she spent a year seeing how things are done in Oregon and New Zealand, and then joined her mother in the adventure. The team was completed by a new, young, shaven-headed *régisseur* named Jean-Claude Bouveret, known to one and all as Kojak.

A re-examination of methods Numerous have been the changes of practice and the refinements in technique, as the new team have re-examined methods in the light of modern oenological knowledge and today's awareness of the errors of the past. Viticulture has become more ecological to protect soils and improve vine health and grape ripeness. Low yields are a priority, naturally enough, and surplus buds are removed once the shoots are out and, if necessary, a green harvest is performed at the moment the fruit turns colour.

The fruit is sorted through on a conveyor belt on arrival at the vatroom, and fermentations are tailored to the *terroirs* and the production of elegant rather than robust, structured wines: maceration at 15° for 5 days, fermentations not exceeding 32° with two *remontages* and two *pigeages* per day, and maturation in second-hand barrels bought from Domaine Méo-Camuzet.

Corton Les Bressandes By far the Nicolays' largest Grand Cru holding, and arguably their best, is the Corton Bressandes, which produces a very powerful wine of superb depth and complexity, which takes time to open up. When it does so, its magnificent bouquet of violets, truffle and undergrowth is perfectly bewitching... and merits several minutes' appreciation, before it makes room on the taster's palate for a haunch of young wild boar.

Côte de Beaune | Savigny-lès-Beaune

• Other red wines:
Grand cru:
Corton Clos du Roi,
Corton Les Maréchaudes.
Premier cru:
Savigny-lès-Beaune
Les Fourneaux, SIB Les
Lavières ; Aloxe-Corton
Les Valozières ; Pernand-
Vergelesses Île des
Vergelesses,
PV Les Vergelesses.
Village:
Savigny-lès-Beaune
• White wines:
Grand cru:
Corton-Charlemagne,
Corton.
Premier cru:
Pernand-Vergelesses Île
des Vergelesses
• Owners: M. & Mme.
A.C. de Nicolay
• Wine-makers: Jean-
Claude Bouveret, Claude
& Nadine de Nicolay
• Oenologist: BIVB,
Beaune
• Combined vineyards:
13 hectares
• Production:
68,000 bottles
• Exports: 70%
• Take-away sales: Yes
• Visits: By appointment.
Closed on Sundays

Wine selected:
Corton Les Bressandes

• Classification:
Grand Cru
• Area cultivated:
1.71 hectares
• Soil type:
Clay and limestone
• Average vine age:
30 years
• Average annual
production:
3,000 bottles

DOMAINE COCHE-DURY

The efforts of a father and his son over the last three decades have given Meursault a new estate of which to be proud, an estate which nowadays has far more clients jostling to buy its wines than it needs. Domaine Coche-Dury has become very *recherché* by top restaurants and specialist retailers, French and foreign, and one imagines that its loyal private clients cling to their allocations like limpets, for these are magnificent wines, which are still sold at uninflated prices.

From humble beginnings to prosperity In the beginning grandfather Coche acquired the first plots of vineyard land after the Great War, when things were depressed and the outlook was grim; Meursault was not the prestigious name that it is today. He sold off the major part of his produce in bulk, but did a little bottling himself. The estate was then left to his children in 1964 and divided equally between the three of them, as the Napoleonic Code requires. One of the three, Jean-François Coche's father Georges, set about enlarging his share by purchase and sharecropping agreements, and increased the amount of bottling. He was proud of his wines and entered them into competitions with great success, which led to their inclusion on the wine lists of the best restaurants.

Jean-François Coche took over from his father in 1972, and over the years has managed to purchase a number of the plots he was looking after as a sharecropper. Recently he has made an excursion into the neighbouring village of Puligny, with the acquisition of half a hectare of Les Enseignères.

Reduced yields and liberal use of oak The key to quality, Coche tells his visitor, is low yields. To that end he keeps half of his Chardonnay vines trained by *cordon de Royat* rather than all by *Guyot simple*, as is more usual, although the reverse is the case for Pinot Noir. Each variety has its preferred form, which leads to smaller bunches of smaller grapes and lower yields. Debudding early in the year is naturally regarded as an essential operation.

After a gentle pressing and settling of the lees, wines – including the Aligoté – are fermented in barrel; for the best wines half of the oak is new, for lesser wines proportionately less. They are given regular *bâtonnage*, and are racked twice before eventual bottling by hand directly off their finings after 20 months, without filtration.

Meursault Perrières Despite having a long list of Village *climats*, Coche has just one Premier Cru, but not any old one: les Perrières, lying above Charmes at the Puligny end of Meursault, is the Meursault *climat* which is generally reckoned to approach Grand Cru quality the most frequently, giving a wine of great liveliness and precision, with a steely, mineral character and little of the overblown heaviness of certain other *climats*. Obviously, the man who makes the wine also makes a lot of difference, and the Coche-Dury Perrières combines this *terroir* personality with the polish and refinement of its maker's style, providing a wine of wonderful concentration, aromatic complexity and harmony. This wine goes very well with lobster *à la crème*.

- Other white wines:
Grand cru:
Corton-Charlemagne.
Village:
Meursault Les Rougeots,
M Les Chevalières,
M Les Vireuils,
M Les Caillerets,
Meursault; Puligny-
Montrachet Les
Enseignères.
Régional:
Bourgogne Chardonnay,
Bourgogne Aligoté
- Red wines:
Premier cru:
Volnay Clos des Chênes,
V Taillepieds.
Village:
Meursault, Monthélie,
Auxey-Duresses.
Régional:
Bourgogne Pinot Noir
- Owner:
Jean-François Coche
- Wine-maker:
Jean-François Coche
- Combined vineyards:
10.5 hectares
- Production:
60,000 bottles
- Exports: 50%
- Take-away sales: No
- Visits: No

Wine selected:
Meursault Perrières

- Classification:
Premier Cru
- Area cultivated:
0.52 hectares
- Soil type:
Clay and limestone
- Average vine age:
45 years
- Average annual
production:
2,100 bottles

1995

Meursault-Perrières

APPELLATION CONTROLÉE

CE VIN N'A PAS SUBI
DE FILTRATION

75 cl.   13% vol.

J.-F. COCHE-DURY

PROPRIETAIRE-VITICULTEUR A MEURSAULT (COTE-D'OR)

There are a fair number of Epenots wines, both Grands and Petits, made by one or other of Pommard's different estates. However Epeneaux, the old French spelling of the same word, denotes one particular wine, the flagship wine of Domaine Comte Armand. Clos des Epeneaux is one of the finest and longest-living red wines of the entire Côte de Beaune.

Nicolas Marey creates the Clos Domaine Comte Armand is unusual for a Burgundian estate, for until recently it made only this one wine, which, equally unusually, comes from a vast *monopole* vineyard. What is more, the vineyard has belonged to the same family since it was pieced together shortly after the Revolution.

It was Nicolas Marey who, following the carving up of the estates of the dispossessed church and nobility, progressively bought up parcels of the Grands and Petits Epenots vineyards. He surrounded his new vineyard with a wall and started using the old French version of the name to differentiate his wine from those of his neighbours. Marey's daughter Clothilde married Jean-François Armand, and the *clos* thus passed into the Armand patrimony. Today, four generations on, it is owned by Comte Gabriel Armand.

A young Canadian takes on a challenge The Armands have traditionally worked far from Burgundy, and the estate has been run by a *régisseur* for most of the last century. In 1984 Comte Armand appointed a 22-year-old Canadian named Pascal Marchand to look after things, an appointment which has proved inspired, for Marchand has been responsible for the increase in quality from usually very good to regularly exceptional.

Marchand's first year was spent looking after the two previous vintages in cask and producing the 1985, which was a success. Thereafter he reflected deeply on how best to attain the finest fruit possible, observing nature at work and taking endless samples of soil for analysis. Initially he started working the vineyard organically, then from 1988 introduced a biodynamic regime, for which the *clos*, being walled, is ideally suited. In the cellar he opted for total destalking of the harvest and started using more new oak than had been habitual up until then for ageing. But equally important was the separate vinification of the fruit of vines of different ages. Marchand makes four wines, and the finely-adapted *élevage* of each and the subsequent blending just before bottling lends great intensity and balance to the final wine.

After 10 vintages Marchand felt ready for the challenge of new *terroirs*, and Comte Armand bought and contracted vineyards in Volnay, Auxey and Meursault. The first vintages of the white Meursault Meix Chavaux are very impressive.

Pommard Clos des Epeneaux Marchand's efforts have given the Clos des Epeneaux breeding and elegance which it lacked before, and have tamed the often brutal Pommard structure to contribute greater finesse. This is still textbook Pommard, but with more refinement than most. Young, it has a mass of black fruit richness, regimented by a corset of ripe tannin and acidity, a combination which destines it for a long and happy life. When its youthful ardour has been calmed, it makes a fine match for a crusty cheek of beef and potato pie.

• Other red wines:
Premier cru:
Volnay Fremiets; Auxey-Duresses Premier Cru.
Village:
Volnay, Auxey-Duresses
• White wines:
Village:
Meursault Meix Chavaux, Auxey-Duresses.
Régional:
Bourgogne Grand Ordinaire
• Owner: Comtes Armand family
• Manager:
Pascal Marchand
• Wine-maker:
Pascal Marchand
• Combined vineyards:
10 hectares
• Production:
40,000 bottles
• Exports: 75%
• Take-away sales: No
• Visits: By appointment

Wine selected:
Pommard
Clos des Épeneaux
(monopole)

• Classification:
Premier Cru
• Vineyard size:
5.2 hectares
• Soil type:
Clay and limestone
• Average vine age:
13-65 years
• Average annual production:
20,000 bottles

L ike all truly devoted wine-makers, Philippe Senard has the habit of ceaselessly reappraising what he has achieved. There came a moment in the middle of the 1980s when a gradual build-up of dissatisfaction with his wines incited him to invite the consultant agronomist and oenologist Guy Accad to advise him on how he could improve things. Accad's involvement led to many changes and a good deal of criticism, yet the end results have been undeniably positive. Thanks to Senard's courage, this domaine is one of Aloxe's finest.

For healthy soil and healthy fruit Guy Accad encouraged Senard to change his methods in a number of radical ways. Firstly the raw material had to be improved, and that could only be achieved by addressing a fundamental problem, for Accad's analyses of the soils revealed deficiencies in their equilibrium, a legacy of chemical treatments and excessive fertilisation which were commonplace on the Côte in the 1950s and 1960s. The unbalanced soils were therefore not able to nourish the vine properly. Re-establishing the equilibrium had to be done by using natural treatments, sparingly, and by weeding by plough or hoe, in such a way the grape quality could be improved. Another factor that needed improving was fruit ripeness: better grape quality would enhance ripeness, and picking later, with its concomitant element of risk, was essential if Senard was really to improve his wines. Taking the bull by the horns he started harvesting 2-3 weeks later than he had previously done.

A new technique for capturing aroma Secondly, there was an alternative way for extracting all the fruit's finest aromas and colour pigments. It involved maceration of the solids in the juice *before* any alcohol had been created, which was desirable because the finest aromatics and colour, Accad advised, are extracted without the presence of alcohol. The maceration takes place at a chilly 10°, after a heavy sulphuring of the must, the two factors combining to enhance extraction and retard the start of fermentation. After some 5 days the fermentation, at a relatively cool 25°, may proceed, and lasts 3 weeks. Thereafter a period of ageing in barrel lasting between 18-24 months, and a light fining but no filtration, gives wines all the essentials for a prolonged life in the bottle.

Corton Clos du Roi Senard received copious and frequently ill-considered criticism from fellow *vignerons* for listening to Accad, yet as vintages from 1988 on progressively mature, it is patently obvious that the criticisms are unfounded.
The Corton Clos du Roi is a triumphant example. Richly fruity, opulent and at the same time muscular, oaky when young, structured and very long, at seven years of age the 1989 was developing a superb, complex personality, which has as much Corton character as one could wish for. This is one of the very best Cortons made today, a definite vindication of Accad's philosophies. Recent vintages are, if anything, more distinguished. At table it begs for a grilled rib of beef, or a roast, stuffed pheasant, to reply to its rousing tune.

• Other red wines:
Grand cru:
Corton, Corton Bressandes, Corton Clos des Meix (monopole).
Premier cru:
Aloxe-Corton Valozières; Beaune Premier Cru.
Village:
Aloxe-Corton
• Owner: Philippe Senard
• Wine-maker: Philippe Senard
• Combined vineyards: 17 hectares
• Production: 95,000 bottles
• Exports: 45%
• Take-away sales: Yes
• Visits: Weekdays, 8-12 a.m., 2-5 p.m., by appointment

Wine selected:
Corton Clos du Roi

• Classification: Grand Cru
• Area cultivated: 0.9 hectares
• Soil type: Clay and limestone
• Average vine age: 30 years
• Average annual production: 3,000 bottles

1995

Mis en Bouteille au Domaine

GRAND CRU
CORTON
CLOS DU ROI
APPELLATION CONTROLEE

SCE DU DOMAINE
Comte Senard
PROPRIETAIRE A ALOXE CORTON COTE-D'OR FRANCE
ESTATE BOTTLED-PRODUCE OF FRANCE

There is one Meursault estate which towers above its peers, making wines which are sought out by connoisseurs the world over. Domaine des Comtes Lafon is the source of wines of supreme richness, purity and character, achieved thanks to excellent vineyard holdings, solid family traditions and the talent and devotion of their wine-maker.

Jules Lafon founds the estate The estate came into being when Jules Lafon, a lawyer and *inspecteur des finances* at Dijon, married a Meursault girl, Marie Boch, in 1894. Marie had inherited a good number of vineyard plots, and the wealthy Lafon, a *bon vivant* and connoisseur, added others to their estate and swapped the lesser of hers for better-quality land. He died in 1940, leaving two sons, Pierre and Henri. Pierre died four years after his father, and Henri, who cared not a jot for the estate, decided to sell up; however he had reckoned without René, Pierre's son, who resisted the sale. René took on the estate, and despite the difficulties of having a job in Paris and financial constraints imposed on him by Henri through the courts, managed to keep it operational, making the wine with the help of a faithful employee on the spot and selling it off in bulk. From 1961 he started bottling it all on the estate.

Letting the wine make itself Today's René's son Dominique is in charge, and this widely-travelled and open-minded young man has proved himself one of Burgundy's greatest and most consistent wine-makers. Although the estate made its name by its white wines, Dominique Lafon has taken pride in increasing the reputation of the red wines – for the estate has large parcels in three of Volnay's finest Premiers Crus – which he has done with great success.

The greatness of Lafon wines may be attributed firstly to their vineyards: thanks to a viticultural regime which is as organic as possible, its healthy soils give healthy vines, which are pruned short and debudded at the start of the season to reduce the yield and give top-quality grapes, which are picked late for maximum aromatic concentration. Little in the way of vinification has changed over the last century, the essential action being to intervene as little as possible and let the wine make itself. Long ageing in the Lafon cellars, reputed the coldest in Burgundy, then precedes bottling with careful fining and no filtration.

Montrachet With one third of a hectare of the precious stony russet soil of Le Montrachet, bought by his great-grandfather at auction in 1918, Dominique Lafon makes a tiny amount of one of the world's greatest white wines. Deep though it is, its fine golden yellow colour does not really prepare one for the intensely concentrated, fat and opulent mouthful of flavour, stunning in the extent of its dimensions, which has formidable length once swallowed. This Montrachet should not be broached before 10 years of age, and deserves nothing less than a lobster, grilled on a spit, for company – an unforgettable, once in a lifetime experience!

• Other white wines:
Premier cru:
Meursault Perrières,
M Gouttes d'Or,
M Genevrières,
M Charmes; Puligny-
Montrachet Champ Gain.
Village:
Meursault Désirée,
M Clos de la Barre
(monopole), Meursault
• Red wines:
Premier cru:
Volnay Santenots du
Milieu, V Clos des
Chênes, V Champans;
Monthélie Les Duresses
• Owners: Comtes Lafon
• Wine-maker:
Dominique Lafon
• Oenologist: BIVB,
Beaune
• Combined vineyards:
13.5 hectares
• Production:
65,000 bottles
• Exports: 45%
• Take-away sales: No
• Visits: No

Wine selected:
Montrachet

• Classification:
Grand Cru
• Area cultivated:
0.31 hectares
• Soil type:
Clay and limestone
• Average vine age:
55 years
• Average annual
production:
900 bottles

Domaine Étienne Sauzet

Showing a remarkable talent for making wine and a perfect understanding of the various *terroirs* in his charge and of what great white Burgundy is all about, with every new vintage Gérard Boudot fashions beautiful examples of some of the greatest appellations, which are snapped up by a long list of Michelin-starred restaurateurs and loyal French clients. This is a very fine estate.

Love and a change of vocation Gérard Boudot did not come from a wine-making family. This son of Le Creusot, west of the Côte Chalonnaise, was set on working in the Forestry and Lakes Department, yet he failed the necessary exams and had to reset his sights. He enrolled on a course at Beaune's *lycée viticole*. He met Sauzet's granddaughter Jeanine after a rugby match in Beaune in which he was playing, they duly fell in love and married, and when the moment came in 1974 for one of the grandchildren to take charge of the estate, his wife's brothers not being interested, the job fell on him.

A négociant activity replaces lost vineyards Over the years Boudot had his work cut out getting the vineyards into shape, for they had suffered years of potassium-based fertilizer excesses. Patiently he applied small doses of magnesium to neutralize the potassium and had unending analyses carried out, and after a decade the soils were living and breathing again. On the positive side, the experience gave him an intimate knowledge of all his charges!

In 1989 Jeanine's mother officially handed down the estate equitably to her children, and her son Jean-Marc decided unexpectedly to withdraw his portion. The Boudots thus suddenly found themselves with an estate reduced by a third. The logical answer, which is what they did the next year, was to form a négociant company and buy raw material to make up for the shortfall, which was possible thanks to Boudot's relations with a good number of conscientious growers.

Limited yields and peak ripeness His wine-making holds no revolutionary secrets. Severe debudding is carried out in spring to limit yields, and harvesting is delayed until peak ripeness, which is tricky, for the slightest overripeness and accompanying acidity deficiency are undesirable. Fermentation takes place at around 20° in barrel, and there is then a long settling period, so that maturation will take place only on very fine lees, for maximum finesse. Wines are roused with ever-diminishing regularity until the first racking, after a year, and prior to bottling two months later they are transferred to vat for unification and fining, which lasts up to three weeks.

Bâtard-Montrachet Demonstrating Boudot's painstaking thoroughness, the Bâtard-Montrachet, vinified in an equal proportion of new and used barrels for 15 months, is a superbly-fashioned wine of great power and dimension. Despite being concentrated, intense and virile, it is unusually elegant, which is a hallmark of Gérard Boudot's wines, and remarkably long. It needs cellaring for at least 8 years, and at table may be served, suggests Jeanine, with creamy Bresse chicken and morels, or grilled lobster.

• Other white wines:
Grand cru:
Montrachet, Chevalier-Montrachet, Bienvenues-Bâtard-Montrachet.
Premier cru:
Puligny-Montrachet Les Combettes, PM Champ Canet, PM Folatières, PM Perrières, PM Referts, PM La Garenne.
Village:
Puligny-Montrachet, Chassagne-Montrachet
• Manager:
Gérard Boudot
• Wine-maker:
Gérard Boudot
• Combined vineyards:
14 hectares
• Production:
90,000 bottles
• Exports: 70%
• Take-away sales: No
• Visits: No

Wine selected:
Bâtard-Montrachet

• Classification:
Grand Cru
• Area cultivated:
0.6 hectares
• Soil type:
Clay and limestone
• Average vine age:
30 years
• Average annual production:
3,500 bottles

ES
1996

Batard-Montrachet

Grand Cru

Appellation Batard-Montrachet Contrôlée

Mis en bouteilles par

Etienne Sauzet

Alc 13.5 % by Vol.   750 ml

PULIGNY-MONTRACHET - CÔTE-D'OR - FRANCE

Produce of France

DOMAINE FRANÇOIS JOBARD

Finding a bottle of François Jobard's wine is about as difficult as arranging a rendez-vous with the man himself, for his small 5-hectare estate produces a mere 24,000 bottles per year, and he does just about all the work himself. More or less all the wine is accounted for by restaurants, private French clients and foreign agents, who, once they are in the fortunate position of being able to reserve wine, do not fail to snap up their annual allocation.

Transmission and division of the family estate The Jobard family has owned vines around Meursault for approximately a century, progressively building up an estate over four generations. It was split in two in 1971 following the retirement of Pierre Jobard, because his two sons Charles and François each wanted to pursue their *métier* independently, since which time François has added several plots of vineyard to his half, making it sufficiently large to be able to support a family.

This is a man who has a strong sense of tradition, making his wines slowly and carefully in much the same way his father and grandfather did before him. He has a healthy distrust of modern oenological science and a certain contempt for those of his colleagues who no longer dare take decisions themselves.

Traditional wine-making with variations Jobard uses treatments and herbicides in the spring and then looks after his vines more organically in mid-summer, so that by the time the wines are made the grape juice will have no trace of foreign matter in it. While he prunes short to reduce his yields, along with many others he has found that Chardonnay plants can be harvested at a much higher yield than Pinot and still produce great and concentrated wine. Nevertheless, his are low, and one of the reasons for that is that Jobard trains half of his vines by *cordon de Royat*, which produces smaller fruit than the classical *Guyot simple*.

His wine-making is traditional, with several particularities: the must is put straight into barrel after pressing, without any settling, and the wealth of lees therefore means that little *bâtonnage* is necessary; that explains to some extent the wines' initial austerity and reserve, and their finesse. Maturation is extended, generally lasting 12-18 months before racking, followed by another 3 months, before bottling by gravity with neither fining nor filtration. Little new wood is used.

Meursault Poruzot The Premier Cru which one is most likely to meet is the Poruzot, for at 77 ares it is his largest holding. This is a very fine wine which is true to Jobard's style, being restrained and rather dumb in its youth, but with great elegance and purity. Once it has passed a few years in bottle its plump texture becomes accentuated and it expresses itself much more willingly, with wonderful and complex flavours of hazelnut, honey and spice. Its fine balance gives it the prospect of two decades of life at least, while great vintages can surprise by their exceptional longevity. Once summoned to table, this delicious Poruzot is always very happy to find itself in the company of a chicken fricassee *au* Meursault.

- Other white wines:
Premier cru:
Meursault Charmes,
M Genevrières,
M La Pièce sous le Bois.
Village:
Meursault, Puligny-Montrachet.
Régional:
Bourgogne,
Bourgogne Aligoté
- Red wines:
Premier cru:
Blagny La Pièce sous le Bois.
Régional:
Bourgogne
- Owner: François Jobard
- Wine-maker:
François Jobard
- Combined vineyards:
5.18 hectares
- Production:
24,000 bottles
- Exports: 65%
- Take-away sales:
By appointment
- Visits: No

Wine selected:
Meursault Poruzot

- Classification:
Premier Cru
- Area cultivated:
0.77 hectares
- Soil type:
Clay and limestone
- Average vine age:
23 years
- Average annual production:
4,000 bottles

1995

Meursault-Poruzot

APPELLATION CONTROLÉE

WHITE BURGUNDY WINE

François JOBARD

VITICULTEUR A MEURSAULT, COTE-D'OR, FRANCE

PRODUCE OF FRANCE

de Bourgogne

750 ML

From the cellars of their impressively solid castle, lying in its walled grounds on the edge of Chorey-lès-Beaune, the Germain family ship off to home and foreign markets a fine range of wines capped by five red Beaune Premiers Crus and one white. Each has its character, which makes for a very interesting horizontal tasting, and each is among the finest examples of its appellation.

Measures to reduce yields The Germains have owned the Château de Chorey-lès-Beaune since the turn of the century. François Germain, the owner of the castle and the estate today, bought out his brother and sisters following the death of their father in 1968, and proceeded to make many a fine vintage before being joined in 1993 by his eldest son Benoit. At the top of his list of quality priorities are low yields. Germain aims for at most 35 hl/ha for his Premiers Crus and 40 hl/ha for his Villages, and these he obtains by maintaining a high average vine age and also by taking the necessary steps in the vineyard in the spring, pruning short and debudding. If the vines still overproduce then a *saignée* will be performed on the vatted wines, but green harvesting is not considered a serious remedy. The vineyards are run by *lutte raisonnée* for the sake of the vines' health, with ploughing to keep weeds at bay instead of chemicals, and occasionally feeding the soil with doses of organic compost.

Double maceration for maximum richness Grape-skin tannin is preferred to stalk tannin, and since 1993 the father-and-son team have taken to giving their fruit a cold maceration for 3 days before the onset of fermentation, and once fermentation is finished they put lids on the wooden vats and let the new wine and solids macerate for a further week. That way their wines do not risk lacking in matter.

Maturation takes place in oak *pièces*, with a judicious proportion of new wood every year in accordance with each wine's character. The Premiers Crus in an average year are aged in 50% new oak, but that figure can be increased: the Beaune Les Cras for example received 65% in 1996. There are two rackings and a light filtration before bottling.

Beaune Les Cras Each of the five Beaune Premiers Crus has its own style: the Cent-Vignes and the Boucherottes are the lightest, which may be attributed to relatively sandy soils, the former somewhat spicy, the latter supple and succulent; Vignes Franches is rather more consequent, thanks to its clay soil; the Teurons combines structure and finesse and has great longevity; and finally Les Cras is a wonderfully complex, nuanced wine, a blend of power and harmony. This wine can live for two decades or more, and will delight the wine-lover all the more if served with truffled fillet of beef, or indeed *canard aux pêches*.

- Other red wines:
Premier cru:
Beaune Les Teurons,
B Les Vignes Franches,
B Les Cent Vignes,
B Les Boucherottes.
Village:
Chorey-lès-Beaune.
Régional:
Bourgogne
- White wines:
Premier cru:
Beaune Sur les Grèves.
Village:
Pernand-Vergelesses.
Régional:
Bourgogne
- Owners: François & Benoit Germain
- Manager: Benoit Germain
- Wine-maker: François Germain
- Combined vineyards: 16 hectares
- Production: 80,000 bottles
- Exports: 70%
- Take-away sales: Yes
- Visits: 9-12 a.m., 2-7 p.m.

Wine selected:
Beaune Les Cras

- Classification: Premier Cru
- Area cultivated: 1.3 hectares
- Soil type: Clay and limestone
- Average vine age: 50 years
- Average annual production: 6,000 bottles

Domaine Jacques Prieur

F ew estates on the Côte d'Or can be as richly endowed in great vineyards as Domaine Jacques Prieur, in Meursault, which has holdings in or farms parcels of 9 Grands Crus and 12 Premiers Crus, stretching from Chambertin Clos de Bèze all the way down to Le Montrachet. To the regret of connoisseurs everywhere the estate went through a prolonged period of mediocrity in the 1970s and 1980s, but it has arisen determinedly from this in recent years. Today Domaine Jacques Prieur produces wines of magnificent quality.

A great domaine fulfils its potential The prime movers behind the recent renaissance have been Jacques Prieur's grandson Martin and Bertrand Devillard, who represents the consortium headed by the Côte Châlonnais *négociant* firm Antonin Rodet, which since 1988 has owned half of the domaine. Aided by the Rodet oenologist Nadine Gublin, they have introduced many a change, and the improvement in quality has been radical.

Reducing yields was one of the first priorities, along with improving vine health and going for greater fruit ripeness, and these aims have been brought about by shorter pruning, debudding and green harvesting if necessary, by reviewing the way vines are trained in order to increase insolation and aeration, and by working the vineyard in as ecological a way as is possible.

At harvest-time fruit is now transported in receptacles containing 30 kg in order to minimise the risk of damage – this is particularly important for an estate with vineyards so far from base – and a conveyor belt has been acquired for picking through the fruit on arrival. Black grapes are destemmed partially or totally and given some 5 days' cold maceration without crushing, before fermenting in open wooden vats. For colour and tannin extraction they are given 3 serious *pigeages* a day, then are transferred by gravity to cask for ageing. There is none of the former reluctance to invest in new oak, the new team give wines all that they need. Finally, if necessary there is a light filtration, then unification and bottling.

Montrachet Domaine Prieur is one of 17 owners of the 8-hectare Montrachet vineyard, a strip of priceless, russet clay which gives what is undoubtedly the greatest, most complex and most costly dry white wine in the world. Its cosseted fruit is pressed very, very gently in a pneumatic Bucher, and the juice is left to settle at a low temperature in stainless steel overnight before transfer by gravity into new oak casks, in which it ferments at around 22°. The wine is stirred once a week until the alcoholic and malo-lactic fermentations are complete, and is then left untroubled for 19 months, before a light filtration and bottling.

The result is a powerhouse of opulent, concentrated refinement, of utter hedonism, the flavour waves of which are given edge by perfectly calculated acidity, ending with a phenomenal finish. Yet mere words are completely insufficient in describing something which so transcends the palate's usual fare... This great wine is best sipped among friends, reverently, on its own, in order to appreciate its total perfection.

- Other white wines:
Grand cru:
Chevalier-Montrachet,
Corton-Charlemagne.
Premier cru:
Puligny-Montrachet
Les Combettes;
Meursault Perrières;
Beaune Champs Pimont,
Beaune Clos de la
Féguine (monopole).
Village:
Meursault Clos de
Mazeray.
Régional:
Bourgogne Blanc
- Red wines:
Grand cru:
Chambertin Clos de Bèze,
Chambertin, Échézeaux,
Musigny, Clos Vougeot,
Corton Bressandes.
Premier cru:
Chambolle-Musigny
Combe d'Orveau;
Beaune Grèves,
B Coucheriats, B Clos de
la Féguine (monopole),
B Champs Pimont;
Volnay Clos des
Santenots (monopole),
V Champans,
V Santenots.
Village:
Meursault Clos de
Mazeray (monopole)
- Owner: SCI du
Domaine Jacques Prieur
- Directors: Martin Prieur
& Bertrand Devillard
- Wine-maker:
Martin Prieur
- Oenologist:
Nadine Gublin
- Combined vineyards:
20.76 hectares
- Production:
90,000 bottles
- Exports: 80%
- Take-away sales: Yes.
En primeur sales also.
- Visits: By appointment

Wine selected:
Montrachet

- Classification:
Grand Cru
- Area cultivated:
0.58 hectares
- Soil type:
Clay and limestone
- Average vine age:
35 years
- Average annual
production:
2,280 bottles

JACQUES PRIEUR
ANTONIN RODET
Propriétaires
• 1995 •

MONTRACHET

GRAND CRU

APPELLATION MONTRACHET CONTRÔLÉE

Mis en bouteille au domaine

DOMAINE JACQUES PRIEUR

Propriétaire à Meursault (Côte-d'Or) France

PRODUCE OF FRANCE

DOMAINE JEAN CHARTRON

I n 1859 a Puligny cooper, Jean-Edouard Dupard, started putting his savings into vineyard land and accumulated a fine estate, which nowadays bears the name of his grandson. Dupard it was who as mayor persuaded the authorities in 1880 to allow Puligny to couple its name with that of its most prestigious vineyard. Today his great-grandson Jean-René Chartron is at the helm of this fine legacy, and the estate is the flagship of a *négociant* firm set up in 1984 by Chartron in partnership with the Beaune merchant Louis Trébuchet.

A white wine specialist The bulk of the Chartron et Trébuchet wines are white, the range consisting of some 26 different *appellations*, and are, unsurprisingly, centred around Puligny. The purchases for the *négociant* label are in the form either of grapes or must, and, whether it is a Domaine or a *négociant* wine, the house philosophy favours vinifications with as little intervention as possible.

All the Domaine wines are fermented and matured in barrel, and 10-40% new wood is used depending on the wine and the year; barrels, which are made of Allier and sometimes Vosges wood, have a life expectancy of 3 years if they end up in the Chartron cellars. Alcoholic fermentations last between 6-8 weeks and the malos follow hard on their heels, during which phase the wines are given a periodic *bâtonnage*. When all activity is over the wines are separated from their lees by racking, and the maturation in cask can commence; it will last 9-12 months, depending on the wine and the vintage characteristics. Like all others in the village, the Chartron cellars are above ground, for the water table is not far below one's feet, and their well-ordered, neatly aligned rows of barrels and long alleyways are strangely reminiscent of another great wine region, a stone's throw from the Atlantic... Finally, a light fining and then a tangential, or crossflow, filtration are carried out, this last being considered less harmful to wines' aromas.

Chevalier-Montrachet Clos des Chevaliers The finest wine of the Domaine Jean Chartron range is the Chevalier-Montrachet, which comes from a walled parcel in that prestigious vineyard bearing the name Clos des Chevaliers. The *clos* is a *monopole*, and while the wine's *appellation* title is Chevalier-Montrachet, the name of the *clos* may be inscribed beneath it.

The Clos des Chevaliers is a fine example of what that noble vineyard is all about: nervy power combined with elegance, concentrated quality and a certain reserve in its formative years. This wine exhibits the Chartron style, which favours delicacy and balance, and is a very different offering to that of Leflaive, for instance. After a decade's bottle age this wine will be on full song, and will then prove a perfect match for capon *en demi-deuil*, or a truffled fillet of sole.

- Other white wines:
Premier cru:
Puligny-Montrachet Clos du Cailleret (monopole),
PM Clos de la Pucelle (monopole),
PM Les Folatières; Saint-Aubin Les Murgers des Dents de Chien.
Village:
Chassagne-Montrachet Les Benoîtes.
Régional:
Bourgogne Blanc, Bourgogne Aligoté
- Red wines:
Premier cru:
Puligny-Montrachet Clos du Cailleret (monopole).
Village:
Chassagne-Montrachet Les Benoîtes.
Régional:
Bourgogne Rouge
- Owner: Jean-René Chartron
- Wine-maker: Michel Roucher-Sarrazin
- Combined vineyards: 9 hectares
- Production: 30,000 bottles
- Exports: 70%
- Take-away sales: Yes
- Visits: Yes

Wine selected:
Chevalier-Montrachet Clos des Chevaliers (monopole)

- Classification: Grand Cru
- Vineyard size: 0.55 hectares
- Soil type: Clay and limestone
- Average vine age: 28 years
- Average annual production: 3,300 bottles

DOMAINE JEAN-MARC BOILLOT

Côte de Beaune | Pommard

R are is the wine-maker who is as good at making red as white, or vice-versa, yet Jean-Marc Boillot is one such talented individual. At his fine house, La Pommardière, on the outskirts of Pommard, he vinifies a range comprising no less than 20 different wines, equally balanced between the two colours, which are deliciously full of flavour and aroma, and of which some are capable of attaining great age.

An inheritance gives birth to a new domaine Boillot's skills were learnt working with his grandfather Etienne Sauzet, and gained further experience from 1984 as the original manager and wine-maker at the new Olivier Leflaive Frères *négociant* firm. In 1990 his mother, Sauzet's only child, passed down the Sauzet estate to her three children, and Boillot decided to break away with his share and set up on his own, for which no doubt the Leflaive experience proved very useful. Starting off with his inheritance of four Puligny Premiers Crus and some Puligny village land, he has added to these a fine selection, principally of red wine vineyards centred around Volnay and Pommard.

The quest for maximum aroma Surprisingly, Boillot makes all of his whites by a more-or-less unvarying formula, from Bourgogne Blanc through to Premiers Crus, and the same goes for his reds. White grapes are pressed, and the musts cooled, chaptalised and fermented using cultured yeast, following which the wines are aged in wood with *bâtonnage* for one year. Black grapes are destalked and then macerated for 4-5 days at a cool temperature, and then warmed up for fermentation to start. For red wines also cultured yeast are preferred, for they give more reliable results in the eternal quest for maximum aroma. The fermentations take place in closed vats, again to preserve aroma, the lids coming off only to carry out *pigeage* and chaptalisation. After 3 weeks' vatting the wines are run off into barrel, and spend up to 18 months maturing before bottling. Wines across the board receive 20-25% new oak every year, with the exception of the Pommard Rugiens, for which half of the *futaille* is renewed annually.

Boillot is one of the rare wine-makers to sing the praises of the unfashionable practice of filtering wines – and is contemptuous of the many who, he alleges, claim not to filter but do so clandestinely. Carried out carefully, he asserts, filtration enhances a wine's aromatic purity. On the evidence, how can one disagree?

Pommard-Rugiens The russet-coloured clay and limestone soil of Les Rugiens (the name is thought to come from the soil's colour) gives birth to a wine which epitomizes the virile, rich and structured Pommard character. The venerable 80-year-old Boillot vines thrive there, yet in their old age give niggardly yields (27 hl/ha in 1996), which of course have the advantage of contributing great intensity of flavour. This wine has great concentration, richness and structure, and a magnificent long and pure finish. Drink it with pigeon or game, says Jean-Marc Boillot... but first leave it in the cellar for many a year, and let it find its voice.

• Other red wines:
Premier cru:
Pommard Jarollières, Pommard Saucilles; Volnay Pitures, V Carelle sous la Chapelle, V Ronceret; Beaune Montrevenots.
Village:
Volnay, Pommard.
Régional:
Bourgogne Rouge
• White wines:
Premier cru:
Puligny-Montrachet Combettes, PM Champ Canet, PM Referts, PM La Garenne, PM La Truffière; Beaune Montrevenots.
Village:
Puligny-Montrachet, Chassagne-Montrachet, Meursault.
Régional:
Bourgogne Blanc
• Owner: Jean-Marc Boillot
• Wine-maker: Jean-Marc Boillot
• Combined vineyards: 10 hectares
• Production: 50,000 bottles
• Exports: 75%
• Take-away sales: No
• Visits: No

Wine selected:
Pommard-Rugiens

• Classification: Premier Cru
• Area cultivated: 0.15 hectares
• Soil type: Clay and limestone
• Average vine age: 80 years
• Average annual production: 540 bottles

1996

J.M. Boillot

Pommard-Rugiens

Appellation Contrôlée

Mis en bouteille par
Jean-Marc BOILLOT
PROPRIÉTAIRE À POMMARD, CÔTE-D'OR

Produce of France

DOMAINE JEAN-NOËL GAGNARD

Hidden behind high walls, the handsome creeper-covered house in Chassagne's Place des Noyers is the home of Jean-Noël Gagnard, and the cellars underneath it the source of a fine range of white and red Chassagnes. The quality on offer here has, unsurprisingly, not gone unnoticed, and three quarters of these wines now end up in faraway countries.

A sense of tradition and a youthful eye The proprietor officially handed over responsibility for the estate to his daughter Caroline Lestimé in 1989, and since then the domaine has seen one or two experiments as this attractive blonde, who studied wine-making at Beaune's *lycée viticole*, has looked at the way things are done with a fresh eye. Yet long-standing clients need not worry, Caroline has a keen sense of tradition and all that her forebears have achieved – after all, this family's involvement in the vine and wine has stretched over twelve generations – and is not about to change anything without long discussion with her father, who is still very actively involved in the business and regularly found in the cellars. So far, Caroline's modifications have been centred on the red wines, and have involved the introduction of new wood for ageing and the cessation of filtering. The wines have undeniably gained in richness and structure as a result.

Rigueur, Tradition et Joie de Vivre The domaine is inordinately well-furnished in quality land, and makes 3 red Premiers Crus. The fruit is entirely destalked, and after 10 days' cold maceration the must ferments at an unexcessive 32° or so for 8-10 days, without any *pigeage*; after racking, the wines are aged in barrel, one quarter of which is new, for a relatively short 12-14 months, "to retain their fruit", and have since 1993 been bottled without filtration. The net result is succulence and structure, with elegance where often in these wines one finds rusticity.

It is however its white wines which have made the estate's name. Jean-Noël Gagnard's range – no less than 8 Premiers Crus crowned by the Grand Cru Bâtard-Montrachet – make for a tasting which is a veritable education in the influence of *terroir* on wine: three vineyards on the Puligny side of the village, four below and on the Santenay side of the village, and the lone Morgeot, in richer soil near the border with Santenay... nuances of the mineral, the flowery and the exotic, and austerity, plumpness, delicacy and power, all these characterize one or other of the wines. Faced with the yearly task of creating and maturing these and then eventually enjoying them, small wonder the family motto is Rigueur, Tradition et Joie de Vivre!

Bâtard-Montrachet Like the other whites, the king of the roost is fermented in Allier casks and spends 18 months maturing, interrupted by the odd *bâtonnage*; three quarters of his casks are new. The step up in majesty is noticeable, the weight, breadth and length of this wine have different dimensions. Like all the Gagnard whites the Bâtard is "a little severe when young", and needs 10-15 years to show all its innate magnificence. This is a great wine, and calls for fare to match: lobster *à l'américaine* is eminently suitable.

- Other white wines:
Premier cru:
Chassagne-Montrachet Les Caillerets,
CM Morgeot, CM Clos de la Maltroye,
CM Maltroie,
CM Les Champs Gain,
CM Blanchot Dessus,
CM Les Chaumées,
CM Les Chenevottes.
Village:
CM Les Masures
- Red wines:
Premier cru:
CM Morgeot, CM Clos Saint-Jean; Santenay Clos de Tavanne.
Village:
CM Cuvée L'Estimée
- Owner: Jean Noël Gagnard
- Wine-maker: Caroline Lestimé
- Combined vineyards: 9 hectares
- Production: 60,000 bottles
- Exports: 75%
- Take-away sales: Yes
- Visits: By appointment

Wine selected:
Bâtard-Montrachet

- Classification: Grand Cru
- Area cultivated: 0.36 hectares
- Soil type: Clay and limestone
- Average vine age: 35 years
- Average annual production: 2,400 bottles

The *négociant* house Joseph Drouhin has for long been a purveyor and champion of authentic Burgundy, unafraid of periodically reviewing its methods and innovating in the quest for self-improvement. This is a house which continues to provide the finest quality available, in a style which encapsulates fragrance, elegance and balance, a style eminently suited to the Pinot Noir and the Chardonnay.

A century of growth and diversification The house has existed since 1880, when Joseph Drouhin bought up a merchant business in Beaune and gave it his name. His son Maurice gave the firm its 20th-century vocation by deciding to specialize in the wines of Burgundy and to invest in vineyards. After the Second World War the house made concerted efforts on the export market and laid the foundations of its international reputation. Robert Drouhin succeeded Maurice in 1957 and, foreseeing the increasing demand for fine Burgundy, continued the policy of vineyard acquisitions, from 1960 expanding northwards into the Côte de Nuits, then in 1968 north-west to take in a Chablis estate. Finally in 1988 the expansion culminated in the creation of Domaine Drouhin in Willamette Valley, Oregon. Drouhin's daughter Véronique is in charge of this American estate, and the wines are very promising.

Experimentation in the vineyard Following the general trend among the more conscientious and thoughtful growers in Burgundy, the house has recently become aware of shortcomings in its viticultural practices in relation to vineyard soils and environments, and Philippe Drouhin, in charge of all the firm's vineyards since 1988, has adopted practices far more friendly to these and to the vine. They have included reintroducing hoeing to eliminate weeds instead of spraying, using organic compost, using biological products to defend the vine against certain illnesses, grassing the steeper vineyards, using bacteria and natural predators to combat cryptogamic illnesses and insect enemies of the vine... and since 1996 the firm has been trying out biodynamics, which involve administering the biological methods in accordance with the planetary calendar.

All this experimentation is driven by Drouhin's persistent quest for finer fruit, which will enable them to make even finer wines.

Musigny Some prefer the Drouhin whites, and it is easy to see why, for they are wines of dazzling purity, definition and finesse. The reds also are exemplary in their respective appellations, perhaps the finest being the Musigny. That great *terroir* certainly lends itself to the Drouhin style. The ethereal and bewitching fragrance and the silky, delicate yet intense palate provide a stunningly eloquent reflection of the famous *climat*. A wine of such seduction that is difficult to resist drinking in its youth, yet the wine-lover who manages to resist the temptation for a dozen years is very amply compensated! Stuffed turkey or roast leg of lamb will have sufficient respect to allow this diva to sing out to her heart's content, to the absolute rapture of all present.

• Other red wines:
Grand cru:
Chambertin Clos de Bèze, Griotte-Chambertin, Bonnes-Mares, Clos de Vougeot, Grands Échézeaux, Échézeaux, Corton Bressandes.
Premier cru:
Chambolle-Musigny Les Amoureuses; Vosne-Romanée Les Petits Monts; Beaune Clos des Mouches, B Grèves; Volnay Clos des Chênes.
Vins de village et régionaux également
• White wines:
Grand cru:
Corton-Charlemagne, Bâtard-Montrachet, Montrachet Marquis de Laguiche, Chablis Les Clos, Chablis Vaudésir.
Premier cru:
Beaune Clos des Mouches; Puligny-Montrachet Folatières; Chassagne-Montrachet Marquis de Laguiche; Meursault Perrières; Chablis Montmains, Chablis Vaillons.
Vins de village et régionaux également
• Owner: Robert Drouhin
• Wine-makers: Robert Drouhin, Laurence Jobard
• Combined vineyards: 60 hectares
• Exports: 85%
• Take-away sales: No
• Visits: By appointment

Wine selected:
Musigny

• Classification: Grand Cru
• Area cultivated: 0.7 hectares
• Soil type: Clay and limestone
• Average vine age: 25
• Average annual production: 2,500 bottles

GRANDS VINS DE BOURGOGNE
1995

Joseph Drouhin

RÉCOLTE DU DOMAINE

MUSIGNY
GRAND CRU

APPELLATION CONTROLÉE
MIS EN BOUTEILLE PAR JOSEPH DROUHIN NÉGOCIANT
ÉLEVEUR À BEAUNE, CÔTE - D'OR, FRANCE, AUX CELLIERS
DES ROIS DE FRANCE ET DES DUCS DE BOURGOGNE

13% vol.

FRANCE

DOMAINE JOSEPH MATROT

I n no French wine region is the notion of *terroir* so hallowed as in Burgundy, where the infinite nuances of geological variation make for very different wines, even between neighbouring vineyards. While every single Burgundian grower will profess an absolute respect for *terroir*, a great number of their wines are unfortunately coloured more by personal wine-making style, in which *bâtonnage* and new oak often play an excessive part. The Matrot establishment in Meursault is one where *terroir* is respected and given full voice.

Espousing the terroir philosophy Joseph Matrot, the founder, had a sales background, and when he set up in Meursault before the Great War it was second nature to him to bottle his own produce and sell it directly to clients, rather than selling it in bulk to the *négociants*. His son Pierre played an important role in gaining the estate a reputation for quality, for he realized as early as the 1950s the value of clones in quality wine production.

Pierre's son Thierry, having as a lad followed his father around the vineyards and cellars and then studied wine-making at Beaune, made his first vintage in 1983, and has espoused the *terroir* philosophy wholeheartedly. That explains his intense dislike of new oak flavours in wine: "All those exotic flavours are better suited to rum!" Matrot breaks in his barrels with his generic Chardonnay. He also disapproves of *bâtonnage*, which reduces a wine's finesse, although his wines enjoy long lees contact. Richness, finesse and reserve are what he aims for.

Refreshing, lively wines for matching with food A self-confessed Epicurean since his youth, he has also not lost sight of the fact that good wine, even the richest Meursault, should be refreshing to drink, and this unclouded sense of priorities has had an undeniable influence on his wine-making. While low yields are naturally a priority at the domaine, harvesting at optimum ripeness is another. Overripeness is scrupulously avoided, for Matrot detests overly heavy wines, such as many of those produced in what many reckon 'great' years such as 1989. All his wines have good, natural *nervosité*. Another fact of today's world that Matrot regrets is that growers and wine professionals alike are too fixated with wine's quality *per se*, and that the important "user's handbook" for each wine is nearly always neglected. Not so at Domaine Matrot, where conversation in our Epicurean's cellar unfailingly turns to the seasons, circumstances and dishes for each wine; indeed the domaine's wine list suggests dishes to accompany each of the wines.

Meursault Blagny The La Pièce sous le Bois vineyard, lying in the commune of Blagny yet entitled to the AOC Meursault Blagny when the wine is white, lies on a slope with very poor soil, which gives a wine which, vinified by Matrot, is austere and mineral in its youth, with a pungent, rich bouquet. After 10 years it develops intriguing vegetal aromas of undergrowth, mushroom and fern and a fine honeyed quality on the palate, and has a long mineral finish. Young vintages may be enjoyed with fish in a rich sauce, Matrot advises, while older bottles even appreciate feathered game.

- Other white wines:
Premier cru:
Meursault Charmes,
M Perrières; Puligny-
Montrachet Les
Chalumeaux,
PM Les Combettes.
Village:
Meursault.
Régional:
Bourgogne Chardonnay,
Bourgogne Aligoté
- Red wines:
Premier cru:
Volnay Santenots; Blagny
La Pièce sous le Bois.
Village:
Auxey-Duresses
- Owner: Matrot family
- Wine-maker:
Thierry Matrot
- Combined vineyards:
20 hectares
- Production:
120,000 bottles
- Exports: 60%
- Take-away sales: No
- Visits: No

Wine selected:
Meursault Blagny

- Classification:
Premier Cru
- Area cultivated:
1.8 hectares
- Soil type:
Clay and limestone
- Average vine age:
35 years
- Average annual
production:
10,000 bottles

1996

Meursault-Blagny

APPELLATION MEURSAULT 1ER CRU CONTROLÉE

MIS EN BOUTEILLES PAR LE

Domaine Joseph Matrot Propriétaire à Meursault

PRODUCT OF FRANCE

For connoisseurs around the world the name Puligny-Montrachet is inseparable from that of Leflaive, and images of the Domaine's label, its heavy yellow lead capsule and the rich, opulent and heady nectar in the bottle get the saliva flowing and the memory casting back to the last blissful occasion... This, in many peoples' book, is the greatest white wine estate in the world.

An implacable belief in the future Domaine Leflaive as we know it was the creation of Joseph Leflaive, descendant of a vineyard-owning family which can trace its lineage back to 1580. Having inherited 2 hectares of vines in 1905 and believing implacably in Burgundy's future, which was at the time going through the dreadful post-phylloxera period when much land was up for sale, Leflaive set about buying up plots, and by 1925 had accumulated a fine estate of some 25 hectares of vineyards.

From the earliest days the wine was by all accounts excellent, and over the century many a great wine has been made, and the great reputation forged. Joseph was succeeded by his sons Jo and Vincent, the *régisseur* François Virot by his son Jean, and in 1973 a *Société Civile d'Exploitation* was founded to accommodate the co-ownership of the numerous descendants. In 1990 the cousins Anne-Claude and Olivier Leflaive were named co-managers of the Domaine, and Pierre Morey, a highly respected Meursault grower, was employed as a replacement for the retired Jean Virot.

A change to biodynamic viticulture Top estates, more than any others, are not allowed to rest on their laurels, and the present generation is doing anything but that. Uneasy about the growing immunity of vines to vineyard treatments and the slow asphyxiation of the soil, Anne-Claude had the courage to envisage a radical change in viticultural practice, and initiated parallel tests of biological and biodynamic methods of culture on certain plots, in the hope of reviving the microorganic life in the soil and enabling the plants to develop their own system of resistance to disease. Eyebrows were raised, and there were no doubt mutterings about youthful irresponsibility with some of Burgundy's greatest vineyards. However since late 1997, after seeing enough improvement to vindicate their action, the estate has gone ahead and conducted all viticultural operations according to biodynamic principles, which necessitate applying organic treatments by the planetary calendar.

Chevalier-Montrachet Among their fabulous patrimony of Grands and Premiers Crus the Leflaives own 2 of the 7 hectares of the Chevalier-Montrachet *climat*, which lies above Le Montrachet itself. This magnificently perfect liquid takes a dozen years to mature, developing infinite depth of flavour, sensuality and refinement, and combining power and elegance with rare success. Clive Coates put it perfectly: "... this is a wine to drink on bended knees and with heart-felt and humble thanks". A Leflaive Chevalier-Montrachet appreciates being served with a noble crustacean, such as lobster, *à l'américaine* or simply grilled, or langoustes thermidor. This must just about be gastronomic perfection!

• Other white wines:
Grand cru:
Montrachet, Bâtard-Montrachet, Bienvenues-Bâtard-Montrachet.
Premier cru:
Puligny-Montrachet Les Pucelles, PM Clavoillon, PM Folatières,
PM Les Combettes.
Village:
Puligny-Montrachet.
Régional:
Bourgogne Blanc
• Red wine:
Premier cru:
Blagny Sous le Dos d'Âne
• Owner: Leflaive family
• Manager: Anne-Claude Leflaive
• Wine-maker:
Pierre Morey
• Combined vineyards:
22 hectares
• Production:
130,000 bottles
• Exports: 70%
• Take-away sales: No
• Visits: No

Wine selected:
Chevalier-Montrachet

• Classification:
Grand Cru
• Area cultivated:
2 hectares
• Soil type:
Clay with limestone
• Average vine age:
27 years
• Average annual production:
8,000 bottles

DOMAINE LOUIS CARILLON & FILS

Their stationery and labels give the date of 1632, but the Carillons have recently unearthed a document attesting to the viticultural activities of Jehan Carillon in 1520, which makes this estate the doyen of Puligny, predating even the Leflaives. Carillon wines have their own style, which might be summed up as medium-bodied, rich and elegant, with just a hint of oakiness. They are made for the long-term, and are delicious.

Time, mortality and continuity A visit to the Carillon estate can induce a bout of reflection on time, mortality and continuity. Here is a family which will soon be able to celebrate its half-millennium, which today comprises three generations: grandfather Robert, retired but always around and ready with advice, father Louis, head of the domaine, and sons Jacques and François, both now taking care of all the day-to-day operations. No doubt in the near future there will be younger heads peaking for the first time around the cellar door, discovering perhaps a little apprehensively the mysterious environment of the wine cellar! And here history is everywhere, here courtyards, nooks and passages all have their story to tell, with much that has survived since the Revolution, yet at the same time history rubs shoulders with the late 20th-century, whose stainless steel vats and other accoutrements of the modern wine-maker's art sit at ease in the cellars of a bygone age.

Indeed the Carillons seem to blend tradition with modernity effortlessly in their aim for uncompromising quality. In the vineyard they are as ecological as is practical, ploughing the soil to keep weeds at bay and using treatments only when examination of vines has informed them that they are necessary. Replanting is carried out parcel by parcel, in order to have a good mixture of vine ages, and the soil is left fallow for a number of years before receiving the young vines; this sacrifice of a few years' crops, to revive the soil for the benefit of following vintages, is indicative of the Carillon spirit. Grapes are harvested by hand at peak ripeness, that is after some and before others, for the Carillons do not want over-ripe any more than underripe fruit.

When it comes to making the wines, after pressing and a short period of settling the better wines are fermented in barrel. Exotic, tropical fruit aromas are not appreciated, and therefore fermentations are carried out at around 25°, *bâtonnage* is not done to excess, and the amount of new wood used each year is at most 20% for Grand and Premiers Crus and 10% for Village wines. In such a way the natural, citrus purity of the fruit and the *terroir* character are never swamped by artificial vinification flavours.

Bienvenues-Bâtard-Montrachet A mere 600 bottles are produced in an average year of the Carillons' greatest wine, Bienvenues-Bâtard-Montrachet. This *seigneur* combines power and delicacy, fragrance and intensity, and, thanks to the flair of its creators manages to avoid the heaviness and dominant oakiness of certain other versions. It should not be broached before its sixth year, for its rich fruitiness takes time to find its voice. A masterpiece of restraint and class, it calls for the noblesse of a lobster *à l'armoricaine*.

- Other white wines:
Premier cru:
Puligny-Montrachet
Les Combettes,
PM Les Champs Canet,
PM Les Champs Gain,
PM Les Perrières,
PM Les Referts.
Village:
Puligny-Montrachet,
Chassagne-Montrachet.
Régional:
Bourgogne Aligoté
- Red wines:
Premier cru:
Saint-Aubin Les
Pitangerets.
Village:
Chassagne-Montrachet,
Mercurey.
Régional:
Bourgogne, Bourgogne
Passetoutgrain
- Owners: Carillon family
- Combined vineyards:
12 hectares
- Production:
65,000 bottles
- Exports: 70%
- Take-away sales: Yes
- Visits: By appointment

Wine selected:
Bienvenues-Bâtard-Montrachet

- Classification:
Grand Cru
- Area cultivated:
0.12 hectares
- Soil type:
Clay and limestone
- Average vine age:
35 years
- Average annual
production:
600 bottles

Wearing the twin caps of merchant and grower with equal ease and distinction, the Beaune firm Louis Jadot makes some 130 wines, the quality of which shines out every year. Fortunately for the world's thirsty Burgundy lovers Jadot has many grower-suppliers and access to large quantities of grapes, and large quantities of the various wines are thus shipped off around the world. That quantity should rhyme with quality is here an undeniable and welcome paradox!

Merchant and grower Louis Jadot founded his firm in 1859, and from the very start invested profits in vineyard land. As the *négociant* business grew, therefore, so the estate expanded. After his death his son Louis-Baptiste continued reinvesting profits in real estate. Louis-Baptiste's son Louis-Auguste spent much time developing sales in export markets, and in 1954 employed the young André Gagey to help him cope with the ever-growing business.

Gagey was to play a greater role in the firm's future than Louis-Auguste could have suspected, for after the latter's death and the premature death of his son Louis-Alain in 1968 Gagey was better equipped than anyone to run the firm, and was duly appointed to the top job. Since then he, and since his retirement his son Pierre-Henry, have directed the firm with rock-steady assurance, and prepared it for the uncertain future in the only way possible for a *négociant*, by continuing to invest in land. Today the firm owns four estates: Domaine Louis Jadot (comprising the former Domaines Clair-Daü and Champy), Domaine Héritiers Louis Jadot, Domaine Duc de Magenta and Domaine André Gagey. In 1985 the Jadot family parted ways with their firm, selling it to the owners of Kobrand, their American importer.

Bringing out terroir characteristics Since 1970 the responsibility for wine-making has been held by Jacques Lardière, who with every new vintage demonstrates once more his talent for bringing out the *terroir* characteristics of each wine – no mean feat with such a long list of wines, where it would be so easy for a house 'style' to speak louder than all these individual voices.

Lardière is a traditionalist, one of the non-interventionist school who prefer to let nature rather than man make the wine. Long vattings, lasting sometimes more than 30 days, and no tampering with fermentation temperatures, which have been known to rise to 40° without any ill effect, these give his wines the body and aromatic depth, and of course the *terroir* personality, which Burgundy lovers so appreciate.

Beaune Clos-des-Ursules The Jadots' very first vineyard holding, Clos-des-Ursules, is an enclave in the Vignes Franches vineyard which was the property of the Ursuline Convent in Beaune in the 17th century. This wine's characteristics are a relative lightness – the soil in the *clos* is very stony at the top end, and this sector has a slightly lower clay content than that of the more full-bodied Premiers Crus nearer Savigny – with great purity, elegance and perfume, and enough structure to make it a wine for laying down for a dozen years in a good vintage. In the succulence of full maturity it makes a fine match for roast guinea-fowl, and is a fine bottle indeed.

• Other red wines (Domaine):
Grand cru:
Chapelle-Chambertin, Chambertin Clos de Bèze, Clos Saint-Denis, Bonnes-Mares, Musigny, Clos Vougeot, Échézeaux, Corton, Corton Grèves, Corton Pougets.
Numerous Premier Cru principally around Gevrey-Chambertin, Chambolle-Musigny, Savigny-lès-Beaune et Beaune
• White wines:
Grand cru:
Corton-Charlemagne, Chevalier-Montrachet Les Demoiselles.
Premier cru:
Puligny-Montrachet Les Referts, PM Champ Gain, PM Clos de la Garenne, PM Les Folatières; Chassagne-Montrachet Morgeot; Santenay Clos de Malte
• Owner: Kopf family
• Chairman & Managing Director:
Pierre-Henry Gagey
• Wine-maker:
Jacques Lardière
• Combined vineyards: 100 hectares
• Exports: 80%
• Take-away sales: Yes
• Visits: By appointment

Wine selected:
**Beaune
Clos-des-Ursules**
(monopole)

• Classification:
Premier Cru
• Vineyard size:
2.2 hectares
• Soil type:
Clay and limestone
• Average vine age:
35 years
• Average annual production:
15,000 bottles

LOUIS JADOT

1995

FONDÉE EN 1859

BEAUNE
CLOS-DES-URSULES
Appellation Beaune 1er Cru Vignes Franches Contrôlée
(Seul Propriétaire)
MISE EN BOUTEILLES PAR
LOUIS JADOT
LOUIS JADOT, NÉGOCIANT-ÉLEVEUR A BEAUNE · COTE-D'OR · FRANCE
Domaine des Héritiers Louis Jadot
75cl e   13,5% vol
PRODUIT DE FRANCE

MAISON LOUIS LATOUR

For some four centuries the Latour family have been active in the vineyards of the Côte de Beaune, during which time they have contributed much to the advancement of Burgundy's wines and renown. Today Maison Louis Latour encompasses both its principal activity as *négociant* and also Domaine Latour, owner of a fabulous vineyard portfolio, and produces an extended and fine range of wines which now even includes a Chardonnay wine from the Ardèche region and a Pinot made in the Var.

A long lineage in the service of Burgundy The Latour family lineage has been traced back as far as Emiliand Latour, a *vigneron-laboureur* in the 17th century. The last seven generations have borne the name Louis, which has led to the quasi-regal use of numbers for identification.

The family and Burgundy as a whole owes a lot to the astute Louis Latour III. He was convinced that the only real solution to the phylloxera crisis which was ravaging France was to graft French plants onto American rootstock. Having built up the family's vineyard holdings around Aloxe and then in 1890 bought the Corton-Grancey estate at what must have been a very low price in those desperate times, he proceeded to replant 17 hectares of vineyards by this manner, and encouraged his fellow growers to observe and do likewise. He it also was who uprooted the Aligoté and Pinot Noir which occupied some of the prime limestone soils of the Corton hill and replanted them in 1891 with Chardonnay, thus effectively creating the Grand Cru Corton-Charlemagne.

Traditional and controversial wine-making White wine production, carried out at a fine, modern vatting centre in Beaune, is traditional at Latour, and produces wines of very high quality. Musts are put into tanks to start off their fermentation, and then all but the least consequent wines are transferred to barrel to continue it. The firm employs a cooper, who uses nothing but top quality Allier oak, air-dried at Aloxe, and the whites spend a year maturing in his barrels, with two rackings, before bottling.

Red wines are entirely destalked and then fermented without previous cold maceration. Fermentation, with regular human *pigeage*, lasts a mere 10 days, after which the wines are transferred to barrel to mature. The rapidity of the whole process gives wines of which structure and concentration have never been the strong points, which has earned the firm a fair amount of criticism. Adding a further point of controversy, Louis IV introduced the practice of flash pasteurization before bottling in order to stabilize the wines, and this is suspected by many to be detrimental to the wines' final quality.

Corton-Charlemagne Domaine Latour has an extraordinary holding of no less than 9.65 hectares of Corton-Charlemagne, enabling them to make some 45,000 bottles of this great wine per year. And great it is, one of the best, initially with typical Charlemagne austerity yet over the years softening up, displaying its richness and power, and at the same time great elegance and style. It is a wine which improves over 15-20 years in great vintages, at the end of which time it makes an admirable partner for foie gras and braised chicken with tarragon.

- Other white wine (domaine):
Grand cru:
Chevalier-Montrachet
Les Demoiselles
- Red wines (domaine):
Grand cru:
Chambertin Cuvée Héritiers Latour,
Romanée-Saint-Vivant Les Quatre Journaux, Corton Clos de la Vigne Au Saint (monopole), Corton Château Corton-Grancey.
Premier cru:
Beaune Vignes Franches, B Perrières, B Clos du Roi, B Les Cras; Pommard Épenots; Volnay Santenots; Aloxe-Corton Les Chaillots; Pernand-Vergelesses Îles des Vergelesses
- Owner: Louis Latour
- Manager: Louis Latour
- Wine-maker: Denis Fetzmann
- Oenologist: Jean-Pierre Jobard
- Combined vineyards: 50 hectares
- Production: 6 million bottles
- Exports: 92%
- Take-away sales: No
- Visits: No

Wine selected:
Corton-Charlemagne

- Classification: Grand Cru
- Area cultivated: 9.65 hectares
- Soil type: Clay and limestone
- Average vine age: 35 years
- Average annual production: 45,000 bottles

ANS
1997

L:9801142
128

DOMAINE
LOUIS
LATOUR

1996

Corton-Charlemagne
GRAND CRU
APPELLATION CONTROLÉE

MIS EN BOUTEILLE PAR
LOUIS LATOUR, NÉGOCIANT A BEAUNE (CÔTE-D'OR), FRANCE
PRODUIT DE FRANCE

DOMAINE MARQUIS D'ANGERVILLE

A ngerville is one of the great names of Burgundy. Prominent after the Great War in speaking out against the fraudulent practices which were rife in the *négociants*' cellars, and, matching words with actions, one of the first to promote authenticity by bottling and selling directly all of the crop, Angerville is a name which has long been synonymous with top-quality Volnay. Indeed Marquis d'Angerville wines have been amongst Burgundy's finest for just about the entire 20th century.

A number of prime vineyard acquisitions The Marquis d'Angerville estate was founded by the Baron du Mesnil, *sous-préfet* of Autun, in 1804. Around a fine country house which he had built on a prominent position on the northern side of Vollenay, as it was then known, he added a number of prime vineyard acquisitions to form a very fine *ensemble*. His great-grandson Jacques, Marquis d'Angerville, came into the estate in 1906, shortly after the phylloxera louse had wreaked its ravages, and had the task of replanting on a large scale. He did this by taking cuttings from his healthiest vines, an experience which later led him and his son to develop their own strain of Pinot *fin*, which has borne the family name ever since. Clones have never found their way into the Angerville vineyards, and the vines are allowed to grow to a venerable age before being individually replaced. Angerville's son, also named Jacques, made his first vintage in 1945, and inherited the estate on the death of his father in 1952. He is today helped by his son-in-law Renaud de Villette.

Unashamedly conservative wine-making Like his father, the present Marquis is thoroughly conservative in his wine-making practices, believing that it is best to leave well enough alone. Yields are kept well in hand by acting at the start of the growing cycle, and once harvested the fruit is entirely destalked when it arrives at the vatroom. Fermentation thereafter is allowed to proceed much as it wishes, rising as high as 35°, and is followed by 8-10 days' maceration, with *remontages* but no *pigeages*. New barrels are not held in particularly high esteem on the estate, the highest proportion used being 35%, for the top wines, and even then the wines are transferred to older wood once the malo-lactic fermentations are over. When maturation is complete the wines are fined and lightly filtered before bottling, which takes place 15-18 months after the harvest.

Volnay Clos des Ducs The wine for which the Angervilles are perhaps best known is their Clos des Ducs, a fine *monopole* vineyard lying on the north side of the family residence, which was once part of the estate of the Dukes of Burgundy. This wine is somewhat firmer than the Taillepieds, Cailleret and Champans, more Pommard than Volnay in style, yet has a remarkably harmonious and fragrant personality, enhanced by great volume and richness. Like all the D'Angerville wines the Clos des Ducs proves that Volnays can age with as much grace as many a Côte de Nuits, and can make a fine match for refined dishes such as fillet of beef *en brioche*.

- Other red wines:
Premier cru:
Volnay Champans,
V Frémiet, V Cailleret,
V Taillepieds, V L'Ormeau,
V Les Angles, V Pitures.
Village:
Pommard Les Combes
- White wine:
Premier cru:
Meursault Santenots
- Owner: Marquis
Jacques d'Angerville
- Wine-makers: Marquis
Jacques d'Angerville &
Renaud de Villette
- Combined vineyards:
14 hectares
- Production:
60,000 bottles
- Exports: 75%
- Take-away sales:
By appointment
- Visits: By appointment

Wine selected:
Volnay Clos des Ducs
(monopole)

- Classification:
Premier Cru
- Vineyard size:
2.4 hectares
- Soil type:
Clay and limestone
- Average vine age:
30 years
- Average annual
production:
10,000 bottles

Côte de Beaune | Volnay

158

Every year some 4,500 cases of white Burgundy of Village level and better leave the Chassagne estate of Michel Colin-Deléger & Fils to seduce the palates of the world's wine-lovers. Among their number may be found no less than 6 different Premiers Crus from the village and 2 more from neighbouring Puligny, one of which is the rare and exquisite Les Demoiselles. There is also one majestic Grand Cru, Chevalier-Montrachet. These wines are fine ambassadors for the region, and a delight for anyone who is interested in tasting *terroir* rather than grape.

The convolutions of a Burgundy wine estate The Colins have been in the village since 1878, and with time the original estate has become three. Michel Colin learnt his trade working from 1964 to 1975 alongside his father, and has built up his business considerably since 1975. He is now helped by his sons Philippe and Bruno.

While some of the vineyards were inherited from his father and others came from his wife's family, a good number are either leased or sharecropped, and some wines are made from both owned and leased or sharecropped fruit in the same vineyard; on the other hand the top wine, Chevalier-Montrachet, is made from grapes bought from his wife's uncle, and another is made from sharecropped grapes which are subcontracted to another *métayer* in the village... Such are the convolutions of a Burgundy wine estate!

Unceasing attention to detail The Colins set out to make aromatic, pure wine which contains the different *terroirs'* signatures; elegant and fruity, nothing too heavy or overblown. Their method of making wine is unexceptional, it is just the unceasing attention to detail which makes the difference between these and less distinguished offerings from the village. Firstly the quality of the raw material is checked twice, in the vineyard and on arrival at base. Then the fruit is pressed gently but insistently in a pneumatic press, which leaves only the finest of lees, eliminating the need for *débourbage*. Fermentation of the smaller quantities takes place in barrel, while the larger quantities are initially put into stainless steel vats with temperature control. Colin renews one fifth of his stock of barrels each year, and the wines spend 10-12 months maturing on their lees with weekly *bâtonnage* up until the malo-lactic fermentation. Bottling is carried out in the September following the vintage.

Chassagne-Montrachet Les Chaumées As might be hoped, while they share the language of the Chardonnay grape, Colin's 6 Premiers Crus all have different accents. The four on the Puligny side of the village have greater finesse than the Maltroie and Morgeot, which are more robust and spicy. Les Chaumées is perhaps the most elegant, a beautiful, refined and flowery wine of great balance and breeding, which benefits from 6-8 years in bottle to round it out. Apart from making a wonderful aperitif wine this complements starters as diverse as baked eggs in a creamy, curry sauce, fresh fish dishes such as salmon served *en croute*, and indeed numerous white meat dishes.

• Other white wines:
Grand cru:
Chevalier-Montrachet.
Premier cru:
Chassagne-Montrachet
Les Vergers,
CM Les Chenevottes,
CM En Rémilly,
CM La Maltroie,
CM Morgeot;
Puligny-Montrachet
Les Demoiselles,
PM La Truffière;
Saint-Aubin Les Combes,
SA Charmois.
Village:
Chassagne-Montrachet,
CM Clos Devant.
Régional:
Bourgogne, Bourgogne
Aligoté, Crémant de
Bourgogne
• Red wines:
Premier cru:
Chassagne-Montrachet
La Maltroie,
CM Morgeot; Santenay
Gravière; Maranges
Premier Cru.
Village:
Chassagne-Montrachet,
CM Clos Devant;
Santenay.
Régional:
Côte de Beaune,
Bourgogne
• Owners: M. et Mme.
Colin-Deléger
• Wine-makers: Michel,
Philippe & Bruno Colin
• Combined vineyards:
18.8 hectares
• Production:
120,000 bottles
• Exports: 90%
• Take-away sales: No
• Visits: No

Wine selected:
**Chassagne-Montrachet
Les Chaumées**

• Classification:
Premier Cru
• Area cultivated:
1.5 hectares
• Soil type:
Clay and limestone
• Average vine age:
25 years
• Average annual
production:
10,000 bottles

After Michel Gaunoux's death in 1984 his widow looked around for someone to take charge of wine-making operations. No one suitable could be found, so the lady knew what she had to do, and set about learning how her husband had made his magnificent Pommards, aided by their cellar hand. There was scarcely a hiccup in quality, and since that difficult period this coura-geous lady has steered the domaine with absolute self-assur-ance and resoluteness. Gaunoux Pommards have always been, and thanks to her are today, wonderfully virile and authentic wines.

A domaine with its own traditions The estate, which was founded in 1895 by Michel Gaunoux's grandfather, has always had its own way of doing things, and refuses to be swayed by fashions or other such external influences. Madame Gaunoux is not keen on publicity and does not push sales of her wines, much of which is bought by well-known restaurants. The estate has a policy of never letting the visitor taste out of the barrel, and does not put wines on sale until they have had at least two years in bottle. There are always a half-dozen or so vintages on sale, and for regular clients there are small stocks going back over several decades! Proving a sincere desire – voiced but not proved by many others – to produce nothing but the finest, the estate has been known to sell off in bulk an entire vintage if it is not up to standard.

Wines of power and structure The power and structure of these wines is achieved by vinification methods which are utterly traditional. A large proportion of the vines are of a venerable age, and the necessary measures are taken to ensure that yields do not exceed 35 hl/ha. if possible. Total vatting time lasts 17-18 days, during which there is regular *pigeage* by foot inside the wooden vats, and the fermentation temperature is allowed to attain relatively high levels. Use of sulphur is kept to the strict minimum necessary at all stages of the process. Madame Gaunoux shares her late husband's indifference to new oak, regarding it as mere fashion, a devi-ation from tradition, and for *élevage* uses at the very most 50% for her best wines in the best vintages. Wines receive a good traditional ageing of up to two years in cask, before a light fining and filtering and then bottling.

Pommard Grands Epenots Pommard has no Grand Cru vineyards, yet its two finest *climats*, Les Grands Epenots, on the Beaune side of the village, and Les Rugiens Bas, on the Volnay side, in the right hands frequently attain the top level of quality. The Gaunoux versions of both are classy exam-ples, the former perhaps having a touch more power and muscle, the latter more elegance... yet both are unmistakably true Pommard, tannic and unyielding when young, but gradually over the years softening up to reveal generous, complex characters, rich in alcohol, in short fine wines for a winter evening. The Grands Epenots requires at least 10 years before one should even contemplate broaching it, and has the staying power of 3 decades if well stored. When its day comes it benefits from decanting, and is enhanced by tasty fare such as jugged hare or a grilled rib of beef.

- Other red wines:
Grand cru:
Corton Renardes.
Premier cru:
Pommard Rugiens, P Les Arvelets, P Premier Cru.
Village:
Beaune.
Régional:
Bourgogne
- Owner: Domaine Michel Gaunoux
- Manager: Jacqueline Gaunoux
- Wine-makers: Michel Durand & Alexandre Gaunoux
- Combined vineyards: 7 hectares
- Production: 40,000 bottles
- Exports: 50%
- Take-away sales: Yes
- Visits: By appointment

Wine selected:
Pommard Grands Épenots

- Classification: Premier Cru
- Area cultivated: 2 hectares
- Soil type: Clay and limestone
- Average vine age: 40 years
- Average annual production: 9,000 bottles

1993

Mis en bouteilles
au Domaine

POMMARD GRANDS ÉPENOTS

Appellation POMMARD PREMIER *CRU* Contrôlee

>·>·<·<·

DOMAINE Michel GAUNOUX

PROPRIÉTAIRE - VITICULTEUR
à POMMARD (COTE - D'OR)

PRODUIT DE FRANCE

DOMAINE MICHEL LAFARGE

T he quiet little village of Volnay, tightly hemmed in by its surrounding vineyards, is home to some 95 growers, and the general standard of their output is high. There are a handful of exceptional producers, however, who manage to produce yardstick wines year in, year out, in which the exquisite finesse and delicacy of Volnay's *terroir* sings out. Domaine Michel Lafarge is one of them.

Father and son perpetuate a tradition The Lafarge family is an integral part of the village fabric, having been very active in Volnay's affairs during the last century; Michel Lafarge, his father and grandfather were all mayor of the village. They go much further back than that, having been vineyard labourers, toiling for the important landholders of the 18th century, and having gradually started buying plots of land and taking their destinies into their own hands. A section of the Clos des Chênes was bought in the late 19th century, and the Clos du Château des Ducs soon after. Lafarge's father bought some Beaune Grèves in 1954 and he himself has added his stone to the edifice with some Beaune Teurons and Pommard Pézerolles and more Village land.

Continuity, and the handing-on of received and acquired expertise, is all-important to the family. Michel learnt his trade working with his father, and his eldest son Frédéric, having studied oenology and gained experience in other wine regions, has been working alongside him for the last dozen years. Yet this is not just a simple case of 'teaching the next generation how to do it'; here there is teamwork, two minds each contributing their own ideas and working together to make the best use of what nature brings them each year. As at all great estates, every year sees a review of what has been done in the past, and with what degree of success, the better to use what the new vintage brings.

Bringing out terroir characteristics For the Lafarges their responsibility is to cultivate their vines in such a way as to bring out the finest characteristics of each *climat*; if a wine lacks *typicité* then they have failed in their mission. That fact then makes this domaine a fine one to get to know if one wishes to learn the essential differences in character between the wines of Volnay, Pommard and Beaune – the finesse, fragrance and delicacy of the first, the power and structure of the second and the flesh, robustness and spice of the third.

Volnay Clos des Chênes The 15-hectare *climat* Clos des Chênes lies at the southern end of Volnay at some 300 metres altitude, and enjoys a perfect south and south-east orientation. Here the Lafarge vines, of a high average age of 45 years, produce a wine of wonderful purity and finesse. It is deceptively easy to drink when young, for the tannic structure is invariably hidden in the seductive and ample flesh of the wine, yet the Clos des Chênes is made for keeping, and the best vintages need a good dozen years to open up fully. Even the difficult years, such as 1994, in the hands of the Lafarges reflect with great talent the quality of the *terroir*, and when ready express themselves with great eloquence – and if there is a fattened and truffled bird on the table, so much the better!

• Other red wines:
Premier cru:
Volnay Clos du Château des Ducs (monopole),
Volnay Premier Cru;
Beaune Grèves, Beaune Teurons; Pommard Pézerolles.
Village:
Volnay.
Régional:
Côte de Beaune Villages,
Bourgogne Pinot Noir,
Passetoutgrain
• White wines: *Village*:
Meursault.
Régional:
Bourgogne Aligoté
• Owner: Lafarge family
• Wine-makers:
Michel & Frédéric Lafarge
• Combined vineyards:
10 hectares
• Production:
53,000 bottles
• Exports: 50%
• Take-away sales: Yes
• Visits: By appointment

Wine selected:
Volnay Clos des Chênes

• Classification:
Premier Cru
• Area cultivated:
0.9 hectares
• Soil type:
Clay and limestone
• Average vine age:
45 years
• Average annual production:
3,500 bottles

1994

Volnay

Clos des Chênes

APPELLATION D'ORIGINE VOLNAY 1er CRU CONTRÔLÉE

Domaine Michel Lafarge

Propriétaire à Volnay (Côte-d'Or) France

Mis en bouteilles à la Propriété

The village of Monthélie is frequently overlooked by tourists and wine-lovers as they rush from one prestigious Côte de Beaune village to the next, to their great loss. Although small, Monthélie has a number of fine *climats,* and growers who coax from them wine of great refinement and delicacy, rivalling better-known and more costly Volnay offerings from nearby. Eric de Suremain is one such.

Viticulture at one with the environment De Suremain's operations are based in the fine old Château de Monthélie. Looking down on the village, the somewhat dilapidated-looking château is one of the rare constructions of consequence on the Côte, and parts of it go back as far back as the 14th century. Eric de Suremain took over from his father Robert in 1983, and works tirelessly, refining and experimenting, to improve the lot of his vines and by consequence the quality of his small range of wines.

Viticultural methods have long been governed by a respect for the environment, the soil and the vine, and since 1996 have embraced the principles of biodynamics, which dictate the most favourable time for the various vine-growing and wine-making operations according to the planetary calendar. For the moment the biodynamic angle is experimental. Yields are kept ruthlessly in check by the use of low-yielding rootstock and by making the necessary use of secateurs in spring and summer, and also be grassing the vineyard; this *enherbement* also prevents soil erosion and reduces humidity and thus rot. Compost is organic, and where grassing is not employed, weeding is carried out by hand.

A fine Monthélie comes into being Once the fruit has been harvested, white grapes destined for the white Rullys are immediately pressed and left to settle for 24 hours before being transferred to barrel to ferment. As for the reds, after a light crushing the fruit is given a mere 8 days *cuvaison* in wooden vats, during which Eric de Suremain climbs in twice a day to tread the solid matter for a better extraction of its contents. The unfinished wine is then run off the solids and left to settle, and at the same time finish its fermentation. It is then put into the cellar to undergo its malo-lactic fermentation, and during the summer following the vintage is racked and all the barrels mixed in vat for homogeneity before returning to barrel. Thereafter it spends 16-20 months ageing, depending on the quality of the vintage, before Kieselguhr filtration and bottling by gravity. Roughly one fifth new oak is used.

Monthélie Sur la Velle De Suremain's best vineyard is Sur La Velle, a fine 3-hectare holding contiguous with Volnay's Clos des Chênes, which, thanks to its east-facing, sloping and well-drained soil gives a wine of great finesse, elegance and perfume. When young it has pure black fruit flavours and a noticeable structure, into which animal, spice and vegetal nuances creep with age. Silkiness and refinement are what this delicious bottle is all about, and it adores the company of leg of lamb, followed by creamy cheeses such as Brillat-Savarin.

- Other red wines:
Premier cru:
Rully Préaux, Rully
Agneux.
Village:
Monthélie
- White wines:
Premier cru:
Rully Meix Caillet, Rully
Premier Cru
- Owner: Eric de
Suremain
- Wine-maker:
Eric de Suremain
- Combined vineyards:
10 hectares
- Production:
40,000 bottles
- Exports: 50%
- Take-away sales: Yes
- Visits: 9-12 a.m.,
2-6 p.m.

Wine selected:
Monthélie Sur La Velle

- Classification:
Premier Cru
- Area cultivated:
3 hectares
- Soil type:
Clay and limestone
- Average vine age:
Up to 40 years
- Average annual
production:
10,000 bottles

Côte de Beaune | Monthélie

1995

CHÂTEAU DE MONTHELIE

MONTHELIE 1ER CRU SUR LA VELLE

Appellation Monthelie 1er Cru Contrôlée

ERIC DE SUREMAIN

Propriétaire à Monthelie (Côte d'Or) France

PRODUCE OF FRANCE

The wines of Volnay do not have a reputation for great longevity, that is more the preserve of its neighbour Pommard. Yet the Volnays produced by the de Montille estate belie this reputation and require long cellaring before they show themselves in their finest light. Needless to say, the same goes for the estate's Pommards. Whichever one chooses, de Montille wines are among the very finest of their kind.

Responsibility from a tender age Hubert de Montille was throw in at the deep end after his father died while he was young, and made his first vintage in 1947 at the age of 17, then took on entire responsibility for the estate 4 years later. However, times being hard and the estate covering a mere 2.5 hectares, the young man trained as a lawyer. Thereafter, until his recent retirement, his entire professional life was devoted to his practice in Dijon, with extended presence on site only during the vintage season. De Montille's son Etienne has been progressively shouldering responsibilities since 1988, and his two daughters Isabelle and Alix despite having their own careers are also on hand when help is needed.

Pure fruit and long life expectancy De Montille wines favour finesse, relative lightness of body, rich fruit and good structure. One year the young de Montille miscalculated the amount of chaptalisation necessary for one of them, and the wine, with merely 11.5° of alcohol, turned out far better than the others of the vintage. Therein lay a lesson which he did not miss, and minimal chaptalisation has been one of his rules ever since, and delicacy one of his wines' trademarks.

His aim has always been to produce wines in which the pure Pinot Noir flavour dominates, and vinifications are adapted to this end. The manually harvested fruit is partially destalked and then fermented in wooden vats at a fairly high temperature, with lots of *pigeage*. De Montille is not convinced of the worth of cold pre-fermentation maceration for his wines. After the fermentation is finished however there follows a two-week maceration of the made wine, which is then run off into wooden casks. New oak is considered to mask the true Pinot character, and he is thus heartily disdainful of it; even the greatest vintages are matured for the most part in used casks. *Elevage* lasts in all some 22 months, during which it has long been the custom to rouse the lees in the barrel from time to time, then when ready the wines are bottled with fining but without filtration.

Volnay Les Taillepieds The three named Volnay Premiers Crus are among the finest examples produced by anyone in Burgundy. Each has its own character, but all have the unmistakable de Montille elegance and refinement, beautiful balance and sumptuous perfume. Taillepieds is perhaps the most elegant of the three, irresistible when young yet needing two decades to reveal the stunning complexity of tertiary aromas that it develops after sufficient time in bottle. This is a remarkably fine bottle, well suited to white meats such as roast turkey with chestnut stuffing.

- Other red wines:
Premier cru:
Volnay Champans,
V Mitans, V Premier Cru;
Pommard Rugiens,
P Grands Épenots,
P Pézerolles.
Village:
Volnay.
Régional:
Bourgogne
- Owner: Hubert de Montille
- Wine-maker:
Etienne de Montille
- Combined vineyards:
7 hectares
- Production:
25,000 bottles
- Exports: 50%
- Take-away sales: Yes
- Visits: No

Wine selected:
Volnay Les Taillepieds

- Classification:
Premier Cru
- Area cultivated:
0.78 hectares
- Soil type:
Clay and limestone
- Average vine age:
28 years
- Average annual production:
3,500 bottles

Récolte 1994

Volnay
Les Taillepieds

1er CRU
APPELLATION VOLNAY 1er CRU CONTROLÉE

Hubert de MONTILLE
Propriétaire à Volnay - France

12% vol.   75 cl

A s at many of Burgundy's top estates, excessive demand has for many years been a problem at Domaine Leflaive, and a source of frustration for would-be clients. The situation led one of the younger generation of Leflaives to create a *négociant* business in 1984, in order to satisfy what would otherwise simply have been lost custom. Olivier Leflaive Frères is now well established and making commercial quantities of very fine wines.

As it would have been done at the Domaine From the start Leflaive's idea was to buy grapes or must, but never fermented wine, and treat the raw material in exactly the way he would have treated it had it been grown on the family estate. Sourcing high-quality Puligny grapes is of course not that easy, yet Olivier Leflaive was in the fortunate position of having contacts and good relations with many a grower in the white wine villages of the Côte de Beaune, thanks to his family's long history and important role in the region.

He took on the talented Jean-Marc Boillot as *régisseur* and wine-maker, and together the two of them got down to making the wines. The business started thriving, then in 1991 Boillot left in order to take in hand an inheritance, and Franck Grux, who had previously been with Jean-Marc Roulot, took his place. Unsurprisingly, given that he was brought up seeing things from the grower's point of view, Leflaive has started buying vineyard plots, and Olivier Leflaive Frères is now a Domaine as well as a Maison...

Traditional wine-making and respect for terroir Wine-making is carried out in the most traditional manner and with all due respect for *terroir* characteristics. After a gentle pneumatic pressing and a day's settling, musts are fermented in oak *pièces*, some 20-25% of which are new, depending on the quality of the vintage. The oak comes from the Allier forests and is given a light toasting, making it thoroughly suitable for long periods of *élevage*, interspersed with lots of *bâtonnage*. The wines' development is monitored by regular tasting, and the first racking takes place at one moment or another after some 12-15 months, following which the various barrels are unified in vat. Several weeks later the wines are fined, and thereafter bottled, sometimes with, sometimes without a light filtration.

Montrachet The most impossible task for any *négociant* is finding a source of the supremely desirable Montrachet, yet Olivier Leflaive has one, enabling him in 1996 to make 4 *pièces*, giving 1,200 bottles. This is a very great bottle of wine, concentrated, rich and powerful, fat on the tongue yet with a high level of acidity to keep its opulence in check; yet rigid and unformed after two years, it really needs at least another ten to soften up and develop all its inherent complexity. In *jambon persillé* it will find a soul-mate who speaks with the same accent, yet when mature it will demand more refined company; sweetbread, or a noble crustacean, will be eminently suitable.

Côte de Beaune | Puligny-Montrachet

• Other white wines:
Grand cru:
Chevalier-Montrachet, Bâtard-Montrachet, Criots-Bâtard-Montrachet, Bienvenues-Bâtard-Montrachet, Corton-Charlemagne.
Numerous premiers crus and village wines from Puligny, Chassagne, Meursault, Saint-Aubin et Rully
• Red wines:
Premiers crus and village wines from Volnay, Pommard et Monthélie
• Owner: Olivier Leflaive
• Wine-maker:
Franck Grux
• Oenologist:
Philippe Grillet
• Combined vineyards:
12 hectares
• Production (négoce and domaine):
750,000 bottles
• Exports: 70%
• Take-away sales: Yes
• Visits: By appointment

Wine selected:
Montrachet

• Classification:
Grand Cru
• Soil type:
Clay and limestone
• Average vine age:
30 years
• Average annual production:
1,200 bottles

Montrachet

GRAND CRU

APPELLATION MONTRACHET CONTRÔLÉE

1996

VINIFIÉ, ÉLEVÉ ET MIS EN BOUTEILLES PAR

Olivier Leflaive

SEVIB S.A. 21190 PULIGNY-MONTRACHET

DOMAINE PAVELOT

The vineyards of Savigny-lès-Beaune are the source of some deliciously thirst-quenching and fruity wines. One has to choose carefully, for there are many examples which are excessively lean and unripe, yet those from the best producers are well worth their modest prices. Some of the very best come from Jean-Marc Pavelot.

Living soils, healthy vines and perfect grapes The Pavelots are anything but new to the region, having been growers there since 1640. Over the years the family accumulated a fine estate of five Savigny Premiers Crus and one at Pernand, as well as a fair amount of Village land. In the time of Pavelot *père* this was mostly sold off in bulk, yet now the contrary is the case, with 90% of the production sold in bottle.

Pavelot runs his vineyards by *lutte raisonné*, sharing the conviction of many of his peers that top quality fruit only comes from perfectly healthy vines, which in turn require healthy, living soil, teeming with its millions of microorganisms, to provide them with all the necessary nutrients. Weeds are kept at bay by spring ploughing, which has the added advantage of obliging vines to bury their roots deeper under the soil to avoid the plough's blades, leading thus to stronger plants and greater *terroir* character in the wines. There are no systematic vineyard treatments, yet nor is there an idealistic refusal on principal to use chemicals; sprays may be used with care if there is no other way of saving the harvest from any of the various diseases or attacks with which Nature presents it from time to time.

User-friendly and succulently fruity The style of Pavelot wines has changed with the last change of generation, and they are now definitely more user-friendly and succulently fruity, though that is not to say that they have become more simple. The change is probably the result of a greater awareness of the importance of grape ripeness, destalking, temperature control and duration of *élevage,* and of the impact of new oak... and an understandable desire for greater quality in a wine on which one sticks one's own label.

The range provides a variety of characters, for Pavelot's parcels are spread all over the two sides of the valley. One characteristic they all seem to have in common is a fine, fleshy texture, indicative of a *vigneron* who does not rush out to harvest at the first instant.

Savigny-lès-Beaune La Dominode The *climat* La Dominode is one of the vineyards down onto which one looks from the Savigny *aire* of the A6 motorway. This side of the valley, facing north-east, is less disposed to making fine wine than the far side, yet La Dominode proves an exception to the rule, particularly in Pavelot's hands. By doggedly hanging on for peak ripeness of the old vines' fruit, he fashions a wine of delicious aroma, which is succulent and fleshy on the palate, and nicely concentrated. Yet it is a wine for laying down, and is inexpressive for a handful of years after bottling. But once it has come of age the wait is amply rewarded. It makes a good match for kidney fricassee.

- Other red wines:
Premier cru:
Savigny-lès-Beaune
Les Narbantons,
SIB Aux Guettes,
SIB Aux Gravains,
SIB Les Peuillets;
Pernand-Vergelesses
Les Vergelesses.
Village:
Savigny-lès-Beaune
- White wine:
Village:
Savigny-lès-Beaune
- Owner:
Jean-Marc Pavelot
- Wine-maker:
Jean-Marc Pavelot
- Oenologist: SGS
Oenologie, Beaune
- Combined vineyards:
12 hectares
- Production:
65,000 bottles
- Exports: 50%
- Take-away sales: Yes
- Visits: 9-12 a.m.,
2-6 p.m. by appointment

Wine selected:
**Savigny-lès-Beaune
La Dominode**

- Classification:
Premier Cru
- Area cultivated:
2 hectares
- Soil type:
Clay, silt and sand
- Average vine age:
45 years
- Average annual
production:
10,000 bottles

GRAND VIN   DE BOURGOGNE

SAVIGNY-LES-BEAUNE

LA DOMINODE - 1ᵉʳ CRU
APPELLATION CONTRÔLÉE

75 cl   13% vol

Mis en bouteille par
Jean-Marc PAVELOT
PROPRIÉTAIRE A SAVIGNY-LES-BEAUNE (CÔTE-D'OR) FRANCE
PRODUIT DE FRANCE

Given the number of wines he makes these days, it is not easy to see how Pierre Morey manages to dedicate sufficient time to each one, yet he does. Be they from his own estate, from his *négociant* business or those of Domaine Leflaive, his touch is sure, and the wines masterpieces of their respective appellations.

An ultimatum to look after the estate Morey's family is distantly related to the many Moreys in Chassagne, for during the Terror which followed the Revolution in 1793, an ancestor named Alexis Morey met a local girl, married her and settled in the village. He built up a small viticultural property, but over the years and the changes of generation it was subdivided several times until the pieces were too small to support a family.

Morey's father Auguste Morey-Genelot duly inherited his share in 1930, but seeing no future in wine-making he left to become a travelling salesman. After a couple of years Auguste's father, an invalid veteran of the Great War who was getting on in years, gave him an ultimatum to come back and look after the estate or he would sell it. Auguste came back. Although he did not have enough faith in the future to buy land, he took on 4 hectares of prestigious appellations – Meursault Perrières, Genevrières and Charmes, and 35 ares of Le Montrachet – on a sharecropping basis for the Lafon family, and later on some Bâtard-Montrachet and Pommard Epenots.

Compensation for lost vineyards Pierre Morey started working with his father at the age of 18, and total responsibility passed to him on his father's retirement 6 years later, in 1972. After some 15 years he saw all the magnificent Lafon holdings reclaimed by Dominique Lafon as the contracts expired, leaving rather a dearth of quality appellations in his cellar. To compensate for these losses, in 1990 he set up a *négociant* business named Morey-Blanc, enabling him to buy grapes or must and make wine, and has since found sources of Genevrières, Charmes and Montrachet itself, as well as Bouchères, Les Narvaux and Saint-Aubin Les Combes.

Morey's talent and devotion to his *métier* was rewarded in 1988 with an invitation to understudy Jean Virot as winemaker at Domaine Leflaive with a view to succeeding him on his retirement, and he was duly offered and took up that post in 1990. Critics have noted a clear improvement in quality at the domaine in the 1990s.

Meursault Perrières In 1987 Morey managed to buy a half-hectare parcel of Les Perrières which he had operated as sharecropper since 1973, since which time some 2,500 bottles of a wonderfully concentrated, mineral-flavoured wine have epitomized his style of wine-making and graced his cellar every vintage for a short time before being snapped up by eager clients. It is to be hoped that they all have cellars and patience, for perhaps more than any other of his wines this individual needs time to develop. Some 8-10 years at least, but preferably two decades or more, thanks to its excellent acidity and balance, are required for it to express itself to the full. It makes a fine partner at table for sea-perch *en croûte*.

Côte de Beaune | Meursault

• Other white wines (Domaine):
Grand cru:
Bâtard-Montrachet.
Village:
Meursault Les Tessons, Meursault.
Régional:
Bourgogne Chardonnay, Bourgogne Aligoté
• Red wines:
Premier cru:
Pommard Grands Épenots.
Village:
Meursault Les Durots, Monthélie.
Régional:
Bourgogne Pinot Noir
• Owner: Pierre Morey
• Wine-maker: Pierre Morey
• Combined vineyards: 8 hectares
• Exports: 70%
• Take-away sales: No
• Visits: No

Wine selected:
Meursault Perrières

• Classification: Premier Cru
• Area cultivated: 0.52 hectares
• Soil type: Limestone
• Average vine age: 30 years
• Average annual production: 2,500 bottles

PRODUCE

OF FRANCE

1994

1994

MEURSAULT PERRIÈRES

APPELLATION MEURSAULT 1er CRU CONTROLÉE

Mis en bouteille à la Propriété par

Pierre MOREY

A MEURSAULT (COTE D'OR) FRANCE

A nyone wanting to taste the very best in white Burgundy, to see where the limits lie in what can be done by fermenting Chardonnay juice, should just open up a bottle of Ramonet. This is one of the Côte d'Or's two or three mythical estates, and for good reason.

From humble origins to international acclaim Ramonet's story could be said to start with the marriage of Pierre Ramonet, a young vineyard worker of humble origins, and Lucie Prudhon, whose father was a *chef de culture*. Pierre, born in 1906, had left school at the age of 8 to help his father, a *tâcheron*, and he and Lucie undoubtedly knew the meaning of hard work and saving. With their savings they bought a parcel of the Chassagne Premier Cru Ruchottes in the 1930s, and his 1934 vintage was imported into the United States, newly emerged from Prohibition, making it one of the first Burgundy estates to be exported and, rapidly, to gain an international reputation. Over the years Pierre displayed an uncommon genius for fashioning magisterial wines, and the Ramonets invested in vineyard land when there were savings available, in 1955 buying their parcels of Bâtard- and Bienvenue-Bâtard-Montrachet, and in 1978 25 ares of Le Montrachet itself.

Pierre and Lucie had a son, André, who in turn sired two boys, Noël and Jean-Claude. Throughout his life André had precarious health, and never entirely took over from his father. The two together made their last vintage in 1983, after which the young brothers took over. Since then these two have upheld the family name with consummate talent, going about the numerous tasks that occupy a wine-maker with unerring instinct, for it is empiricism, not oenology diplomas, that makes the wines at Ramonet.

White wines for the long term The whites are made for long term ageing, which in the case of Ramonet means several decades, while the reds, which should on no account be ignored, are ready after 6 years or so. Old vines receive great respect (any vine under 18 years old is considered young) and low yields are the cornerstone of quality.

The white wines are fermented with their gross lees, initially in tank and subsequently in barrel, with no real temperature control, and then remain on them until the first racking becomes essential. All this solid matter obviates the need for anything but the occasional *bâtonnage*, and then when the *élevage*, generally in 35% new wood with a light toasting, has run its course, the wines are given a light fining and filtration and are then bottled.

Bienvenue Bâtard-Montrachet While the domaine's range of Premiers Crus is of breathtaking quality, the three Grands Crus mark a distinct climb into a higher orbit. The Montrachet is usually the finest of the three, but there is never a great deal to separate them. The Bâtard is invariably firmer and more austere than the Bienvenue, which, Noël states, is a question of different wood. The Bienvenue is a majestic display of opulent seduction, a triumph of extraordinary dimensions and complexity, with an unbelievably long finish. Parsleyed frogs' legs, or a *chaud-froid* of chicken with tarragon, these are suitable dining companions for this great wine.

- Other white wines:
Grand cru:
Montrachet, Bâtard-Montrachet.
Premier cru:
Chassagne-Montrachet Ruchottes, CM Morgeot, CM Les Caillerets, CM Les Chaumées, CM Les Vergers, CM La Boudriotte; Puligny-Montrachet Champ-Canet; Saint-Aubin Le Charmois.
Village:
Chassagne-Montrachet, Puligny-Montrachet.
Régional:
Bourgogne Aligoté
- Red wines:
Premier cru:
Chassagne-Montrachet Morgeot, CM Clos de la Boudriotte, CM Clos Saint-Jean.
Village:
Chassagne-Montrachet.
Régional:
Bourgogne Grand Ordinaire
- Owner: Ramonet family
- Wine-makers: Noël & Jean-Claude Ramonet
- Combined vineyards: 17 hectares
- Production: 80,000 bottles
- Exports: 70%
- Take-away sales: No
- Visits: No

Wine selected:
Bienvenue Bâtard-Montrachet

- Classification: Grand Cru
- Area cultivated: 0.5 hectares
- Soil type: Clay and limestone
- Average vine age: 50 years
- Average annual production: 2,500 bottles

RAMONET

1996

Grand Cru
BIENVENUE
BATARD-MONTRACHET
APPELLATION CONTRÔLÉE

S.C.E. DOMAINE RAMONET
VITICULTEUR A CHASSAGNE-MONTRACHET
COTE-D'OR, FRANCE

13,5% vol.

DOMAINE ROBERT AMPEAU & FILS

Few Meursault producers, indeed few white Burgundy producers at all, are as consistent as Domaine Robert Ampeau, turning out wines which defy climatic variation and the host of other problems which fickle Nature throws up from time to time. What is more, the wines are not just consistent but are also of absolutely splendid quality.

Keeping the vineyard in perfect condition Before the wines the vines, for splendid quality is not achieved without splendid raw material. Michel Ampeau, who took over on his father Robert's retirement in 1985, is a very dedicated grower whose vines are kept in such perfect condition that they regularly attract the admiration of his neighbours. Like his father before him, Ampeau swears by clones, and selects them with extreme care in order to create perfect matches with their rootstocks and the various soils of their vineyards, using several different clones in each vineyard to give complexity to its wine. Yields are ruthlessly controlled by very short pruning and debudding in the spring, and ripeness and aeration are enhanced by stripping away excess foliage before the summer. Also as his father did before him, every year Ampeau plants grass in between the rows of vines in order to prevent soil erosion and to encourage vines to bury their roots deeper, thus bringing out more intense *terroir* characteristics... and then, at the end of every year he gets rid of it!

Destined for long years in bottle In the cellar the Ampeau tradition has always been to make wines which last a long time, and this is as true for the whites as the reds. After a pneumatic pressing, Chardonnay musts are fermented in barrel; some 10-25% of these are renewed each year, yet so rich are the musts, for they are stirred very often, that new wood flavours are never particularly visible in the wines. Red wines are usually entirely destemmed. Chaptalisation is left until near the end of fermentations in order to prolong them, which always presents the risk of residual sugar in the finished wine. One rather unusual factor that Ampeau has introduced into the domaine's ways is short maturation times of 9-10 months for both whites and reds, for he wants above all to protect the wines' fresh fruitiness and acidity, essential if wines are to remain fresh and crisp over long years.

And long years are what the wines are destined for. The domaine has a policy of not releasing them for sale until they are considered ready to drink, which often means 10 years or more after the vintage, and not necessarily in chronological order at that. Yet they go on to live distinguished lives for many a year after that.

Meursault Perrières Generally recognized as Meursault's finest *climat*, in Michel Ampeau's hands the Perrières is a wine of lean, muscular athleticism, radiating health and vigour. Yet behind this classy front it is also very profound, and what is more can reveal a wealth of irresistible charm if born in a warm vintage. At table it makes friends easily, and is drawn to great eloquence in the company of an asparagus and frogs' leg turnover, or indeed a noble lobster, roasted on a spit.

• Other white wines:
Premier cru:
Meursault Charmes, M La Pièce sous le Bois; Puligny-Montrachet Les Combettes.
Village:
Meursault
• Red wines:
Premier cru:
Beaune Clos du Roi; Blagny La Pièce sous le Bois; Auxey-Duresses Les Écusseaux; Volnay Les Santenots; Savigny-lès-Beaune Les Lavières.
Village:
Pommard, Savigny-lès-Beaune
• Owner:
Robert Ampeau & Fils
• Wine-maker: Michel Ampeau
• Oenologist: BIVB, Beaune
• Combined vineyards: 9.5 hectares
• Production: 50,000 bottles
• Exports: 90%
• Take-away sales: No
• Visits: No

Wine selected:
Meursault Perrières

• Classification: Premier Cru
• Area cultivated: 0.56 hectares
• Soil type: Clay and limestone
• Average vine age: 40 years
• Average annual production: 3,500 bottles

DOMAINE ROUGEOT

I n the cellar under a handsome 17th-century house in a quiet street in Meursault lies a range of sumptuous white wines, ageing in the cold, dark tranquillity until the day when Marc Rougeot decides that they are ready for bottling and sale. When that day comes, they will be much sought after by French and foreign connoisseurs, for although there is only one white and one red Grand Cru among the wines produced, the range consists of beautifully crafted examples of their respective appellations.

Three generations do it their way Rougeot is the third generation of his family to make wine. When he made his first vintage in 1975, the estate was regularly selling off its output in bulk, but he knew that the future lay in building up a private clientèle and export markets, and started bottling progressively more of the production each year. From the outset his wines were good, and the point was eventually reached where demand reached supply, and in ungenerous years even outstripped it. Once sales were more or less guaranteed he could put all his efforts into aiming for even greater quality!

Now that quality measures are firmly in place, the entrepreneurial Rougeot is not sitting back on his laurels: in 1990 he and his wife founded Rougeot-Dupin, a *négociant* business dealing principally in Côte de Nuits Grands Crus. More recently he has become the French agent for a Port shipper and a Moselle wine estate, and he has also acquired Domaine des Forges, another Meursault estate. This is not a man for letting the grass grow under his feet!

Soil, nature and man must give of their utmost Experience has taught Rougeot that to make the finest wine possible all three essential elements – soil, nature and man – must give of their utmost, and that at every stage operations should be as natural as possible. The soil must be given free rein to express itself by means of the grape, and must therefore be cultivated as respectfully as possible; nature, in the form of the vine, must be allowed to give of its finest quality, by suitable training, pruning, yield reduction, and harvesting at the right moment; and man, who can so easily spoil everything, must know when and how to intervene before, during and after fermentation, and must know when to leave the wine alone, for the less manipulations it suffers the better it generally turns out!

Meursault Charmes Rougeot's most prestigious wine is a superlative example of its appellation, rich, concentrated and full-bodied, with all the intensity of flavour of 50 year-old vines and the sheer quality that only comes from excellent fruit vinified slowly and naturally. Perhaps its greatest quality though is its balance, for despite its richness and heady alcohol, the taster is left with an overriding impression of crispness and liveliness, of purity and breed. This Charmes is a classic Meursault, to be savoured with pike and prawn *mousseline*, or asparagus and frogs' legs in puff-pastry.

- Other white wines:
Village:
Meursault Les Grandes Gouttes, M Sous la Velle, Meursault, Saint-Romain.
Régional:
Bourgogne Chardonnay, Bourgogne Aligoté
- Red wines:
Premier cru:
Volnay Santenots.
Village:
Pommard, Ladoix, Saint-Romain.
Régional:
Bourgogne Rouge, Bourgogne Passetoutgrain
- Owner: Marc Rougeot
- Wine-maker: Marc Rougeot
- Combined vineyards: 19 hectares
- Production: 100,000 bottles
- Exports: 60%
- Take-away sales: No
- Visits: No

Wine selected:
Meursault Charmes

- Classification: Premier Cru
- Area cultivated: 0.46 hectares
- Soil type: Clay and limestone
- Average vine age: 50 years
- Average annual production: 2,700 bottles

RÉCOLTE DU **1997** DOMAINE

MEURSAULT-CHARMES

PREMIER CRU

APPELLATION MEURSAULT-CHARMES CONTROLÉE

Mis en Bouteille au Domaine

DOMAINE ROUGEOT

PROPRIÉTAIRE-RÉCOLTANT A MEURSAULT, COTE-D'OR, FRANCE

PRODUCT OF FRANCE
L MC 06

DOMAINE ROULOT

S uch are the nuances of geology and microclimate in Burgundy that a mere few metres separating one plot from its neighbour can make a noticeable difference in the glass. This is as true at Meursault as anywhere, and its village *climats* are often vinified and sold as such. The Domaine Roulot has an extensive list, each with its own personality, which is crowned by three immaculate Premiers Crus.

The growing pains of a young estate It was Guy Roulot who put together the nucleus of the estate in the post-war decades, with the dowry from his marriage and with a number of purchases. However continuity has not been a luxury that the estate has enjoyed in recent times, for Roulot died prematurely in 1982, and his son Jean-Marc, a classical actor, was not free to step into his father's shoes. For two years the estate was run by a Californian named Ted Lemon, and then for the following four years Franck Grux was in charge, before going on to make Olivier Leflaive's wines.

Jean-Marc Roulot returned for good to the estate in 1988. His father had been one of the first to start bottling the produce of different plots independently of each other, and his son wholeheartedly embraced this policy. He set about making his range of wines in an unostentatious, traditional manner, quietly taking the pains and looking after the details which separate the best wine-makers from the rest.

Low yields and stringent selection Great wine may only be made from restricted yields, and to this end Roulot takes great care in reducing the number of buds on stems, as well as suckers, in the spring; green harvesting before the fruit turns colour in August is a second chance of correcting quantities, yet it should not be necessary, some maintain, if sufficient *ébourgeonnage* and *évasivage* has been carried out earlier on in the year, and if the timing is not right its efficacy is questionable. Roulot cultivates his vines and treats his vineyards as naturally as possible, keeping weeds at bay by hoe rather than herbicide and spraying as little as possible.

After a thoroughly serious sorting, grapes are gently pressed in a pneumatic press; this is not as protracted as is usual, and musts are of a correspondingly higher quality. A little maceration follows, so as not to miss certain aromas that lie just under the skin, then fermentation in barrel may proceed. Once its malo-lactic fermentation is over the wine is ready for maturation, and this always lasts for some 11 months. Unlike most Meursault producers Roulot is not a great exponent of *bâtonnage*, feeling that it causes loss of purity, and therefore stirs the lees less often than many.

Meursault Perrières The Perrières vineyard, lying at the southern end of the commune at a little under 300 metres, is the source of what most consider Meursault's finest wine. Ample yet firm, rich yet steely, its mineral flavours mingle with those of hazelnuts and butter to give an impression of great drive and authority. The Roulot Perrières is pure, classy and direct, a very fine example, which reaches its peak after a decade, a sumptuous golden nectar. Enjoyed with sweetbread terrine, it leaves a lasting impression on the fortunate taster.

Côte de Beaune | *Meursault*

- Other white wines:
Premier cru:
Meursault Charmes,
M Bouchères.
Village:
Meursault Tessons Clos
de Mon Plaisir,
M Luchets, M Meix
Chavaux, M Vireuils,
M Tillets.
Régional:
Bourgogne Blanc
Chardonnay, Bourgogne
Aligoté
- Red wines:
Premier cru:
Auxey-Duresses Premier
Cru.
Village:
Monthélie.
Régional:
Bourgogne Pinot Noir
- Owner: Roulot family
- Manager:
Jean-Marc Roulot
- Wine-maker:
Jean-Marc Roulot
- Combined vineyards:
11 hectares
- Production:
60,000 bottles
- Exports: 60%
- Take-away sales: No
- Visits: No

Wine selected:
Meursault Perrières

- Classification:
Premier Cru
- Area cultivated:
0.26 hectares
- Soil type:
Clay and limestone
- Average vine age:
30 years
- Average annual
production:
1,400 bottles

1995

MIS EN BOUTEILLES A LA PROPRIÉTÉ

Meursault-Perrières

APPELLATION MEURSAULT 1er CRU CONTROLÉE

DOMAINE ROULOT

PROPRIÉTAIRE A MEURSAULT, COTE-D'OR, FRANCE

L ittle is predictable at the large Savigny estate of Simon Bize apart from the quality of the wines, which can itself be attributed to the very lack of the systematic, and the readiness to try out new ideas. Adapting themselves to the vine's demands every season, the Bize family makes a fine list of Savigny-lès-Beaunes, interspersed with a few other appellations, in which the character of each vineyard shines through.

A healthy disrespect for wine schools Three generations of Bizes, all named Simon, made wines in the village before responsibility for the estate settled on the shoulders of Patrick Bize in 1988. Patrick learnt his trade at his father's side and received invaluable advice on all sides of the business from such luminaries as Henri Jayer, Aubert de Villaine and the Marquis d'Angerville, which has stood him in good stead ever since. He has a healthy disrespect for wine schools and the inflexible theory which they cram into the heads of their students.

Bringing out the best of each vintage While the Bize philosophy embraces respect for the soil, the estate does not sit firmly in any particular camp as regards viticultural regime; Patrick Bize knows his plots and treats each according to the needs presented by the vintage. Old vines and low yields are the principal quality factors of the wines – 25-40 hl/ha is the aim for the red wines – and harvesting never takes place until peak ripeness has been attained.

Once the fruit has arrived at the vatroom all the young wines (less than 20 years of age!) are destalked, while the adults are vatted whole. Fermentation, carried out by indigenous yeast, takes place in open wooden vats and starts in its own good time, without preliminary cold maceration. Temperatures are not allowed to rise beyond 33°, and three *pigeages* per day enable sufficient extraction of aroma, colour and tannin. In all, vatting can last up to 21 days. Then it is tasting, and not any analysis in the laboratory, which tells Bize when to run off the wine into barrel. The pulp is not used at this estate, the wines consisting exclusively of free-run wine.

The first racking takes place after some 8-10 months, when the malo-lactic fermentations have finished, and during this period the Premiers Crus will have been lodged in 50-100% new oak, depending on the vintage. Generally the wines are unified before being fined and filtered – tasting again decides whether these operations will take place or not – and subsequently bottled.

Savigny-lès-Beaune Aux Vergelesses Of the 5 Premiers Crus made by Bize, the south-east-facing Aux Vergelesses, on the eastern side of the village at the Pernand-Vergelesses extremity, produces probably the most distinguished wine, which combines structure, finesse and elegance, and invariably has great complexity and intensity thanks to the advanced average age of its vines and, needless to say, low yields. This, it could be argued, is Savigny's finest wine, which takes a dozen years to reveal all its character. When it does, it is enhanced by the accompaniment of partridge *à la mode bourguignonne*.

• Other red wines:
Grand cru:
Latricières-Chambertin.
Premier cru:
Savigny-lès-Beaune
Les Marconnets,
SlB Aux Guettes,
SlB Les Fournaux,
SlB Les Serpentières.
Village:
SlB Aux Grands Liards,
SlB Les Bourgeots;
Aloxe-Corton Le Suchot.
Régional:
Bourgogne Les Perrières
• White wines:
Grand cru:
Corton-Charlemagne.
Village:
Savigny-lès-Beaune.
Régional:
Bourgogne Les Perrières,
Bourgogne Les
Champlains
• Owner:
Domaine Bize & Family
• Wine-maker:
Patrick Bize
• Combined vineyards:
22 hectares
• Production:
110,000 bottles
• Exports: 60%
• Take-away sales: Yes
• Visits: 8-12 a.m.,
2-6 p.m.

Wine selected:
**Savigny-lès-Beaune
Aux Vergelesses**

• Classification:
Premier Cru
• Area cultivated:
3 hectares
• Soil type:
Clay and limestone
• Average vine age:
50 years
• Average annual
production:
14,000 bottles

1996

Savigny-les-Beaune 1er Cru

"Aux Vergelesses"

APPELLATION CONTROLÉE

750 ml e
ALC 12.5 % BY VOL

Simon Bize & Fils

Négociant Propriétaires à Savigny-lès-Beaune (Côte d'Or)

PRODUIT DE FRANCE

Lovers of the northern Côte de Beaune wines have long gone to Domaine Tollot-Beaut to replenish their cellars, for it is one of the finest sources of Beaune, Savigny, Chorey and Aloxe, and offers great reliability whatever the climatic conditions of the vintage. These wines are all about harmony and finesse, and are never overly structured, being made for the medium-term.

A tightly-knit family Harmony seems to apply to the Tollot family as much as to its wines, for the current generation, owning and running the estate, consists of three brothers working side by side, aided by their offspring (one child each). Jacques, Alain and François are the 5th generation to exploit the family estate, which was founded in 1880. Standards have always been high, and the desire for authenticity was very positively demonstrated back in the 1920s by the brothers' grandmother Beaut, who took the revolutionary decision to risk the ire of the Beaune merchant houses and bottle her own unadulterated production.

An ecological yet practical outlook It is not surprising, given the family dedication to authenticity, purity and finesse, to learn that the vineyards are worked in a thoroughly ecological manner, with a *lutte raisonnée* attitude – that is, there are no systematic vineyard treatments, but neither is there a stubborn and unrealistic refusal on principal to use chemicals; sprays may be used with care if there is no other way of saving the harvest from any of the various diseases or attacks with which Nature presents it from time to time. Weeds are kept at bay by physical effort, and rather than blindly manuring the vineyard soils, they are monitored by regular analysis, and deficiencies in nutritional elements rectified.

Yields are kept down by serious and repeated debudding, for the brothers believe that the problem must be dealt with at the start of the vine's cycle, and are contemptuous of those who make a song and dance about their mid-summer green harvests, which have very limited influence on yields unless practised expertly and at the right moment.

Low yields and old vines Vinifications are tailored to the aim of producing soft, aromatic wines without excessive structure, and that involves relatively short fermentations without maceration, for concentration and colour can be better achieved, the brothers are adamant, by low yields and old vines. Some 75% of the bunches are destalked, and the fruit is crushed before being loaded into the cement and stainless steel vats. Once fermentations are over, maturation takes place in Tronçais oak, with one third of the casks renewed annually for Premier Cru wine and half for the Grands Crus.

Corton Bressandes Power combined with finesse is how the Tollot Bressandes may be succinctly described. This wine is rich, robust and fleshy, with a fine aromatic mix, yet restraint and refinement are also part of its make-up, making of it a very accomplished wine indeed. Its balance is irreproachable, its savour intense, and its finish very long. Partridge makes a fine partner at table, and considering the wine's origin, why not partridge *à la mode bourguignonne*?

• Other red wines:
Grand cru:
Corton.
Premier cru:
Aloxe-Corton Les Vercots,
AC Les Fournières;
Beaune Grèves, B Clos du
Roi; Savigny-lès-Beaune
Les Lavières, SlB Champ
Chevrey (monopole).
Village:
Aloxe-Corton, Beaune
Les Blanches Fleurs,
Savigny-lès-Beaune,
Chorey-lès-Beaune.
Régional:
Bourgogne
• White wines:
Grand cru:
Corton-Charlemagne.
Régional:
Bourgogne,
Bourgogne Aligoté
• Owner: Tollot family
• Wine-maker:
Tollot family
• Combined vineyards:
22 hectares
• Production:
120,000 bottles
• Exports: 60%
• Take-away sales: Yes
• Visits: 9-12 a.m.,
2-6 p.m., by appointment

Wine selected:
Corton Bressandes

• Classification:
Grand Cru
• Area cultivated:
0.91 hectares
• Soil type:
Clay and limestone
• Average vine age:
40 years
• Average annual
production:
4,000 bottles

The name of Santenay unfailingly suggests *santé*, health, and bathers at the village's spa have long found that a visit there works wonders, particularly those suffering from gout and rheumatism. The wine made at Santenay, like all other good Burgundy, can also leave one with a feeling of both physical and mental health if it is well made. It pays to be selective however, for certain *climats* are undeniably better than others, and not all the village's wine-makers are equally conscientious and talented. One of the very best is Vincent Girardin.

Expansion and critical acclaim Girardin inherited his vines in 1982, one quarter of his parents' estate, which amounted to 3 hectares. He has come a long way since then, widening his portfolio with several purchases and with contracts to farm others' land, and above all as a wine-maker, which has not gone unnoticed by the world's wine critics, nor by its top chefs, a good number of whom feature his wines on their *carte*. He has also set up his own *négociant* business, and proposes red and whites of very fine quality from just about every village on the Côte de Beaune.

Two local viticultural particularities Soils at Santenay are among the richest of the Côte d'Or, and in order to limit their productivity Pinot Noir vines are trained by the Cordon de Royat method, which is thought better-suited to this soil, yet which is dangerously conducive to over-production. Interestingly there is a variant here of the Pinot Noir known as Pinot Fin de Santenay, which is well-adapted to the local soils, although clones are much more prevalent than this strain today.

Difficulties for the Santenay wine-maker Santenay provides a very good litmus test of a wine-maker's talents. Its wines were invariably – and often still are – dense, solid, burly or rustic in character compared with other Côte de Beaune villages, and lacking their elegance and finesse. The limestone strata, at the surface on the Côte de Nuits but deeper buried south of it, which reappear at Chassagne and Santenay and contribute structure more typical of the Côte de Nuits, are one explanation for their solidity.

None of the rusticity, coarseness or undue muscle are to be found in Girardin's wines. Apart from the quality of his vineyard sites, the usual quality factors are respected here: viticulture by *lutte raisonnée*, low yields picked at peak ripeness and sorted for quality in the vineyard, then total destalking followed by traditional vinification. White wines get lots of *bâtonnage* and a light fining and filtration, while reds get neither fining nor filtration and are matured in up to one third new oak.

Santenay Les Gravières The south-east-facing Les Gravières, at the Chassagne end and heart of the village's vineyards, is the source of one of Girardin's greatest wines, which needs a good decade to develop all its bouquet and displays remarkable silkiness and elegance as it ages. Rich and concentrated, with an obvious yet judiciously dosed oak component when young, it is perfectly suited to roast duck served with blackcurrants.

- Other red wines:
Premier cru:
Santenay La Maladière ; Maranges Clos des Loyères; Pommard Les Chanlins; Beaune Le Clos des Vignes Franches.
Village:
Pommard Les Vignots, Pommard Le Clos des Lambots
- White wines:
Premier cru:
Santenay Le Beaurepaire, Santenay Clos du Beauregard; Chassagne-Montrachet Morgeot.
Village:
Meursault Les Narvaux
- Owner:
Vincent Girardin
- Wine-maker:
Vincent Girardin
- Combined vineyards:
15 hectares
- Production:
90,000 bottles
- Exports: 85%
- Take-away sales: No
- Visits: No

Wine selected:
Santenay Les Gravières

- Classification:
Premier Cru
- Area cultivated:
1.5 hectares
- Soil type:
Clay and limestone
- Average vine age:
40 years
- Average annual production:
9,000 bottles

PRODUCT OF FRANCE

GRAND VIN DE BOURGOGNE

Vieilles Vignes

Domaine Vincent Girardin

1996

SANTENAY

PREMIER CRU " LES GRAVIÈRES "

APPELLATION CONTROLEE

12,5% vol.   750 ml

Mis en bouteille à la propriété par
Vincent GIRARDIN, Propriétaire-Récoltant à Santenay (Côte d'Or)

PRODUCERS

The addresses and telephone numbers of companies referred to by their initials under the heading Sales Outlets are given in the separate Sales Outlets list.

Prices indicated correspond to the specific wine photographed, and are those asked at the property, except in cases where there are no on-site sales, in which case they represent the average price charged by sales outlets. The star notations represent the following price ranges:

*	Less than 150 F.
**	150 F. - 300 F.
***	300 F. - 500 F.
****	500 F. - 800 F.
*****	In excess of 800 F.

Domaine François Raveneau
9, rue de Chichée -
89800 Chablis -
Tel. 03 86 42 17 46
Sales Outlets: BAD, LSV, VIN, CR, LGC, LFF, CDC, CT, PER
Price: *

Domaine Jean-Paul Droin
8, bd. de Ferrières -
89800 Chablis -
Tel. 03 86 42 16 78
Directions: Boulevard de Ferrières stretches from Place Lafayette down to Quai Voltaire and the river. Domaine Droin is on the right-hand side as one goes downhill.
Sales Outlets: LSV, VIN, PER
Price: *

Domaine Louis Michel & Fils
9-11, bd. de Ferrières -
89800 Chablis -
Tel. 03 86 42 88 55
Directions: Boulevard de Ferrières stretches from Place Lafayette down to Quai Voltaire and the river. Domaine Louis Michel is on the left-hand side as one goes downhill.
Sales Outlets: PER
Price: *

Domaine de la Maladière
14, rue Jules Rathier -
89800 Chablis -
Tel. 03 86 42 12 51
Directions: From Place Lafayette proceed along Rue Jules Rathier. Domaine de la Maladière, fronted by its chic shop, is on the right-hand side.
Sales Outlets: VGJ
Price: *

Domaine René & Vincent Dauvissat
8, rue Emile Zola - 89800 Chablis - Tel. 03 86 42 11 58
Directions: From Place Lafayette proceed along Rue Jules Rathier and in front of the Les Clos hotel follow the bend to the right. Dauvissat is some 20 metres along on the right-hand side.
Sales Outlets: CA, LSV, CM, MIL, LG, IM, CLT, RB, CR, LGC, LFF, PER
Price: *

Domaine Alain Burguet
18, rue de l'Eglise -
21220 Gevrey-Chambertin -
Tel. 03 80 34 36 35
Sales Outlets: PER
Price: *

Domaine Alain Hudelot-Noëllat
21220 Chambolle-Musigny -
Tel. 03 80 62 85 17
Directions: When driving south on the RN74 take the slip-road on the right-hand side just before arriving at the Vougeot roundabout. Domaine Hudelot-Noëllat is roughly 100 metres along on the right-hand side.
Sales Outlets: MIL
Price: *

Domaine Alain Michelot
6, rue Camille-Rodier -
21700 Nuits-Saint-Georges -
Tel. 03 80 61 14 46

Directions: The estate lies on the main road through Nuits-Saint-Georges, next to the municipal library.
Sales Outlets: At the estate, otherwise telephone for details of the nearest stockists.
Price: **

Domaine de l'Arlot
21700 Prémeaux -
Tel. 03 80 61 01 92
Directions: As one drives south through Prémeaux on the RN74, the Domaine de l'Arlot is on the right-hand side.
Sales Outlets: PER
Price: *

Domaine Armand Rousseau
1, rue de l'Aumonerie -
21220 Gevrey-Chambertin -
Tel. 03 80 34 30 55
Directions: The estate is at the top of the village on the corner of Rue de l'Eglise and Rue de l'Aumonerie, which leads out of the village towards the Combe de Lavaux.
Sales Outlets: LCI, CR, LGC, PER
Price: ***

Domaine Bachelet
Rue de la Petite Issue -
21220 Gevrey-Chambertin -
Tel. 03 80 51 89 09
Directions: If driving north up the RN74, turn right at the first traffic lights on entering Gevrey, or if heading south, left at the third lights. Domaine Bachelet's unmarked wooden door is 20 metres along on the left-hand side.
Sales Outlets: At the estate
Price: **

Domaine Bernard Dugat-Py
Rue de Panteligone - BP.31 -
21220 Gevrey-Chambertin -
Tel. 03 80 51 82 46
Sales Outlets: CLT, LGC, PER
Price: **

Domaine Bruno Clair
5, rue de Vieux Collège - BP.22 -
21160 Marsannay-la-Côte -
Tel. 03 80 52 28 95
Directions: From the RN74 take the road to Marsannay. Turn right at the first set of lights, and left at the first turning. Domaine Clair is several metres along, on the right-hand side.
Sales Outlets: CA, CB, RB, PER
Price: **/***

Domaine du Clos de Tart
21220 Morey-Saint-Denis -
Tel. 03 80 34 30 91
Directions: When arriving in Morey head for the church. The Domaine du Clos de Tart is just above it.
Sales Outlets: MIL, PER
Price: **/***

Domaine Comte Georges de Vogüé
Rue Sainte-Barbe -
21220 Chambolle-Musigny -
Tel. 03 80 62 86 25
Directions: Rue Saint-Barbe is the last on the right before Chambolle's church.
Sales Outlets: CA, LSV, LCI, CM, MIL, IM, CGC, PER, NIC
Price: ****

Domaine Confuron-Cotétidot
10, rue de la Fontaine -
21700 Vosne-Romanée -
Tel. 03 80 61 03 39
Directions: As one goes down the RN74 Rue de la Fontaine is the last street on the right-hand side before leaving Vosne in the direction of Nuits-Saint-Georges. Domaine Confuron-Cotétidot is on the left-hand side.
Sales Outlets: CT, GVF
Price: **

Domaine Daniel Rion & Fils
Prémeaux - 21700 Nuits-Saint-Georges - Tel. 03 80 62 31 28 -
E-mail: Patrice.Rion@wanadoo.fr
Directions: As one drives north through Prémeaux on the RN74, Domaine Daniel Rion is on the

main road on the right-hand side.
Sales Outlets: At the estate
Price: **

Domaine Denis Mortet
22, rue de l'Eglise -
21220 Gevrey-Chambertin -
Tel. 03 80 34 10 05
Sales Outlets: Telephone for details of the nearest stockist.
Price: **

Domaine Dujac
7, rue de la Bussière -
21220 Morey-Saint-Denis -
Tel. 03 80 34 32 58
Directions: From the church proceed down Grande Rue until Rue de la Bussière and turn right. Domaine Dujac is 200 metres along on the left.
Sales Outlets: LCI, MIL, PER
Price: ***

Domaine Emmanuel Rouget
18, route de Gilly -
21640 Flagey-Echézeaux -
Tel. 03 80 62 83 38
Sales Outlets: LSV, CM, LGC, CT
Price: **

Domaine Faiveley
B.P.9 -
21701 Nuits-Saint-Georges Cedex - Tel. 03 80 61 04 55
Sales Outlets: FIC, CAP, LCI, CB, IM, CLT, CGC, CR, LFF, LV, GVF, PER, VGJ, NIC
Price: **/***

Domaine Forey
2, rue Derrière-le-four -
21700 Vosne-Romanée -
Tel. 03 80 61 09 68
Directions: Follow Rue du Château, on the left-hand side of Vosne's church. Rue Derrière-le-four is the second on the right. Domaine Forey is on the right-hand side.
Sales Outlets: PER
Price: *

Domaine François Lamarche
9, rue des Communes -
21700 Vosne-Romanée -
Tel. 03 80 61 07 94
Directions: Domaine Lamarche is on the left-hand side as one drives along Rue des Communes from the church to the mairie.
Sales Outlets: MIL, PER
Price: ***

Domaine Frédéric Esmonin
12, rue du Chêne -
21220 Gevrey-Chambertin -
Tel. 03 80 34 37 25
Directions: Rue du Chêne is the last on the right-hand side before leaving Gevrey along the Route des Grands Crus towards Morey. The estate is at the junction at the top, level with the fountain.
Sales Outlets: PER
Price: **

Domaine Georges Mugneret
5, rue des Communes -
21700 Vosne-Romanée -
Tel. 03 80 61 01 57
Directions: Domaine Georges Mugneret is on the left-hand side as one drives along Rue des Communes from the church to the mairie.
Sales Outlets: LGC, CT, PER
Price: **/***

Domaine Georges Roumier
21220 Chambolle-Musigny -
Tel. 03 80 62 86 37
Sales Outlets: LSV, LCI, CB, CLT, CR, LGC, CT
Price: **/***

Domaine Ghislaine Barthod
Rue du Lavoir -
21220 Chambolle-Musigny -
Tel. 03 80 62 80 16
Directions: Rue du Lavoir is on the left-hand side as one enters Chambolle from Morey-Saint-Denis. Domaine Barthod is on the bend as the road turns towards the vineyards.
Sales Outlets: LGC
Price: */**

Domaine Guy Coquard
55, route des Grands Crus -
21220 Morey-Saint-Denis -
Tel. 03 80 34 38 88
Directions: The estate is one of the first on the right-hand side as one enters the village on the Route des Grands Crus from Gevrey.
Sales Outlets: At the estate.
Price: *

Domaine Henri Gouges
7, rue du Moulin -
21700 Nuits-Saint-Georges -
Tel. 03 80 61 04 40
Directions: Domaine Gouges is on the junction of Rue de la Duchesse and Rue du Moulin, opposite Quai Fleury in the centre of the town.
Sales Outlets: LCI, CB, PER
Price: **

Domaine Hubert Lignier
45, Grande Rue -
21220 Morey-Saint-Denis -
Tel. 03 80 34 31 79
Directions: Grande Rue leads from the RN74 up to the church.
Sales Outlets: LSV, MIL, CB, LGC, PER
Price: ***

Domaine Jacques-Frédéric Mugnier
Château de Chambolle-Musigny - 21220 Chambolle-Musigny -
Tel. 03 80 62 85 39
Directions: Proceed into Chambolle, drive past the church, and at the end turn right. The château is on the left-hand side.
Sales Outlets: LSV, CLT, LGC, PER
Price: ***

Domaine Jayer-Gilles
21700 Magny-lès-Villers -
Tel. 03 80 62 91 79
Sales Outlets: CGC, LGC, LFF, CDC, CT, PER
Price: ***

Domaine Jean Grivot
6, rue de la Croix-Rameau -
21700 Vosne-Romanée -
Tel. 03 80 61 05 95
Directions: Rue de la Croix-Rameau runs northwards from the Place de l'Eglise. Domaine Grivot is on the right-hand side.
Sales Outlets: MIL
Price: ****

Domaine Jean-Jacques Confuron
Les Vignottes - 21700 Prémeaux-Prissey - Tel. 03 80 62 31 08
Directions: The estate lies on the main road on the right-hand side as one approaches Prémeaux from Comblanchien.
Sales Outlets: CM, MIL, PER
Price: ****

Domaine des Lambrays
31, rue Basse - 21220 Morey-Saint-Denis - Tel. 03 80 51 84 33
Directions: The domaine's fine building is easily identified from the RN74, thanks to its name, which features in large letters on one of the estate walls.
Sales Outlets: CAP, LG, PER
Price: **

Domaine Leroy
15, rue de la Fontaine -
21700 Vosne-Romanée -
Tel. 03 80 21 21 10
Sales Outlets: CLT, LFF, PER
Price: *****

Domaine Méo-Camuzet
11, rue des Grands Crus -
21700 Vosne-Romanée -
Tel. 03 80 61 11 05
Directions: Follow Rue du Château, on the left-hand side of Vosne's church. Rue des Grands Crus is the third on the right.
Sales Outlets: LSV, CT, PER
Price: *****

Domaine Michel Gros
3, rue des Communes -
21700 Vosne-Romanée -
Tel. 03 80 61 04 69
Directions: Domaine Michel Gros

is on the left-hand side as one drives along Rue des Communes from the church to the mairie.
Sales Outlets: CLT, PER
Price: **

Domaine Mongeard-Mugneret
14, rue de la Fontaine -
21700 Vosne-Romanée -
Tel. 03 80 61 11 95
Directions: As one goes down the RN74 Rue de la Fontaine is the last street on the right-hand side before leaving Vosne in the direction of Nuits-Saint-Georges. Domaine Mongeard-Mugneret is on the left-hand side.
Sales Outlets: CM, MIL, CB, LG, PER
Price: **

Domaine Pierre Gelin
2, rue du Chapitre - 21220 Fixin -
Tel. 03 80 52 45 24
Directions: Follow the Route des Grands Crus from Gevrey into Fixin. Rue du Chapitre is the first street on the left-hand side, and Domaine Gelin is several metres along on the right.
Sales Outlets: PER
Price: *

Domaine Ponsot
17-21, rue de la Montagne -
BP.11 - Tel. 03 80 34 32 46 -
Internet: www.domaine-ponsot.com
Sales Outlets: LSV, LCI, CLT, CGC, LGC, PER
Price: ***

Domaine René Engel
3, place de la Mairie -
21700 Vosne-Romanée -
Tel. 03 80 61 10 54
Directions: Domaine René Engel is in front of the mairie on the left-hand side.
Sales Outlets: CB, PER
Price: **

Domaine Robert Arnoux
3, Route Nationale -
21700 Vosne-Romanée -
Tel. 03 80 61 09 85
Directions: Domaine Arnoux is the last domaine on the right-hand side as one follows the RN74 through Vosne in the direction of Nuits. It is well sign-posted.
Sales Outlets: BAD, CLT, PER
Price: ****

Domaine Robert Chevillon
68, rue Félix Tisserand -
21700 Nuits-Saint-Georges -
Tel. 03 80 62 34 88
Directions: At the fountain turn along Quai Fleury, then turn left at Place Marie Maignot into Rue Félix Tisserand. Domaine Chevillon is on the right-hand side.
Sales Outlets: CLT, PER
Price: */**

Domaine Robert Groffier Père & Fils
3, route des Grands Crus -
21220 Morey-Saint-Denis -
Tel. 03 80 34 31 53
Directions: Domaine Groffier is near the entry to the village on the left-hand side as one arrives from Chambolle-Musigny.
Sales Outlets: LSV, CLT, PER
Price: ***

Domaine de la Romanée-Conti
1, rue Derrière-le-Four -
21700 Vosne-Romanée -
Tel. 03 80 61 04 57
Directions: Follow Rue du Château, on the left-hand side of Vosne's church. Rue Derrière-le-four is the second on the right. The Domaine de la Romanée-Conti is on the left-hand side.
Sales Outlets: FIC, CA, LSV, LCI, CM, MIL, CB, LG, CLT, GVF, PER
Price: *****

Domaine Rossignol-Trapet
Rue de la Petite Issue -
21220 Gevrey-Chambertin -
Tel. 03 80 51 87 26
Directions: If driving north up the RN74, turn right at the first traffic lights on entering Gevrey, or if heading south, left at the third lights. The estate is 100 metres along on the right-hand side.
Sales Outlets: PER
Price: **

Domaine Sérafin Père & Fils
7, place du Château -
21220 Gevrey-Chambertin -
Tel. 03 80 34 35 40
Sales Outlets: LGC, PER
Price: **

Château de la Tour
Clos de Vougeot -
21640 Vougeot -
Tel. 03 80 62 86 13
Directions: From Vougeot's main street follow the road up to the Château du Clos de Vougeot. In front of the entrance turn left. Château de la Tour is on the right-hand side some 100 metres along.
Sales Outlets: at the estate
Price: ***

Domaine Trapet Père & Fils
53, route de Beaune -
21220 Gevrey-Chambertin -
Tel. 03 80 34 30 40 - E-mail: domTRAPET-CHAMBERTIN@plan-etb.fr
Directions: The large ochre-coloured Trapet building is on the RN74, on the right-hand side as one heads through Gevrey southwards.
Sales Outlets: LCI, CT
Price: ***

Domaine Albert Morot
Château de la Creusotte -
21200 Beaune -
Tel. 03 80 22 35 39
Directions: Château and cellars are located on the Avenue Charles Jaffelin, next to the lycée viticole.
Sales Outlets: LSV, PER
Price: *

Domaine Bernard Morey & Fils
21190 Chassagne-Montrachet -
Tel. 03 80 21 32 13
Directions: Follow the Santenay road below the village of Chassagne. Domaine Bernard Morey is in the hamlet of Morgeot.
Sales Outlets: CLT, CGC, CT
Price: *

Domaine Bitouzet-Prieur
Rue de la Combe - 21190 Volnay - Tel. 03 80 21 62 13
Directions: If coming from Meursault take the first turning left off the Route des Grands Crus into Volnay. The estate is on the right-hand side on the junction at the top of the road.
Sales Outlets: MIL
Price: *

Domaine Blain-Gagnard
15-17, route de Santenay -
21190 Chassagne-Montrachet -
Tel. 03 80 21 34 07
Directions: Take the Santenay direction on arriving in Chassagne. The estate is several yards along, on the left.
Sales Outlets: CT
Price: ***

Domaine Bonneau du Martray
21420 Pernand-Vergelesses -
Tel. 03 80 21 50 64
Directions: Proceed to the Pernand church. Carry on for 50 metres up the Rue de Frétille. The domaine is on the right-hand side.
Sales Outlets: BAD, LCI, MIL, CGC, LGC, NIC
Price: **

Maison Champy Père & Cie
5, rue du Grenier-à-sel - BP.53 -
21202 Beaune Cedex -
Tel. 03 80 24 97 30
Directions: The firm is in the north-west sector of town, behind the Hôtel de Ville. Rue du Grenier-à-Sel is accessed by way of Rue du Travail.

Sales Outlets: On the premises
Price: **

Domaine Chandon de Briailles
1, rue Sœur Goby -
21420 Savigny-lès-Beaune -
Tel. 03 80 21 52 31
Directions: Indications to the domaine are given at the entrance to the village.
Sales Outlets: At the estate
Price: **

Domaine Coche-Dury
9, rue Charles Giraud -
21190 Meursault -
Tel. 03 80 21 24 12
Sales Outlets: PER
Price: **

Domaine Comte Armand
Place de l'Eglise -
21630 Pommard -
Tel. 03 80 24 70 50
Directions: The domaine is on the left-hand side of the church. Peering into the courtyard one can see a carved sign reading "Clos des Epeneaux".
Sales Outlets: BAD, LSV, LCI, CB, CLT, LGC, LFF, PER
Price: **

Domaine Comte Senard
7, rempart Saint-Jean -
21200 Beaune -
Tel. 03 80 24 21 65
Directions: Enter the old town by way of Rue du Château. Rempart Saint-Jean is the first on the left.
Sales Outlets: FIC
Price: **

Domaine des Comtes Lafon
Clos de la Barre -
21190 Meursault -
Tel. 03 80 21 22 17
Sales Outlets: BAD, LSV, MIL, IM, RB, CR, LGC, CT
Price: *****

Domaine Étienne Sauzet
11, rue de Poiseul -
21190 Puligny-Montrachet -
Tel. 03 80 21 32 10
Sales Outlets: BAD, CA, MIL, CLT, LGC, CT, PER
Price: ***

Domaine François Jobard
2, rue de Leignon -
21190 Meursault -
Tel. 03 80 21 21 26
Directions: Take the main turning from the N74 towards Meursault, turn right at the junction and follow the road for 100 metres. Turn right into Rue des Santenots and then take the first left. Rue de Leignon is the first street on the right.
Sales Outlets: CT, PER
Price: **

Domaine Germain Père & Fils
Château de Chorey-lès-Beaune -
21200 Beaune -
Tel. 03 80 22 06 05
Directions: The Château lies at the entrance to the village on the left-hand side as one approaches from the RN74.
Sales Outlets: PER
Price: **

Domaine Jacques Prieur
6, rue des Santenots -
21190 Meursault -
Tel. 03 80 21 23 85
Directions: The Prieur estate lies at the bottom of the Lafons' Clos de la Barre. Take the main turning from the N74 towards Meursault, turn right at the junction and follow the road for 100 metres. Rue des Santenots is on the right.
Sales Outlets: CAP, LSV, CPM, RB, VIN, LV, PER
Price: ****/*****

Domaine Jean Chartron
13, Grande Rue - 21190 Puligny-Montrachet - Tel. 03 80 21 32 85
Directions: Grande Rue leads into the village from the RN74. Chartron et Trébuchet's offices and tasting cellar are on the left-hand side.
Sales Outlets: MIL, CLT, CGC,

CPM, EV
Price: ****

Domaine Jean-Marc Boillot
La Pommardière -
21630 Pommard -
Tel. 03 80 22 71 29
Sales Outlets: CT, PER
Price: **

Domaine Jean-Noël Gagnard
9, place des Noyers -
21190 Chassagne-Montrachet -
Tel. 03 80 21 31 68
Directions: On arriving at Chassagne, follow the road towards Santenay. Take the last road on the right leading up to Chassagne, called Rue Notre Dame, which leads into Place des Noyers.
Sales Outlets: CLT, CT, PER
Price: ***

Maison Joseph Drouhin
7, rue d'Enfer - BP.29 -
21201 Beaune Cedex -
Tel. 03 80 24 68 88 - Internet: http://www.drouhin.com
Directions: Visitors to Drouhin should present themselves at the cellar entrance in Place Général Leclerc, in front of the Notre Dame church.
Sales Outlets: DP, MIL, LG, CLT, CGC, LV, GVF, PER, NIC
Price: ****

Domaine Joseph Matrot
12, rue Martray -
21190 Meursault -
Tel. 03 80 21 20 13
Sales Outlets: CM, MIL, CPM, RB, LGC, PER
Price: */**

Domaine Leflaive
Place des Marronniers -
21190 Puligny-Montrachet -
Tel. 03 80 21 30 13
Sales Outlets: BAD, CA, LSV, LCI, CM, MIL, CLT, CGC, CPM, CR, LGC, LFF, CT, PER
Price: ****

Domaine Louis Carillon & Fils
21190 Puligny-Montrachet -
Tel. 03 80 21 30 34
Directions: On entering Puligny from Meursault Domaine Carillon is on the right-hand side, well indicated, just before the church.
Sales Outlets: MIL, CLT, CPM, LGC, PER
Price: ***

Maison Louis Jadot
21, rue Eugène Spuller -
21200 Beaune -
Tel. 03 80 22 10 57
Directions: Enter the old town by way of Rue de Lorraine, and take the first left, Rue Emmanuel. Turn left, then right, cross Place Morimont and proceed along the one-way Rue Spuller. Jadot is on the right.
Sales Outlets: DP, LCI, MIL, LG, IM, CLT, BR, PER, NIC
Price: **

Maison Louis Latour
18, rue des Tonneliers -
21204 Beaune -
Tel. 03 80 24 81 00 - Internet: http://www.LouisLatour.com
Sales Outlets: DP, BAD, LSV, CLT, CGC, LV, PER
Price: **

Domaine Marquis d'Angerville
21190 Volnay -
Tel. 03 80 21 61 75
Directions: Pass on the right-hand side of the church up Rue Derrière l'Eglise, then turn right at the junction. The estate is several metres along, on the right.
Sales Outlets: CA, CLT, RB, VIN, LGC, CT, PER
Price: **

Domaine Michel Colin-Deléger & Fils
3, impasse des Crêts -
21190 Chassagne-Montrachet -
Tel. 03 80 21 32 72
Sales Outlets: MIL, CLT, CGC, LGC, PER
Price: */**

Domaine Michel Gaunoux
Rue Notre Dame -
21630 Pommard -
Tel. 03 80 22 18 52
Directions: Rue Notre Dame leads
off Place de l'Eglise. Domaine
Michel Gaunoux is on the corner.
Sales Outlets: MIL, CT
Price: **

Domaine Michel Lafarge
21190 Volnay -
Tel. 03 80 21 61 61
Directions: From behind the
church head along Rue de la
Combe. Domaine Lafarge is
some 100 metres along on the
left-hand side.
Sales Outlets: CB, CLT, LGC
Price: **

Château de Monthélie
21190 Monthélie -
Tel. 03 80 21 23 32
Directions: On entering
Monthélie from Meursault pro-
ceed a little way up Grande Rue.
The Château de Monthélie is on
the left-hand side.
Sales Outlets: At the château
Price: *

Domaine de Montille
Rue de Pied de la Vallée -
21190 Volnay -
Tel. 03 80 21 62 67
Directions: From behind the
church head along Rue de la
Combe. Domaine de Montille is
on the right-hand side just past
Rue Derrière la Cave.
Sales Outlets: CA, LCI, CM, MIL,
CLT, LGC, CT, PER
Price: **

Olivier Leflaive Frères SA
Place du Monument -
21190 Puligny-Montrachet - Tel.
03 80 21 37 65
Directions: The firm is at number
3, next to the village grocer and
baker.
Sales Outlets: FIC, CB, CGC,
CPM, VIN, PER
Price: *****

Domaine Pavelot
1, chemin des Guettottes -
21420 Savigny-lès-Beaune -
Tel. 03 80 21 55 21
Directions: Find Rue Chanson-
Maldant, north of the church.
Chemin des Guettottes may be
found between nos. 27 and 29,
and the Pavelot estate indicated
by signs.
Sales Outlets: LGC
Price: *

Domaine Pierre Morey
9, rue Comte Lafon -
21190 Meursault -
Tel. 03 80 21 21 03
Sales Outlets: LSV, CLT
Price: **

Domaine Ramonet
4, place des Noyers -
21190 Chassagne-Montrachet -
Tel. 03 80 21 30 88
Sales Outlets: MIL, CLT, CGC,

VIN, LGC
Price: ***

**Domaine Robert Ampeau
& Fils**
6, rue du Cromin -
21190 Meursault -
Tel. 03 80 21 20 35
Sales Outlets: LGC, PER
Price: **

Domaine Rougeot
6, rue André Ropiteau -
21190 Meursault -
Tel. 03 80 21 20 59
Sales Outlets: CLT
Price: **

Domaine Roulot
1, rue Charles Giraud -
21190 Meursault -
Tel. 03 80 21 21 65
Sales Outlets: CLT, PER
Price: **

Domaine Simon Bize & Fils
12, rue du Chanoine Donin -
21420 Savigny-lès-Beaune -
Tel. 03 80 21 50 57
Directions: When arriving in
Savigny from Beaune, pass the
entrance to the château, cross
the square and continue. Take
the first street on the left.
Domaine Bize is 100 metres
along on the right-hand side.
Sales Outlets: PER
Price: *

Domaine Tollot-Beaut
Rue Alexandre Tollot -
21200 Chorey-lès-Beaune -
Tel. 03 80 22 16 54
Directions: On arriving at Chorey
from the RN74 turn right at the
crossroads, then take the first
left. Continue into Rue des
Moutons. The domaine's offices
are on the left-hand side.
Sales Outlets: CA, LSV, LCI, CM,
MIL, CR, LGC, CT, PER
Price: **

Domaine Vincent Girardin
Château de la Charrière -
21590 Santenay -
Tel. 03 80 20 64 29
Sales Outlets: CB, CLT, CGC, VIN,
LGC
Price: *

SALES OUTLETS

BAD: Badie
62, allée de Tourny
33000 Bordeaux
Tél.: 05 56 52 23 72

CA: Caves Augé
116, boulevard Haussmann
75008 Paris
Tél.: 01 45 22 16 97

CAP: La Cave d'Annie Paule
9, rue de l'Hôpital-Militaire
59800 Lille
Tél.: 03 20 54 74 83

CB: Le Cavon de Bacchus
19, rue Crébillon

21700 Nuits-Saint-Georges
Tél.: 03 80 61 15 32

CDC: La Cave du Château
17, rue Raymond-du-Temple
94300 Vincennes
Tél.: 01 43 28 17 50

CGC: Caveau les Grands crus
4, place de l'Europe
21190 Chassagne-Montrachet
Tél.: 03 80 21 96 06

CLT: Caveau de la Tour
7, place de la République
21190 Meursault
Tél.: 03 80 21 66 66

CM: La Cave à Millésimes
180, rue Lecourbe - 75015 Paris
Tél.: 01 48 28 22 62
Minitel: 3615 Alacavamil

CPM: Caveau de Puligny-
Montrachet
1, rue de Poiseuil
21190 Puligny-Montrachet
Tél.: 03 80 21 96 78

CR: Caves Royales
6, rue Royale - 78000 Versailles
Tél.: 01 39 50 14 10

CT: Les Caves Taillevent
199, rue du Faubourg-Saint-
Honoré - 75008 Paris
Tél.: 01 45 61 14 09

DP: Denis Perret
40, rue Carnot
21200 Beaune
Tél.: 03 80 22 35 47

EV: Enclave Vinothèque
11, avenue Charles-de-Gaulle
84600 Valréas
Tél.: 04 90 35 17 96

FIC: Ficofi
16-20, rue des Menus
92100 Boulogne-Billancourt
Tél.: 01 41 31 70 00

GVF: Aux Grands Vins de France
3, rue de l'Argenterie
33000 Montpellier
Tél.: 04 67 60 75 48

IM: Inno Montparnasse
35, rue du Départ - 75014 Paris
Tél.: 01 43 20 69 30

LCI: La Cave de l'Ill
6, rue de l'Ill - 68350 Brunstatt
Tél.: 03 89 06 01 06

LFF: Legrand Filles & Fils
1, rue de la Banque - 75002 Paris
Tél.: 01 42 60 07 12

LG: Lafayette Gourmet
48, boulevard Haussmann
75009 Paris
Tél.: 01 42 81 25 61

LGC: Les Grandes Caves
76, boulevard Jean-Jaurès
92110 Clichy
Tél.: 01 47 37 87 13

LSV: Le Saint-Vincent

Rue Saint-Étienne
89450 Vézelay
Tél.: 03 86 33 22 08

LV: Le Vintage
1, cours Anatole-France
51100 Reims
Tél.: 03 26 40 40 82

MIL: Millésimes
Verger d'Entreprises de la
Capelette - 13520 Maussane
Tél.: 04 90 54 49 45

NIC: Ets Nicolas (headquarters)
2, rue Courson - 94320 Thiais
Tél.: 01 41 73 81 81

PER: Pérardel Grands Vins de
France
Avenue Charles-de-Gaulle
21200 Beaune
Tél.: 03 80 24 08 09

RB: Le Repaire de Bacchus
(headquarters)
31, avenue de l'Opéra
75001 Paris
Tél.: 01 53 29 97 97

VGJ: Les Vins Guy Jeunemaître
(headquarters)
BP 19 - Le Portmontain
77114 Noyen-sur-Seine
Tél.: 01 64 01 81 23

VIN: La Vinothèque
9, rue Pointin - 80000 Amiens
Tél.: 03 22 91 44 31
Minitel: 3615 Alavinothèque

BIBLIOGRAPHY

Jean-François Bazin
Le Vin de Bourgogne,
Hachette, Paris, 1996

Clive Coates M.W.
The Vine (monthly),
Clive Coates M.W., London,
various editions

Roger Dion
*Histoire de la vigne et du vin en
France,*
Flammarion, Paris, 1977

Anthony Hanson
Burgundy (2nd edition)
Faber & Faber, Londres, 1995

Hugh Johnson
Wine Companion (2nd edition)
Mitchell Beazley, London, 1987

Remington Norman
The Great Domaines of Burgundy
(2nd edition)
Kyle Cathie Ltd., London, 1996

Richard Olney
Romanée-Conti
Flammarion, Paris, 1991

Bourgogne (monthly)
Éditions Freeway, Clermont-
Ferrand, various editions

Acknowledgement
The author would like to express his gratitude to all the growers and estate managers
for the warm welcome and hospitality extended to him during the preparation of this book,
for the time they devoted to answering his questions, and for very kindly providing
him with the necessary documentation and a bottle to be photographed.

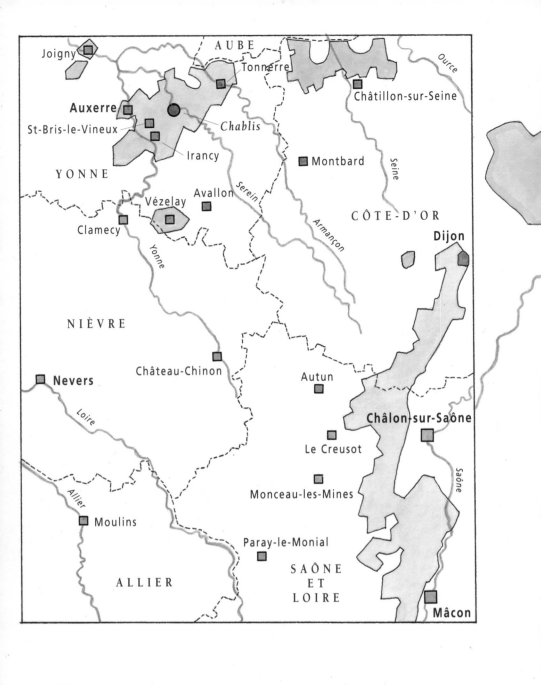

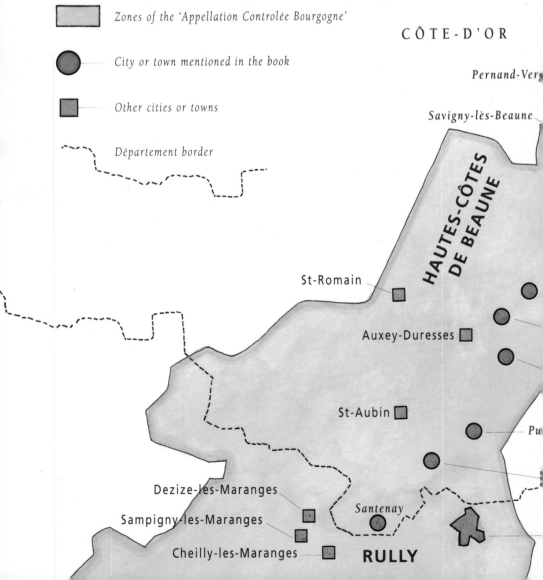

Joigny

AUBE

Tonnerre

Châtillon-sur-Seine

Auxerre

St-Bris-le-Vineux

Chablis

Irancy

Montbard

Seine

Ource

YONNE

Vézelay

Avallon

Serein

Armançon

CÔTE-D'OR

Dijon

Clamecy

Yonne

NIÈVRE

Nevers

Château-Chinon

Autun

Châlon-sur-Saône

Loire

Le Creusot

Saône

Monceau-les-Mines

Allier

Moulins

Paray-le-Monial

SAÔNE
ET
LOIRE

ALLIER

Mâcon

Zones of the 'Appellation Controlée Bourgogne'

City or town mentioned in the book

Other cities or towns

Département border

CÔTE-D'OR

Pernand-Ver

Savigny-lès-Beaune

HAUTES-CÔTES
DE BEAUNE

St-Romain

Auxey-Duresses

St-Aubin

Pu

Dezize-les-Maranges

Santenay

Sampigny-les-Maranges

Cheilly-les-Maranges

RULLY